Pocket ☑ P9-CQV-445

BERLIN

written and researched by

PAUL SULLIVAN

Contents

<< EAST SIDE GALLERY
< BADESHIFF

INTRODUCTION TO

BERLIN

Of all today's European capitals, Berlin carries the biggest buzz. In the two and a half decades since it was reunified, the city has developed into a heady meld of grit and glamour that's vastly different from anywhere else in Germany – or the rest of the world for that matter. Its edgy cultural and fashion scenes, burgeoning nightlife and radical anti-gentrification agenda regularly make global headlines, as does its reputation as "poor but sexy" – a term coined by former mayor Klaus Wowereit and quickly adopted as the city's unofficial motto.

HACKESCHE MARKT

Best place for a Currywurst

Berliners argue endlessly over where to find the best *Currywurst* – sliced pork sausage covered with a unique blend of ketchup and curry powder. While everyone has their favourite *Currywurst* outlet, ours is *Konnopke's Imbiss*, underneath the Eberswalder Str. U-Bahn.
> See p.94

The crackle of youthful energy that characterizes much of the inner city – especially areas such as trendy Mitte (Spandauer Vorstadt and around), student-heavy Friedrichshain and artist and expat haven Neukölln – mingles incongruously with the scars of Berlin's less glamorous past. Holocaust memorials, concentration camps and a wealth of thought-provoking museums, such as Daniel Libeskind's celebrated Jewish Museum, join bullet holes and empty spaces to provide visitors with constant reminders of the horrors of National Socialism and World War II. The fragments of the Berlin Wall, scattered around the city like broken concrete teeth, testify to its painful division – sometimes still reflected in the mindsets of the city's formerly divided neighbourhoods, many of which have retained their pre-reunification identities.

So overwhelming is Berlin's twentieth-century history and its twenty-first century grab for the future that it's easy to forget that the city has a longer and more illustrious history. Originally two cities – Cölln, an island in the middle of the city, now the site of the Museum Island, and Alt Berlin, formerly a fishing village – Berlin was formed in 1237. Located at the intersection of significant trade routes, it quickly prospered, rising to power as the seat of the Hohenzollern dynasty following the Thirty Years' War. During the eighteenth century, Frederick the Great (1712–86) established Berlin – and neighbouring Potsdam, with its magnificent summer palace Sanssouci – as a grand capital for the Prussian monarchy; it was during this time that many of the buildings on Unter den Linden were constructed. When Germany was united in 1871, Berlin became its capital.

Following the defeat of World War I, during the Weimar Republic (1919–33) the city rivalled Paris as a centre for the cultural avant-garde, the legacy and spirit of which live on in contemporary Berlin. World War II reduced seventy percent of the city to ruins, and it was partitioned into American, British and French zones in the West and a Soviet zone in the East. The three Western-occupied zones eventually merged into West Berlin, while the Soviet zone in the East remained defiantly

HOUSE OF WEEKEND CLUB AND FERNSEHTURM

When to visit

Berlin is a great city to visit at any time of year with plenty to do and see – but like most places, it really comes alive in the warmer months. If you're not a fan of cold weather, be warned that the winter months can be brutally chilly thanks to winds blowing in from the east. In general though, the city enjoys a cool and humid climate with an average summer temperature of around 25°C as well as the occasional heat wave. Spring and autumn are often lovely seasons.

separate – the city's division was fully realized with the building of the Berlin Wall in August 1961 by the East German government.

The fall of the Wall in 1989 provided a rare opportunity for a late twentieth-century rebirth. Berlin still carries an unfinished air and change remains an exciting constant in the city, though it's not without its growing pains, with gentrification a red-hot topic: Prenzlauer Berg and Mitte have been yuppified beyond recognition and in Friedrichshain, Kreuzberg and Neukölln cars are torched, windows smashed in and hip cafés spray-painted with graffiti in an effort to resist.

Political forces and ideals continue to battle it out in Berlin, rendering the city a vibrant and vertiginous place to be: an irresistible combination of entrepreneurial possibility and creative energy rubbing shoulders with a fully developed tourist destination overflowing with museums, sights and events. What's not to like?

CYCLISTS AT TEMPELHOFER PARK

BERLIN AT A GLANCE

>> SHOPPING

Despite Karl Lagerfeld's public dismissal of it in 2010, Berlin's fashion scene has been going from strength to strength in the past decade or so, with a string of local designers constantly upping the ante. The city is awash with small boutiques, with clusters around Neue Schönhauser Strasse and Munzstrasse in Spandauer Vorstadt (Mitte) and between Kantstrasse and Ku'damm in Charlottenburg, while Kreuzberg and Friedrichshain have a surfeit of street fashion stores. More commercial shopping can be found around Hackescher Markt and along Ku'damm.

>> DRINKING

The majority of bars are independent and relaxed licensing laws means they can usually close when they like. Though there are a decent spread of bars everywhere, the biggest concentration is around Mitte, Prenzlauer Berg, Kreuzberg and Neukölln, with many operating as cafés during the day serving snacks and light meals, and then as bars later on, staying open all the way through to the early hours.

>> EATING

The dining scene in Berlin has come on leaps and bounds since the Wall fell. Cheap eats are abundant all over the city, with snack stalls – *Imbisses* – hawking everything from burgers and *Currywurst* to Asian food. At the other end, you can dine in style at a decent selection of high-end, Michelin-starred spots – particularly in upscale areas such as Unter den Linden, Potsdamer Platz and Charlottenburg. The area in between – mid-priced restaurants – make up the majority of eating options, again all over the city, and vary from authentic and traditional German restaurants to stylish dens of cool. A particular Berlin favourite is the weekend brunch buffet, served in cafés across the city – Prenzlauer Berg is a good bet for these.

>> NIGHTLIFE

Berlin's nightlife scene is the envy of, well, most of the world, and its large creative scene means that people have fairly flexible schedules. The city's nightclubs not only stay open later than most (some don't close for days) but also purvey some of the most cutting-edge house and techno around, attracting clubbers from around the globe who come to the city just to party the weekend away at heavyweight places like *Berghain*, *Watergate* and *Tresor*. There's a strong concentration of clubs in Friedrichshain and East Kreuzberg, particularly along the river Spree, which divides these two neighbourhoods.

OUR RECOMMENDATIONS FOR WHERE TO EAT, DRINK AND SHOP ARE LISTED AT THE END OF EACH PLACES CHAPTER.

Day One in Berlin

Breakfast > p.53. The café of the Deutsches Historisches Museum is a refined and classic place to start the day before throwing yourself into the museum.

1 Deutsches Historisches Museum > p.52. Check out two thousand years of German history neatly and thoughtfully arranged throughout this beautiful museum.

2 Neue Wache > p.53. Visit Schinkel's famous Neoclassical monument and its emotive Käthe Kollwitz sculpture *Mother with her Dead Son*.

Lunch > For a budget option in the area try sushi at *Ishin* (p.61); for classic Austrian dishes opt for *Café Einstein* (p.62).

3 Berlin Story > p.60. Pop into this sprawling shop to pick up books, souvenirs, DVDs or just about anything else on Berlin.

4 Brandenburg Gate > p.57. Berlin's foremost landmark and one of its biggest tourist attractions. A must see for first-time visitors.

5 Reichstag > p.58. Climb the dome of this historic building to find great views across the city. Make sure you book a tour ahead.

6 Memorial to the Murdered Jews of Europe > p.58. Visit the controversial memorial with its rows of stelae above ground and sobering visitor centre below.

Dinner > p.60. End the day with high-quality Italian cuisine at *Bocca di Bacco*.

Day Two in Berlin

🍴 **Breakfast** > p.139. West Berlin's *Schwarzes Café* is a vaguely bohemian 24-hour café with a wonderful interior (upstairs) and decent breakfasts.

1 Berlin Zoo and Aquarium > p.128. One of the biggest zoos in Europe, with an equally comprehensive aquarium right around the corner.

2 Kaiser-Wilhelm-Gedächtnis-Kirche > p.132. Don't let the shattered spire put you off, this memorial church has a wonderful interior to investigate.

3 Käthe Kollwitz Museum > p.132. The biggest collection of work from Berlin's pre-eminent sculptor displayed in a lovely villa.

🍴 **Lunch** > p.138. Linger over coffee or lunch right next door at elegant café/restaurant *Café im Literaturhaus*.

4 Story of Berlin > p.132. This museum does precisely what it says on the tin, in an insightful and impressive manner.

5 Shopping on Ku'damm > p.134. Since you're on the mighty Kurfürstendamm it'd be a shame not to indulge in some retail therapy. Don't forget to check the side streets too for a host of excellent, independent boutiques.

🍴 **Dinner** > p.137. Try some thoroughly old-fashioned Silesian and Pomeranian food at *Marjellchen*, a wonderful timewarp.

GDR Berlin

Take an "Ostalgie" tour through former East Berlin, its monumental sights, kitsch icons and memorials to the city's divided past.

1 DDR Museum > p.66. Get hands on with GDR culture at this interactive museum, which evokes both the lighter and darker sides of life in communist East Germany. Nearby stand statues of Marx and Engels, tucked into a corner of the Marx-Engels-Forum park.

2 The Fernsehturm > p.65. Gape at the bleak GDR architecture of Alexanderplatz before taking a trip up the Fernsehturm for tremendous views over the city.

3 Karl-Marx-Allee > p.101. Admire the Soviet architecture along this impressive historical boulevard, formerly known as Stalinallee, including the original Kino International, as featured in the film *Good Bye Lenin!*

Coffee > p.105. Grab coffee and cake (or ice cream) at *Café Sybille*, which also hosts a small but informative museum about Karl-Marx-Allee.

4 East Side Gallery > p.100. Finish up at the largest remaining section of the Berlin Wall, also one of the world's largest open-air galleries.

Sleep > p.155. For a complete Ostalgie experience, book a night at the GDR-themed *Ostel* in Friedrichshain, which is also well placed for the neighbourhood's nightlife.

Budget Berlin

Berlin's not necessarily an expensive city, and there are plenty of fun ways to explore the city on the cheap.

1 Take the bus > p.160. Public buses #100 and #200 will give you a guided tour of some of the city's main sights at a fraction of the cost.

2 Free art > p.74 & p.54. For free contemporary art, check out Daimler Contemporary (always free) and DB Kunsthalle (free Mon).

Lunch > p.81. *Joseph Roth Diele*, a charming restaurant near Potsdamer Platz, is dedicated to the Jewish author and has excellent lunch deals.

3 Topography of Terror > p.110. Built on the grounds of the former SS Headquarters, this memorial of Gestapo horrors will leave you reeling.

4 Gedenkstätte Berliner Mauer > p.84. The Wall memorial on Bernauer Strasse has fascinating indoor and outdoor exhibitions for free.

5 Cheap and quirky museums > p.117 & p.34. You can access the delightful Museum der Dinge (Museum of Things; above) for just €5 while the Ramones Museum (€3.50) is the only one of its kind in the world.

Drinks > p.43. Drink and make merry at one of the *Weinerei* bars, low-key, hipster hangouts where you pay what you feel is fair for the wine.

BEST OF BERLIN

Big sights

1 The Reichstag Having survived fascism, revolution, bombardment and neglect, the Reichstag is today a symbol of the city's reunification. **> p.58**

2 East Side Gallery The largest section of the Berlin Wall still standing is also the world's largest open-air art gallery. **> p.100**

3 Memorial to the Murdered Jews of Europe Nineteen thousand square metres of dramatic, disorienting concrete stelae, plus a highly emotive underground museum. **> p.58**

4 The Museum Island A treasure trove of ancient and modern art spread over five world-class museums. **> p.46**

5 Brandenburg Gate This imposing former city gate is one of Berlin's most recognizable symbols. **> p.57**

Architecture

1 Jewish Museum Daniel Libeskind's Jewish Museum is notable not only for its content but also for its complex structural prowess. > **p.111**

2 Schloss Charlottenburg The largest palace in Berlin is also a fine example of Prussian-era architecture, built in stunning Rococo and Baroque style. > **p.132**

3 Tempelhof airport One of the last remaining examples of Nazi architecture is now an expansive leisure area. > **p.112**

4 Berliner Dom Berlin's towering neo-Renaissance cathedral has much to admire both inside and out. > **p.46**

5 Neue Nationalgalerie This beautiful "temple of light and glass" was designed by Bauhaus maestro Ludwig Mies van der Rohe. > **p.77**

Museums and galleries

1 Hamburger Bahnhof This former train station now houses Berlin's largest collection of cutting-edge international art. > **p.36**

2 Topography of Terror Located where the SS headquarters used to be, this museum unflinchingly explores the rise of the Nazi party and its atrocities. > **p.110**

3 Gemäldegalerie The undisputed heavyweight of the Kulturforum boasts hundreds of exquisite Old Masters. > **p.74**

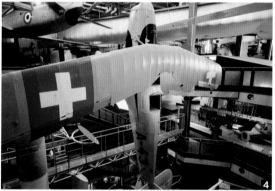

4 Deutsches Technikmuseum A jaw-dropping ensemble of German technical innovations, past and present. > **p.111**

5 Pergamonmuseum If you only get to see one of the Museum Island's big guns, make sure it's this one. > **p.49**

Berlin nightlife

1 Salon zur Wilden Renate An artist-run, two-floor space inside an otherwise abandoned house, dedicated to unbridled hedonism. > **p.107**

3 Clärchens Ballhaus Harking back to an earlier era of Berlin nightlife, *Clärchens* brilliantly mixes live bands, cheesy disco and ballroom dancing. > **p.44**

2 King Size Bar Compact it may be but this tiny bar is a heavyweight draw for Berlin's scenesters. > **p.45**

4 Tresor The third version of one of Berlin's most pioneering clubs offers three floors of muscular techno action. > **p.123**

5 Club der Visionaere This popular, floating summer hangout often has unannounced sets from big-name DJs like Ricardo Villalobos. > **p.121**

Family and kids

1 Kiezkind Try one of Berlin's "kindercafés", a place to enjoy a proper coffee while the little ones roam free. > **p.96**

2 Strandbad Wannsee The most popular lakeside retreat in the city, Wannsee also has one of the largest lidos in Europe. > **p.149**

4 Legoland Play with as much Lego as you can get your hands on down in Potsdamer Platz. > **p.72**

3 Tiergarten Formerly the hunting grounds of Friedrich I, this vast urban park is a great place to kick back or run around with the family. > **p.79**

5 Berlin Zoo and Aquarium One of the largest zoos in Europe, with pandas, elephants, giraffes and more – plus a comprehensive aquarium around the corner. > **p.128**

Kaffee und Kuchen

1 Anna Blume Poetry, flowers and cake mingle harmoniously in this Art Deco Prenzlauer Berg favourite, with attractive outdoor seating as well.
> **p.94**

3 Café Buchwald This place has been serving up *Baumkuchen* and more for 160 years. Needless to say, they're quite good. **> p.82**

2 westberlin Delicious home-made cakes, third-wave coffee and a sleek interior at the edgier end of Friedrichstrasse. **> p.115**

5 Café Einstein A taste of old Vienna in a gorgeous villa allegedly once owned by Goebbels. **> p.142**

4 Barcomi's Cynthia Barcomi's cheesecake is very difficult to beat. Her Berlin-roasted coffees are pretty special too. **> p.41**

Viewpoints

1 Siegessäule The viewing platform at the top of the Victory Column offers vistas across Tiergarten and beyond. **> p.80**

2 Panoramapunkt The lift at the Kollhoff Tower will whisk you up to the 24th floor in no time. It's worth the ride. > **p.73**

3 The Reichstag There's a restaurant in the Reichstag but the views from the glass dome are – quite literally – the highlight. > **p.58**

4 Fernsehturm Buy a timed ticket online to beat the queues to the top of this Berlin landmark for superb views across the whole city. > **p.65**

5 Viktoriapark At 66m, the cross at the top of Schinkel's monument in this Kreuzberg park is officially the highest point in Berlin. > **p.112**

PLACES

Spandauer Vorstadt

Arcing elegantly above the Spree between Friedrichstrasse and Alexanderplatz, the Spandauer Vorstadt was an eighteenth-century suburb that today serves as Berlin's primary "downtown" area, and is the heart of the Mitte district. Before World War II it was a significant hub for Jewish and French Huguenot exiles; after the Wall fell it became an artists' enclave, playing a vital role in the transferral of the city's art scene from West to East. Two decades of commercialization have resulted in a vibrant but touristic part of the city that's dense with boutiques, bars and restaurants, mainly around Hackescher Markt and the adjacent Oranienburger Strasse, as well as galleries, along Auguststrasse and Torstrasse. Key insights into local Jewish life remain at the Neue Synagoge, the Jewish cemetery on Grosse Hamburger Strasse, and a trio of museums in the Haus Schwarzenberg.

HACKESCHE HÖFE

Rosenthaler Str. 40/41 & Sophienstr. 6
Ⓢ Hackescher Markt ☎ 030 28 09 80 10,
Ⓦ www.hackesche-hoefe.com. Open various hours (residential parts close 10pm).
MAP P.32–33, POCKET MAP E12

The extensive series of interconnected courtyards known as the Hackesche Höfe, located just across from S-Bahn station Hackescher Markt, are one of the best-known sights in this area. Having formerly hosted a Jewish girls' club, ballroom, factories, apartments – even a poets' society – the courtyards were remixed post-Wall into a more commercial enterprise, albeit with a vaguely arty twist. Today you'll find a cinema, several theatres, a jumble of smart restaurants and shops – and a throng of tourists, attracted by the impressive Art Nouveau restoration.

THE HAUS SCHWARZENBERG MUSEUMS

Rosenthaler Str. 39 Ⓢ Hackescher Markt
Ⓦ www.haus-schwarzenberg.org. MAP P.32–33,
POCKET MAP E12

Haus Schwarzenberg is the grungy alternative to gentrified Hackesche Höfe, located just a couple of doors away. It has only been minimally refurbished and at least part of its allure are its wonderful crumbling facades. Inside is an aptly unpretentious selection of

cafés, bars and shops plus a cinema and galleries (street art lovers will want to visit Neurotitan Gallery), as well as the **Monsterkabinett**, a collection of moving mechanical monsters (Ⓦ www .monsterkabinett.de; check website for opening times; €8). Of particular interest is a trio of small museums that explore Jewish life in the area during the Third Reich. The **Gedenkstätte Stille Helden** (Ⓣ 030 23 45 79 19, Ⓦ www.gedenkstaette -stille-helden.de; daily 10am–8pm; free) commemorates local residents who risked their lives to rescue persecuted Jews, documenting both heroic successes and tragic failures via photographs, documents and oral testimonies. Among the heroes is Otto Weidt, a German entrepreneur who helped save a number of his blind Jewish employees at his workshop. Now called the **Museum Blindenwerkstatt Otto Weidt** (Ⓣ 030 28 59 94 07, Ⓦ www.museum-blindenwerk statt.de; daily 10am–8pm; free), it preserves photographs and personal mementoes of Weidt and his workers and the claustrophobic, hidden room, located behind a backless wardrobe, where he hid Jewish

families when the Gestapo came knocking. Finally, the **Anne-Frank-Zentrum** (Ⓣ 030 28 88 65 600, Ⓦ www .annefrank.de; Tues–Sun 10am–6pm; €5) is a modern, surprisingly engaging exhibition on her life.

SAMMLUNG HOFFMANN

Sophie-Gips-Höfe, Sophienstr. 21 Ⓢ Hackescher Markt Ⓣ 030 28 49 91 20. Ⓦ www.sammlung-hoffmann.de. By appointment only: Sat 11am–4pm; closed Aug. €10. MAP P.32–33, POCKET MAP D11

Started by avid art collectors Erika and Rolf Hoffmann, this sizeable private museum displays their personal collection of contemporary art, which spans painting, sculpture, photography and video over two floors filled with natural light. Organized subjectively – there are no names, descriptions or over-arching curatorial themes – the exhibition features internationally renowned names such as Jean-Michel Basquiat, Andy Warhol and Bruce Nauman. The collection is changed around every year. Entry is by guided tour (English tours available) – a pleasantly interactive and informative way of experiencing such major works.

Spandauer Vorstadt

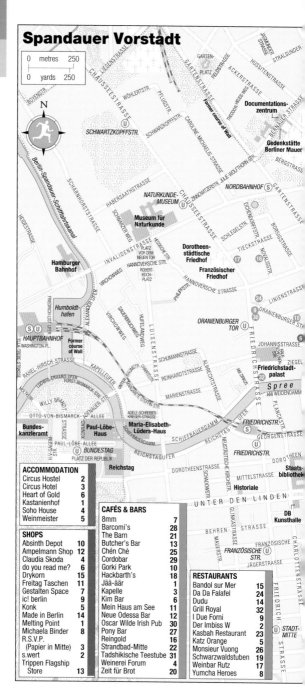

ACCOMMODATION	
Circus Hostel	2
Circus Hotel	3
Heart of Gold	6
Kastanienhof	1
Soho House	4
Weinmeister	5

SHOPS	
Absinth Depot	10
Ampelmann Shop	12
Claudia Skoda	4
do you read me?	6
Drykorn	15
Freitag Taschen	11
Gestalten Space	7
ic! berlin	9
Konk	5
Made in Berlin	14
Melting Point	1
Michaela Binder	8
R.S.V.P.	
(Papier in Mitte)	3
s.wert	2
Trippen Flagship	
Store	13

CAFÉS & BARS	
8mm	7
Barcomi's	28
The Barn	21
Butcher's Bar	13
Chén Chè	25
Cordobar	29
Gorki Park	10
Hackbarth's	18
Jää-äär	1
Kapelle	3
Kim Bar	6
Mein Haus am See	11
Neue Odessa Bar	12
Oscar Wilde Irish Pub	27
Pony Bar	27
Reingold	16
Strandbad-Mitte	22
Tadshikische Teestube	31
Weinerei Forum	26
Zeit für Brot	20

RESTAURANTS	
Bandol sur Mer	15
Da Da Falafel	24
Dudu	14
Grill Royal	32
I Due Forni	9
Der Imbiss W	2
Kasbah Restaurant	23
Katz Orange	5
Monsieur Vuong	26
Schwarzwaldstuben	19
Weinbar Rutz	17
Yumcha Heroes	8

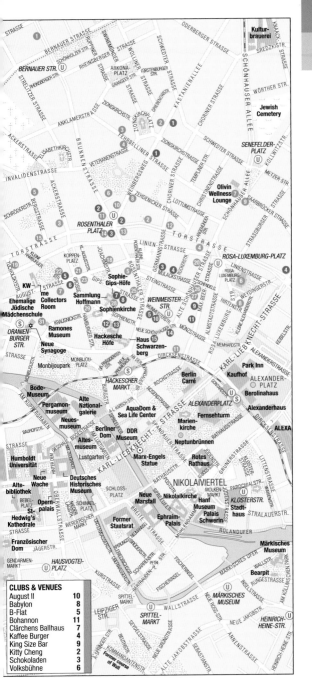

Kultur-
brauerei
Jewish
Cemetery
BERNAUER STR.
SENEFELDER-
PLATZ
Olivin
Wellness
Lounge
ROSENTHALER
PLATZ
ROSA-LUXEMBURG-PLATZ
TORSTRASSE
KW
AUGUST
Ehemalige
Jüdische
Mädchenschule
me
Collectors
Room
Sammlung
Hoffmann
Sophie
Gips-Höfe
WEINMEISTER-
STR.
ORANIEN-
BURGER
STR.
Ramones
Museum
Neue
Synagoge
Sophienkirche
Hackesche
Höfe
Haus
Schwarzen-
berg
Park Inn
Kaufhof
Monbijoupark
HACKESCHER
MARKT
Berlin
Carré
ALEXANDER-
PLATZ
Berolinahaus
Alexanderhaus
ALEXA
Bode-
Museum
Pergamon-
museum
Neues-
museum
Alte
National-
galerie
AquaDom &
Sea Life Center
Berliner
Dom
DDR
Museum
Marien-
kirche
Fernsehturm
Humboldt
Universität
Altes-
museum
Lustgarten
Neptunbrünnen
Neue
Wache
Alte-
bibliothek
Opern-
palais
St-
Hedwig's
Kathedrale
Deutsches
Historisches
Museum
Marx-Engels
Statue
Rotes
Rathaus
NIKOLAIVIERTEL
Nikolaikirche
Hanf
Museum
Stadt-
haus
KLOSTERSTR.
Schloss-
platz
Neue
Marstall
Ephraim-
Palais
Palais
Schwerin
Former
Staatsrat
Französischer
Dom
Märkisches
Museum
Bearpit
HAUSVOGTEI-
PLATZ
GENDARMEN-
MARKT
MÄRKISCHES
MUSEUM
SPITTEL-
MARKT
Former course
of Wall

CLUBS & VENUES	
August II	10
Babylon	8
B-Flat	5
Bohannon	11
Clärchens Ballhaus	7
Kaffee Burger	4
King Size Bar	9
Kitty Cheng	2
Schokoladen	3
Volksbühne	6

RAMONES MUSEUM

Krausnickstr. 23 ⓢ Oranienburger Str. ☎ 030
75 52 88 89, ⓦ www.ramonesmuseum
.com. Daily 10am–10pm. €3.50 (concerts vary
but mostly free). MAP P.32–33, POCKET MAP D11

Berlin's own shrine to the
American proto-punks, the
Ramones Museum was started
by music editor Flo Hayler two
decades ago. Back then the
collection amounted to a few
signed posters and some
T-shirts, but today it has
expanded to over three hundred
items of memorabilia. It's
certainly an eclectic assortment,
ranging from childhood photos
of the group to gig set lists and
flyers. The museum also hosts
film screenings, the odd
acoustic show from artists as
well known as Fran Healy from
Travis and special events.
There's a decent café (*Mania*)
inside selling coffee, beer and
snacks.

NEUE SYNAGOGE

Oranienburger Str. 28–30 ⓢ Oranienburger
Str. ☎ 030 88 02 83 00, ⓦ www.cjudaicum.de.
April–Sept: Mon–Fri 10am–6pm, Sun
10am–7pm; Oct–March Mon–Thurs
10am–6pm, Fri 10am–3pm, Sun 10am–7pm.
€5 (entry to the dome €3). MAP P.32–33,
POCKET MAP D12

Topped with a golden,
glittering dome that almost
rivals the Reichstag's for
prowess and recognition,
the Moorish Neue Synagoge
(New Synagogue) is a building
with a long and largely brutal
history. Consecrated on Rosh
Hashanah in 1866, it quickly
became the most important
synagogue in Berlin; in its
prime it could house over three
thousand worshippers. Its
fortunes changed under the
Nazis and the synagogue was
heavily vandalized during
Kristallnacht (1938), bombed
by Allied planes (1945) and
demolished by the GDR in the

NEUE SYNAGOGE

1950s. Rebuilt and restored in
the 1990s, it stands proudly
today both as a memorial to
Jewish suffering in Germany
and a depository of local
Jewish culture. Sadly it wasn't
possible to restore all of the
synagogue and its interior, so
the front section (or **Centrum
Judaicum**) displays the oldest
surviving elements – original
carvings, entrance vestibules
and anterooms – and hosts
exhibitions, which mostly focus
on the history of the building
and Jewish Berlin. You can get
an idea of the building's former
dimensions by visiting a
gravel-covered area outside,
which marks the original layout
of the synagogue.

ME COLLECTORS ROOM

Auguststr. 68 ⓢ Oranienburger Str. ☎ 030 86
00 85 10, ⓦ www.me-berlin.com. Tues–Sun
noon–6pm. €7. MAP P.32–33, POCKET MAP D11

The latest gallery to join
Auguststrasse's art scene,
Me Collectors Room was
conceived and built by chemist
and endocrinologist Thomas
Olbricht to showcase his
private art collection – which
happens to be among the most
comprehensive in Europe,
including works by John
Currin, Franz Gertsch, Marlene

Dumas and Gerhard Richter – via a series of alternating exhibitions. The "me" here is not misplaced egotism but an acronym for "moving energies": the collection spans painting, sculpture, photography, installation and new media works from the early sixteenth century to the present day. A permanent part of the museum is the **Wunderkammer**, which rekindles an older tradition, popular during the Renaissance and Baroque periods, of bringing together eccentric curiosities and "wonders" from around the world. The spacious café downstairs serves coffee and snacks (Tues–Sun noon–6pm).

KW INSTITUTE FOR CONTEMPORARY ART

Auguststr. 69 Ⓢ Oranienburger Str. ☎ 030 24 34 590, Ⓦ www.kw-berlin.de. Mon–Wed & Fri–Sun noon–7pm, Thurs noon–9pm. €6. MAP P.32–33, POCKET MAP D11

The KW Institute for Contemporary Art was one of the prime movers in the post-*Wende* (reunification) transformation of Auguststrasse into what has been dubbed Berlin's "art mile". Once a nineteenth-century margarine factory, KW was turned into a dedicated art space by Klaus Biesenbach and a group of fellow art-lovers in the early 1990s. The elegant facade leads into a lovely, tree-filled courtyard surrounded by artist studios, the glass-walled *Café Bravo* (designed by American artist Dan Graham) and a series of modern, white spaces that include an exhibition hall by Berlin architect Hans Düttmann. The institute mainly exhibits cutting-edge international works from both up-and-coming and major names such as Doug Aitken,

Dinos and Jake Chapman and Paul Pfeiffer. KW also runs Berlin's immensely popular Biennale for Contemporary Art.

EHEMALIGE JÜDISCHE MÄDCHENSCHULE

Auguststr. 11–13 Ⓢ Oranienburger Str. ☎ 030 33 00 60 70, Ⓦ www.maedchenschule .org. Daily 8am–midnight; specific opening hours vary according to venue. MAP P.32–33, POCKET MAP D11

Built in the late 1920s as one of the last major Jewish structures before the Nazis took over, this charming, former Jewish girls' school opened as a space for art and cuisine in 2012 following a sensitive restoration. The former classrooms and corridors are now used for exhibitions courtesy of galleries such as Camera Work and Michael Fuchs Galerie, and also provide the new principal home for Museum The Kennedys, an exhibition entirely dedicated to JFK and his family. As for cuisine, the one-Michelin star *Pauly-Saal* offers an ambitious menu made from the best of the region, the more relaxed (and affordable) *Mogg & Melzer* Jewish deli brings NYC flavour, and the cultivated *Pauly Bar* provides some evening buzz.

ME COLLECTORS ROOM

HAMBURGER BAHNHOF

FRIEDRICHSTADTPALAST

Friedrichstr. 107 ⑤ Friedrichstr.
☎ 030 23 26 23 26, ⓦ www.show-palace.eu.
MAP P.32–33, POCKET MAP C12

Founded in the 1860s, this theatre has a long and distinguished history, having been a market hall, circus, theatre and, during the Nazi era, the Theater des Volkes when it staged bourgeois operettas. Its current incarnation – an imposing GDR-style block – was opened in 1984. The main hall is a whopping 2800 square metres and holds up to two thousand people for its programme of revue shows and high-profile pop concerts.

MUSEUM FÜR NATURKUNDE

Invalidenstr. 43 ⓤ Naturkundemuseum
☎ 030 20 93 85 91, ⓦ www.naturkundemuseum
-berlin.de. Tues–Fri 9.30am–6pm, Sat & Sun
10am–6pm. €5. MAP P.32–33, POCKET MAP A10

Inaugurated in 1889 by Emperor Wilhelm II, Berlin's natural history museum is the largest of its kind in Germany, counting some thirty million objects within its collections. Highlights include the dinosaur hall, which includes the largest mounted dinosaur in the world – a *Brachiosaurus brancai* composed of fossilized bones recovered by German palaeontologist Werner Janensch from Tanzania in the early 1900s – and a wonderfully preserved Archaeopteryx, the earliest known bird.

HAMBURGER BAHNHOF

Invalidenstr. 50 ⑤ & ⓤ Hauptbahnhof
☎ 030 39 78 341, ⓦ www.hamburgerbahnhof
.de. Tues, Wed & Fri 10am–6pm, Thurs
10am–8pm, Sat & Sun 11am–6pm. €14.
Free guided tours (in English) Sat & Sun noon.
MAP P.32–33, POCKET MAP A11

Occupying a capacious and architecturally interesting space (formerly one of the city's first terminal stations), Berlin's museum for contemporary art (Museum für Gegenwart) is one of the city's major modern art venues. Its permanent collection focuses on the major movements of the late twentieth century up to the present day, with an emphasis on video and film and the expansive Joseph Beuys archive, to which the entire west wing is dedicated. The museum's Marx Collection has works by Anselm Kiefer and Andy Warhol, while Friedrich Christian Flic's collection – donated in 2004 – added 166 works by artists like John Cage, Bruce Nauman and Wolfgang Tillmans. Alongside rotating showcases from these permanent collections, the museum hosts temporary exhibitions by international artists usually at the forefront of their respective fields. The adjacent restaurant, an elegant affair run by German celebrity chef Sarah Wiener, is a good lunch spot.

Shops

ABSINTH DEPOT

Weinmeisterstr. 4 ⓤ Weinmeisterstr.
📞 030 28 16 789. Mon–Fri 2pm–midnight,
Sat 1pm–midnight. MAP P.32–33, POCKET MAP E11

The place not only to find all
kinds of "Green Fairy" liquor
but also a wide variety of props
for the true absinth experience.
You can even have a little taste
should you feel the urge.

AMPELMANN SHOP

Rosenthaler Str. 40–41 ⓤ Weinmeisterstr.
📞 030 44 72 65 15, Ⓦ www.ampelmann.de.
Mon–Sat 9.30am–10pm, Sun 10am–7pm.
MAP P.32–33, POCKET MAP D11

Everything here is based on
the Ampelmännchen – the
distinctive (and stylish) traffic
light men once present on all
East German traffic lights, who
were saved from extinction
after the Wall fell by various
high-profile campaigns.

CLAUDIA SKODA

Mulackstr. 8 ⓤ Weinmeisterstr. 📞 030 40 04
18 84. Mon–Sat noon–7pm. MAP P.32–33,
POCKET MAP E11

This beautiful shop is filled
with Skoda's renowned and
instantly recognizable knitwear.
Unapologetically chic (and
correspondingly expensive),
the clothes are geared mostly
for women but there's a small
men's section too.

DO YOU READ ME?

Auguststr. 28 ⓤ Rosenthaler Platz
📞 030 69 54 96 95, Mon–Sat 10am–7.30pm.
MAP P.32–33, POCKET MAP D11

A magazine lover's paradise,
this multilingual store offers a
vast assortment of magazines
and reading material from
around the world, covering
fashion and photography, art
and architecture. Check the
website for regular readings
and events.

DRYKORN

Neue Schönhauser Str. 14 ⓤ Weinmeisterstr.
📞 030 28 04 56 66. Mon–Fri noon–8pm, Sat
noon–7pm. MAP P.32–33, POCKET MAP E12

Drykorn sells a good range of
smart urban clothing created
by the likes of Grisby, Lagerfeld, Bonser, Cinque and more.

FREITAG TASCHEN

Max-Beer-Str. 3 ⓤ/Ⓢ Alexanderplatz 📞 030
24 63 69 61, Ⓦ www.freitag.ch. Mon–Fri
11am–8pm, Sat 11am–7pm. MAP P.32–33,
POCKET MAP E11

The Mitte flagship store
features concrete, couches and
catwalk lighting – all of which
provides the perfect backdrop
for Markus Freitag's creations:
1600 colourful, durable bags in
every shape imaginable.

GESTALTEN SPACE

Sophie-Gips-Höfe, Sophienstr. 21
ⓤ Weinmeisterstr. 📞 030 20 21 58 21,
Ⓦ www.gestalten.com. Daily except Tues
noon–7pm. MAP P.32–33, POCKET MAP D11

Publisher-run gallery and
bookshop stocking a range of
beautifully produced titles on
subjects such as art, architecture and graphic design. Also
hosts changing exhibitions,
talks and workshops.

AMPELMANN SHOP

IC! BERLIN

Max-Beer-Str. 17 ⓤ Weinmeisterstr. ☎ 030 24 72 72 00. Mon–Sat 11am–8pm. MAP P.32–33, POCKET MAP E11

Internationally famous thanks to owner Ralph Anderl's handmade screwless frames and fantastic designs, the glasses here have been bought by everyone from Tom Cruise to Shakira. They're not cheap, but they are beautiful.

KONK

Kleine Hamburger Str. 15 ⓢ Oranienburger Str. ☎ 030 28 09 78 39. Mon–Fri noon–7pm, Sat noon–6pm. MAP P.32–33, POCKET MAP D11

Featuring collections from many of Berlin's esteemed labels (Anntian, Boessert/Schorn, Marina Hoermanseder), this women's boutique features cutting-edge fashions, jewellery and other glamorous accessories that flit between fashion and art.

MADE IN BERLIN

Neue Schönhauser Str. 19 ⓤ Weinmeisterstr. ☎ 030 21 23 06 01, ⓦ www.kleidermarkt.de. Mon–Sat noon–8pm. MAP P.32–33, POCKET MAP E12

One of four shops in the city that sell cutting-edge, mostly vintage clothes for girls and boys. You'll find everything from hats and shoes to blouses and faintly bizarre appendages. Tuesday noon till 3pm is happy hour (20 percent off all vintage).

MELTING POINT

Kastanienallee 55 ⓤ Rosenthaler Platz ☎ 030 44 04 71 31. Mon–Sat noon–8pm. MAP P.32–33, POCKET MAP E18

Opened in the mid-1990s Melting Point records has stayed true to Berlin's techno and house culture, though it also sells funk, Afro, Latin and more. Masses of vinyl and a small CD section.

MADE IN BERLIN

MICHAELA BINDER

Gipsstr. 13 ⓤ Weinmeisterstr. ☎ 030 28 38 48 69. Tues–Fri noon–7pm, Sat noon–4pm. MAP P.32–33, POCKET MAP E11

Michaela Binder's smart shop stocks her stylish rings, bracelets, ear studs and necklaces in clean, basic shapes, from silver and gold. There's also a line of (cheaper) steel and stone vases.

R.S.V.P. (PAPIER IN MITTE)

Mulackstr. 14 ⓤ Weinmeisterstr. ☎ 030 28 09 46 44. Mon–Thurs noon–7pm, Fri & Sat noon–8pm. MAP P.32–33, POCKET MAP E11

From rare international notebooks to the store's own unique cards and journals, R.S.V.P. sells elegant stationery and related products from international artists. A new shop at no. 26 sells wrapping paper, boxes and envelopes.

S.WERT

Brunnenstr. 191 ⓤ Rosenthaler Platz ☎ 030 40 05 66 55. Mon–Fri 11am–7pm, Sat 11am–6pm. MAP P.32–33, POCKET MAP D18

Interested in special Berliner "architecture pillows", or unique designs of wrapping paper? s.wert sells all this and more, including stylish drinking cups, dresses and curtains, all in a vibrant setting.

TRIPPEN FLAGSHIP STORE

Hackesche Höfe, Hofs 4 & 6, Rosenthaler Str. 40/41 🏠 Hackescher Markt (also Alte Schönhauser str. 45 in Spandauer Vorstadt) ☎ 030 24 63 22 84. Mon–Fri 11am–8pm, Sat 10am–7pm. MAP P.32–33, POCKET MAP D11

Trippen sells men's and women's shoes for every occasion. There are several branches in the city, but this flagship store has the biggest range. Footwear can also be made to order.

Restaurants

BANDOL SUR MER

Torstr. 167 🏠 Rosenthaler Platz ☎ 030 67 30 20 51. Daily 6pm–late. MAP P.32–33, POCKET MAP D11

A former kebab kiosk refurbished into a tiny but casually upmarket French restaurant, *Bandol sur Mer* is hugely popular. The menu, chalked up on the all-black walls, consists of fine French cuisine like snails, entrecote and foie gras. There's not too much innovation for the price (mains around €18) but the food is consistently good.

DA DA FALAFEL

Linienstr. 132 🏠 Oranienburger Tor ☎ 030 27 59 69 27, 🌐 www.dadafalafel.de. Daily 10.30am–3am. MAP P.32–33, POCKET MAP C11

Berlin isn't exactly short of falafels but *Da Da* stands out thanks to their fresh salads and an excellent array of sauces. The Dada Teller (€7.50) will set you up for a day's sightseeing, though you may find a long queue at lunchtimes.

DUDU

Torstr. 134 🏠 Rosenthaler Platz ☎ 030 51 73 68 54, 🌐 www.dudu-berlin.de. Mon–Sat noon–midnight, Sat & Sun 1pm–midnight. MAP P.32–33, POCKET MAP D11

This trendy Asian spot, hidden away behind a walled garden on Torstrasse, draws a cosmopolitan Mitte crowd. The menu includes very good Japanese dishes alongside flavoursome Vietnamese soups, and you can choose to sit inside the chic, minimal interior or at the picnic tables in the cosy garden area.

GRILL ROYAL

Friedrichstr. 105b 🏠 Oranienburger Tor ☎ 030 28 87 92 88, 🌐 www.grillroyal.com. Daily from 6pm. MAP P.32–33, POCKET MAP C12

The steaks are definitely high end at this celeb-friendly restaurant. Some of the best Argentine, German and French cuts in town are served, as well as excellent seafood and wines. In summer try and reserve a seat out on the Spree-facing terrace. Steaks from €24.

I DUE FORNI

Schönhauser Allee 12 🏠 Senefelderplatz ☎ 030 44 01 73 33. Daily noon–midnight. MAP P.32–33, POCKET MAP F10

This famous Italian joint serves up cheap and tasty brick-oven pizzas (€5.50–8.50) and pasta dishes, in an idiosyncratic atmosphere, aided by the punk staff (all Italian) and – in summer – a large beer garden. Service is appropriately blasé.

BANDOL SUR MER

1

DER IMBISS W

Kastanienallee 49 ◎ Senefelderplatz
☏ 030 43 35 22 06, ⊕ www.w-derimbiss.de.
Mon–Thurs & Sun noon–10pm, Fri & Sat
noon–11pm. MAP P.32–33, POCKET MAP H2

Easily identified by its cheekily
inverted *McDonald's* sign (and
orange tables), *Imbiss W* serves
up fusion food that includes
such unusual items as naan
pizza and other bright ideas.
The results can be a bit hit and
miss, but they're generally good
and the reasonable prices
(items begin at €2) and outdoor
seating make this a good
budget option.

KASBAH RESTAURANT

Gipsstr. 2 ◎ Rosenthaler Platz ☏ 030 27 59
43 61, ⊕ www.kasbah-berlin.de. Tues–Sun
6pm–midnight. MAP P.32–33, POCKET MAP D11

One of the few spots in Berlin
to find authentic Moroccan
cuisine, *Kasbah* has the
experience down to a tee, from
the rose-water hand-rinsing
ritual and flickering lanterns to
the tasty tagines and couscous
dishes (from €12). Good
Moroccan wines available.

KATZ ORANGE

Bergstrasse 22 ◎/Ⓢ Nordbahnhof ☏ 030 98
32 08 430, ⊕ www.katzorange.com. Daily from
6pm. MAP P.32–33, POCKET MAP D10

Tucked away in a restored,
nineteenth-century brewery in

Mitte, the (slightly) glamorous
"orange cat" offers a pleasant
blend of casual and fine dining
with an international menu
that spans salads, burgers and
quality fish and meat dishes.
There's also a cocktail bar and a
lovely courtyard terrace for
warmer weather.

MONSIEUR VUONG

Alte Schönhauser Str. 46 ◎ Rosa-
Luxemburg-Platz ☏ 030 99 29 69 24,
⊕ www.monsieurvuong.de. Mon–Thurs
noon–11pm, Fri–Sun noon–midnight. MAP
P.32–33, POCKET MAP E11

The light, simple and cheap
Vietnamese food served at
Monsieur Vuong has made it
one of the most popular dining
spots in Mitte. The menu
changes every few days but
there's always good fresh soups,
noodle salads and fruit
cocktails. You may have to wait
for a table, especially at peak
times. Specials from €7.80.

SCHWARZWALDSTUBEN

Tucholskystr. 48 Ⓢ Oranienburger Str. ☏ 030
28 09 80 84. Daily 9am–midnight.
MAP P.32–33, POCKET MAP C11

This Mitte mainstay doubles as
a casual restaurant serving
hearty Swabian food – think
Sauerkraut, *Maultaschen* (filled
pasta) and *Flammkuchen* (a
type of thin-crust pizza, from
€8.90) – and a friendly bar in
the evenings with decent
German beers on draught.

WEINBAR RUTZ

Chausseestr. 8 ◎ Naturkundemuseum
☏ 030 24 62 87 60, ⊕ www.rutz-weinbar.de.
Tues–Sat: wine bar 4–11pm; restaurant
6.30–10.30pm. MAP P.32–33, POCKET MAP B11

Michelin-starred cuisine on the
second floor and over eight
hundred wines on offer make
this a de rigeur stop for foodies.
It's expensive – multi-course
menus range from €98 to €170
– but the ground-floor bar sells

slightly cheaper (but still great) home-style dishes.

YUMCHA HEROES

Weinbergsweg 8 ⓤ Rosenthaler Platz ☎ 030 76 21 30 35, ⓦ www.yumchaheroes.de. Daily noon–midnight. MAP P.32–33, POCKET MAP E16

With the same owners as nearby Portuguese café *Galao*, *Yumcha Heroes* is *the* place in Mitte for dumplings – steamed, baked or in a tasty broth. The food is handmade and MSG-free, cooked in an open kitchen and served in a small, but stylish interior.

BARCOMI'S

SPANDAUER VORSTADT

Cafés and bars

8MM

Schönhauser Allee 177 ⓤ Senefelderplatz ☎ 030 40 50 06 24, ⓦ www.8mmbar.com. Mon–Fri from 7pm; Sat & Sun from 8pm. MAP P.32–33, POCKET MAP F10

It's just a small, blacked-out room with a small bar, a DJ spinning anything from rock to northern soul and 8mm films projected onto one wall – but it's a superb place for low-key, late-night hedonism.

BARCOMI'S

Sophienstr. 21, Sophie-Gips-Höfe ⓤ Weinmeisterstr. ☎ 030 28 59 83 63, ⓦ www.barcomis.de. Mon–Sat 9am–9pm, Sun 10am–9pm. MAP P.32–33, POCKET MAP D11

This second outlet from American baker Cynthia Barcomi is tucked away in a lovely courtyard (with a new extension) and offers excellent bagels, brunches, coffee and cakes – the cheesecake is justly famous. Reservations essential at weekends.

THE BARN

Auguststr. 58 ⓤ Rosenthaler Platz ⓦ www.thebarn.de. Mon–Fri 8am–6pm, Sat & Sun 10am–6pm. MAP P.32–33, POCKET MAP D11

Wooden shelves stacked with delicious products for sale, and some of the best coffee in town make *The Barn* well worth a visit. The sandwiches, quiches and cakes are all freshly made and organic too. In 2012, the owners opened a spacious roastery-café in Prenzlauer Berg at Schönhauser Allee 8.

BUTCHER'S BAR

Torstrasse 116 ⓤ Rosenthaler Platz ☎ 0176 64328330, ⓦ www.butcher-berlin.de. Wed–Sat from 9pm. MAP P.32–33, POCKET MAP E10

One of Berlin's slew of secret bars, *Butcher's* is cunningly disguised as a *currywurst* shop. Completely devoid of any signage, enter the storefront and turn right at the phone box to find yourself in an intimate, shabby-chic cocktail bar.

CHÉN CHÈ

Rosenthaler Str. 13 ⓤ Rosenthaler Platz ☎ 030 28 88 42 82, ⓦ www.chenche-berlin .de. Daily noon–midnight. MAP P.32–33, POCKET MAP E11

This charming Vietnamese tea room, with its high ceilings and elegant, handmade lanterns, has a small but considered menu featuring a selection of starters and mains as well as great teas and coffees. Try one of the weekend breakfasts for a something a bit different.

41

CORDOBAR

Grosse Hamburger Str. 32 ⑤ Oranienburger Str.
☎ 030 27 58 12 15, Ⓦ www.cordobar.net.
Tues–Sat 6pm–2am. MAP P.32–33, POCKET MAP D11

With Berlin finally overcoming its dearth of serious wine bars, this 2013 arrival is a refreshing mix of high-end viticulture and accessible atmosphere. There are over nine hundred selections on the menu, including many rarities and there's a small, creative food menu.

GORKI PARK

Weinbergsweg 25 ① Rosenthaler Platz
☎ 030 44 04 65 19, Ⓦ www.gorki-park.de.
Mon–Fri 8am–1am, Sat & Sun 9am–1am. MAP
P.32–33, POCKET MAP E10

A network of lounge-style rooms decked out with interesting furniture and retro wallpaper. Despite the Russian theme, mostly evident in the name and the blini and borscht available, there's a distinctly Berlin-esque "Wohnzimmer" (living room) feel to the place.

HACKBARTH'S

Auguststr. 49A ① Rosenthaler Platz ☎ 030 28 27 704. Mon–Sat from 9am. MAP P.32–33,
POCKET MAP D11

With its simple, wooden interior and crowd of regulars, *Hackbarth's* is one of the more casually tasteful options in the area. Snacks and freshly baked cakes offered during the day.

JÄÄ-ÄÄR

Brunnenstr. 56 ① Bernauer Str. Ⓦ www
.jaa-aar.de. Tues–Fri 11am–10pm, Sat
10am–10pm, Sun 10am–9pm. MAP P.32–33,
POCKET MAP G2

Spacious, laidback and friendly, this Estonian-themed café serves open-faced sandwiches, hearty soups and drinks such as Estonian beer and local liqueur Vana Tallinn. Exhibitions, concerts and pop-ups take place too.

KAPELLE

Zionskirchstrasse 22 ① Rosenthaler Platz
☎ 030 44 34 13 00, Ⓦ www.cafe-kapelle.de.
Mon–Fri 10am–late, Sat & Sun 9am–late.
MAP P.32–33, POCKET MAP H2

Taking its name from the Red Orchestra, an anti-capitalist group who held clandestine meetings in the café's basement throughout the 1930s and 1940s, this mellow space serves a solid (and mostly organic) selection of soups, smoothies and cakes, as well as breakfasts and beers.

KIM BAR

Brunnenstr. 10 ① Rosenthaler Platz
Ⓦ www.kim-bar.com. Tues–Sat 8pm–late. MAP
P.32–33, POCKET MAP D10

Art space, bar and locals' hangout, *Kim* is a firm favourite among Mitte's trend-conscious residents. There's no sign on the door, just a glass facade (the entrance is through the adjacent courtyard) onto a perpetually dark, grey-walled space. Also hosts art, film and DJ nights.

MEIN HAUS AM SEE

Brunnenstr. 197–198 ① Rosenthaler Platz
☎ 030 27 59 08 73, Ⓦ www.mein-haus-am
-see.blogspot.com. Open 24hr. MAP P.32–33,
POCKET MAP D16

A spacious café/bar, stumbling distance from Rosenthaler Platz, *Mein Haus am See* is filled with comfy flea-market furnishings and serves as a great spot for some book reading or a chat during the day, and a more upbeat drink late at night when DJs play anything from disco to Latin.

NEUE ODESSA BAR

Torstr. 89 Ⓤ Rosenthaler Platz/
Rosa-Luxemburg-Platz ☏ 030 92 12 57 32,
Ⓦ www.neueodessabar.de. Daily from 7pm.
MAP P.32–33, POCKET MAP E10

Neue Odessa Bar is now something of a place-to-be thanks to a well thought out combination of attractive, swanky interior, reasonably made cocktails and table service. Perpetually busy.

OSCAR WILDE IRISH PUB

Friedrichstr. 112A Ⓤ Oranienburger Tor
☏ 030 28 28 166. Mon–Thurs 4pm–2am,
Fri & Sat noon–3am, Sun noon–midnight.
MAP P.32–33, POCKET MAP C11

Every city's got one, and this is Berlin's quintessential Irish bar. Guinness, Kilkenny and Strongbow on draught (as well as German beers), a good selection of whiskies, Irish breakfasts and televised sporting events make this perennially popular.

PONY BAR

Alte Schönhauser Str. 44 Ⓤ Rosenthaler
Platz ☏ 016 37 75 66 03, Mon–Thurs from
3pm, Fri & Sat from noon, Sun from 7.30pm.
MAP P.32–33, POCKET MAP E11

Just along from *Monsieur Vuong* lies the equally popular *Pony Bar* – a small but perfectly formed drinking spot that serves bottled beers and cocktails (and finger food).

REINGOLD

Novalisstr. 11 Ⓤ Oranienburger Tor
☏ 030 28 38 76 76, Ⓦ www.reingold.de.

REINGOLD

Tues–Sat from 7pm. MAP P.32–33, POCKET MAP C11

Featuring one of the most impressive bars in town – certainly one of the longest – this classy watering hole offers impeccably attired waiters who make meticulous cocktails while you lounge on a leather sofa and listen to 1920s jazz.

STRANDBAD-MITTE

Kleine Hamburger Str. 16 Ⓢ Oranienburger Str.
☏ 030 24 62 89 63, Ⓦ www.strandbad-mitte.de.
Daily 9am–2am. MAP P.32–33, POCKET MAP D11

This laidback café, with breezy, green-tiled, seaside-themed decor, is slightly off the tourist routes and has a correspondingly local vibe. The food and coffee and cakes are good, the staff friendly and there are magazines to read too.

TADSHIKISCHE TEESTUBE

Oranienburger Str. 27 Ⓢ Oranienburger Str.
☏ 030 20 41 112, Ⓦ www.tadshikische
-teestube.de. Mon–Fri 4–11pm, Sat & Sun
noon–11pm. MAP P.32–33, POCKET MAP D11

Though it's moved from its original Unter den Linden location, the delightful "Tajik Tea Room" still features the same Oriental cushions-and-carpets interior, a vast tea menu (tea ceremony around €8) and a kids' storyteller on Mondays spinning fairy-tales in German.

WEINEREI FORUM

Shop: Veteranenstr. 14; bar: Fehrbellnir Str. 57 Ⓤ Rosenthaler Platz ☎ 030 44 06 983, Ⓦ www.weinerei.com. Shop: Mon–Fri 1–8pm, Sat 11am–8pm; bars 10am–midnight. MAP P.32–33, POCKET MAP E10

This "underground" members club-style wine shop and bar operates on an honesty-box system after 8pm: you pay what you feel is fair for your drinks. As such it's popular with a mix of leftie sympathizers, students and freeloaders. The wine is decidedly average but the atmosphere is friendly. The owners run similar ventures nearby.

ZEIT FÜR BROT

Alte Schönhauser Str. 4 Ⓤ Rosa-Luxemburg-Platz ☎ 030 28 04 67 80. Mon–Fri 7.30am–8pm, Sat 8am–8pm, Sun 8am–6pm. MAP P.32–33, POCKET MAP E11

This café offers a mellow, pastel-coloured interior, large windows and an eye-catching assortment of artisanal breads (you can see the bakers working away through a Perspex window). The quiches, sandwiches and sweets are organic and delicious.

Clubs and venues

AUGUST II

Auguststr. 2 Ⓢ Oranienburger Str. Ⓦ www .augustthesecond.de. Mon–Thurs 8pm–2am, Fri & Sat 8pm–5am, Sun 6pm–midnight. MAP P.32–33, POCKET MAP C11

With its chandelier, wooden floors and chintzy armchairs, this clandestine cocktail bar exudes an aura of laidback, in-the-know sophistication. At weekends the tiny bar area becomes a club with soul, funk and house.

BABYLON

Rosa-Luxemburg-Str. 30 Ⓤ Rosa-Luxemburg-Platz ☎ 030 24 25 969, Ⓦ www.babylonberlin .de. MAP P.32–33, POCKET MAP F11

This striking Berlin *Kino* opened in 1929 and remains one of the defining architectural landmarks of Rosa-Luxemburg-Platz. Today the cinema shows a mix of indie, trash and cult movies, as well as hosting concerts and over twenty film festivals annually.

B-FLAT

Rosenthaler Str. 13 Ⓤ Rosenthaler Platz ☎ 030 28 33 123, Ⓦ www.b-flat-berlin.de. Mon–Thurs & Sun from 8pm, Fri & Sat from 9pm. MAP P.32–33, POCKET MAP E11

This cosy jazz club offers a mix of local musicians and the occasional international act. Popular at weekends, there's also a free jam session on Wednesdays (from 9pm) that gets busy.

BOHANNON

Dircksenstr. 40 Ⓢ Hackescher Markt ☎ 030 69 50 52 87, Ⓦ www.bohannon.de. See website for event times. MAP P.32–33, POCKET MAP E12

Named after funk legend Hamilton Bohannon, this club is one of the few places in the city with regular hip-hop, funk

BABYLON

consider its diminutive interior. There's no denying the magnitude of its buzz, though, especially at weekends when local scenesters rub shoulders with well-heeled tourists to a soundtrack of r'n'b, hip-hop and the occasional house/techno set. Most punters dress to impress.

KITTY CHENG

Torstr. 99 ⑪ Rosa-Luxemburg-Platz ☎ 030 89 64 56 55, ⓦ www.kittycheng.de. Tues & Wed 9pm–2am, Thurs–Sat 9pm–5am. MAP P.32–33, POCKET MAP E10

With its vague Renaissance theme – red-and-white-striped walls, regal furnishings – and lengthy drinks list, this slightly under-the-radar spot manages to attract the attention of Mitte's buzzy (and spoiled-for-choice) party crowd. The best parties are at the weekend and the music is refreshingly diverse.

SCHOKOLADEN

Ackerstr. 169 ⑪ Rosenthaler Platz ☎ 030 28 26 527, ⓦ www.schokoladen-mitte.de. Daily from 9pm. MAP P.32–33, POCKET MAP D10

A small live venue (in a former chocolate factory) that is a bit like visiting a private lounge – albeit one with cheap drinks, a friendly atmosphere and a consistently good line-up of indie-pop bands and upcoming singer/songwriters.

VOLKSBÜHNE

Rosa-Luxemburg-Platz ⑪ Rosa-Luxemburg-Platz ☎ 030 24 06 57 77, ⓦ www.volksbuehne -berlin.de. MAP P.32–33, POCKET MAP F11

Built just before World War I, the Volksbühne ("People's Theatre") has its origin in the free people's theatre movement. Damaged during World War II, it was rebuilt in the 1950s and is now established as one of Germany's most experimental theatres. The venue also hosts club nights and concerts.

and dancehall sets, though the sound system could be better.

CLÄRCHENS BALLHAUS

Auguststr. 24 ⑪ Rosenthaler Platz ☎ 030 28 29 295, ⓦ www.ballhaus.de. Daily 11am–late. MAP P.32–33, POCKET MAP D11

This authentic prewar ballroom still hosts dance classes, but at weekends the downstairs is taken over by one of the most diverse crowds (young, old, straight, gay) in Berlin, drawn by the unique atmosphere of a live covers band and an unpretentious good time. Tasty pizzas too.

KAFFEE BURGER

Torstr. 60 ⑪ Rosa-Luxemburg-Platz ☎ 030 28 04 64 95, ⓦ www.kaffeeburger.de. Daily from 9pm. MAP P.32–33, POCKET MAP E11

Kaffee Burger has been throwing parties and events beloved of students and culture vultures for years. The bi-monthly Russian Disco night is most popular; check the website for poetry readings, film screenings and live music.

KING SIZE BAR

Friedrichstr. 112b ⑪ Oranienburger Tor ⓦ www.kingsizebar.de. Wed–Sat 9pm–7am. MAP P.32–33, POCKET MAP C11

The name of this bar/club is somewhat ironic when you

The Museum Island

The world-renowned Museum Island (Museumsinsel) comprises five of Berlin's most famous museums and is an absolute must for any visitor to Berlin, if only to stroll around and take in the lovely buildings and waterside atmosphere. Friedrich Wilhelm III commissioned the Royal Museum (now the Altes Museum) in 1830, but the plan for an island of museums – intended as the embodiment of Enlightenment ideas about culture – came to fruition under Friedrich Wilhelm IV of Prussia. The site was further developed under successive Prussian kings. The range of artwork and architecture is startling, spanning two thousand years and featuring such treasures as the Roman gate of Miletus and the bust of Nefertiti as well as a dizzying range of paintings and sculptures. Though badly damaged during World War II, with the collections divided during the Cold War, sensitive renovations have seen the buildings brought back to life. As well as the main five museums, the island also comprises the Lustgarten park, Berlin Cathedral and the site of the former Stadtschloss.

BERLINER DOM (CATHEDRAL)

Am Lustgarten 1 030 20 26 91 36,
berlinerdom.de. Mon–Sat 9am–8pm,
Sun noon–8pm, Oct–March closes 7pm.
€7, audioguide €3. Guided tours of the
dome are available (030 20 26 91 19).
MAP OPPOSITE, POCKET MAP D13

Designed by Julius Raschdorff in Baroque style with Italian Renaissance influences, Berlin's Protestant cathedral was intended as a counterpart to St Peter's Basilica in Rome. The present structure dates from

BERLINER DOM

1905, but stands on the site of several earlier buildings, including the St Erasmus Chapel and a Neoclassical design by Schinkel dating from 1822. Restoration of the current interior began in 1984 and in 1993 the church reopened. It's a handsome and interesting building to explore, with notable eye candy including Sauer's organ, stained-glass windows designed by Anton von Werner and a marvellous dome intricately decorated with mosaics. You can get an excellent close-up view of the dome – and the entire interior – by climbing the 270 steps to the gallery. The most historically significant feature of the cathedral is its crypt, which holds more than eighty sarcophagi of Prussian royals, including those of Friedrich I and his queen, Sophie Charlotte.

LUSTGARTEN

MAP BELOW, POCKET MAP D13

Berlin's "Pleasure Garden" is a fundamental part of the Museum Island landscape. It's difficult to believe that this charming rectangular park, a great spot for picnics or taking a pause between museum visits, has been used variously as a military parade ground (for Wilhelm I and Napoleon), mass protests (a huge anti-Nazi demo here in 1933 prompted the banning of demonstrations) and rallies (Hitler addressed up to a million people here). Bombed in the War and renamed Marx-Engels-Platz by the GDR, its current incarnation harks back to Peter Joseph Lenné's early nineteenth-century design with a central 13m-high fountain, as re-envisioned by German landscape architect Hans Loidl.

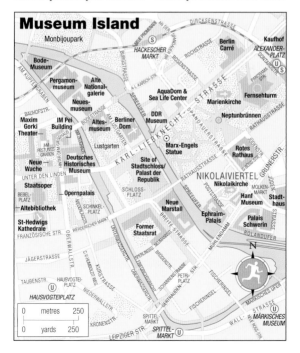

Museum Island practicalities

The **phone number** and **website** for all Museum Island enquiries are: ☎ 030 26 64 24 242 (Mon–Fri 9am–4pm), ⓦ www.smb.museum. The nearest **station** for all museums is ⓢ Hackescher Markt.

Three-day tickets for all state museums (including those in the Kulturforum, see p.72) and a wealth of private museums can be bought for €24 (discounted €12), though these do not include special exhibitions. Note that entrance is always free for anyone under 18.

The **Berlin Welcome Card Museum Island** includes admission to many museums including the Museum Island, travel for up to 72 hours and up to 50 percent discount on many top attractions in Berlin for €40.50. See ⓦ www.visitberlin.de.

A new visitor centre, the **James Simon-Galerie**, is planned for the island (between the Neues Museum and Kupfergraben), though is unlikely to open until at least 2017.

ALTES MUSEUM

Am Lustgarten. Tues–Sun 10am–6pm (Thurs till 8pm). €10. Guided tours by arrangement. MAP P.47, POCKET MAP D13

The Altes Museum, built between 1823 and 1830 after a design by Karl Friedrich Schinkel, is Berlin's oldest museum. It's also one of the city's most important Classicist statements and a marvellous piece of architecture, all fluted Ionic columns, a beautiful rotunda filled with sculptures of Greek gods and a grand staircase that more than nods to Athens and Rome. As well as Greek statues downstairs, the upper floor contains a colossal range of Roman and Etruscan Art – urns, shields, sarcophagi, friezes – all chronologically and thematically arranged.

NEUES MUSEUM

NEUES MUSEUM

ⓦ www.neues-museum.de. Daily 10am–6pm (till 8pm Thurs). €12. MAP P.47, POCKET MAP D13

One of the Museum Island's undoubted highlights, the misleadingly named Neues Museum was opened in 1859 to cater for the overspill of the by-then over-crowded Altes Museum. Largely destroyed during World War II, it was only reopened in 2009, fully restored by British architect David Chipperfield, whose distinguished makeover has melded the old with the new, maintaining traces of war damage. Over three floors you'll find no less than twenty exhibition halls, each impressively designed and connected via a stunning

winding staircase. As well as the archeological collections of the Egyptian museum and papyrus collection, there's plenty of pre- and early history, as well as works from classical antiquity. The big draw is the bust of Egyptian Queen Nefertiti – famously described as "the world's most beautiful woman" – but you could happily spend an entire day absorbing the endless exhibits. Note that due to the popularity of the exhibitions you need to reserve a time slot, either by purchasing one from the nearby sales cabin or on the museum's website in advance.

PERGAMONMUSEUM

Am Kupfergraben 5. Daily 10am–6pm (Thurs till 8pm). €12. Guided tours by arrangement.
MAP P.47, POCKET MAP D12

The Pergamonmuseum was built by Alfred Mussel in 1930 to house the artefacts from the nineteenth-century excavations of German archeologists in Pergamon and Asia Minor, perhaps most famously the controversial "Priam's treasure" – a cache of gold and other artefacts discovered by classical archeologist Heinrich Schliemann, but whose authenticity and relationship to Homeric king Priam has long been in doubt. Essentially three museums in one, the museum offers a collection of Classical antiquities (part of which is also on display in the Altes Museum); the museum of the Ancient Near East; and the museum of Islamic Art. As with the Neues Museum, you can spend a day here easily, though some of the main highlights – specifically the reconstructed (and mind-bogglingly large) Pergamon Altar from the second century BC and the Gallery of Hellenistic Art – have been affected by current renovations that are expected to last until 2019. Depending on what's on display at the time, check out the facade of the throne hall of King Nebuchadnezzar, the Market Gate of Miletus (an important example of Roman architecture) or the bright blue, glazed-brick Ishtar Gate of Babylon from the sixth century BC instead.

ALTE NATIONALGALERIE

Bodestr. 1–3. Tues–Sun 10am–6pm (Thurs until 8pm). €12. MAP P.47, POCKET MAP D12

The Neoclassical Alte Nationalgalerie (Old National Gallery), designed to resemble a Greek temple, houses one of the country's most significant collections of nineteenth-century painting. Built between 1866 and 1876, the museum re-opened in 2001 to showcase its wealth of Classical, Romantic, Impressionist and early Modernist masterpieces. Highlights include the Goethe-era landscapes, works by Jakob Philipp Hackert and Anton Graff and Romantic paintings by the likes of Caspar

Schlossplatz

The reconstruction of Berlin's **Stadtschloss** (City Palace) is just one of the many controversial components of Berlin's cityscape – not least because of its projected €590-million cost. The original palace, which featured architectural elements designed, built and inspired by Schlüter, Stüler, Schinkel and Goethe, among others, was the seat of the Prussian rulers (Hohenzollerns) from the fifteenth century onwards. The Stadtschloss was at the centre of the Revolution of 1848 and its last resident, Kaiser Wilhelm II, quit the palace and throne in 1918 following Germany's surrender in World War I.

The palace was damaged during World War II and pulled down in 1950 by the GDR, who replaced it with their own **Palast der Republik**, a bronze-tinted, blocky behemoth that became surprisingly popular with many East Germans. Nonetheless, after reunification this building was also pulled down, leaving a vast empty space and a lot of heated discussion about whether to rebuild the original palace or something more suited to the modern city. In 2007, the Bundestag (parliament) reached a compromise of sorts by deciding to rebuild the exterior facade with a modern interior – the new building is to be called the **Humboldt Forum** and will house parts of Humboldt University, the city library and various shops and restaurants. The empty space will remain for a while yet, however, since budget cuts have delayed the project until at least 2019, several years later than planned.

David Friedrich and Karl Friedrich Schinkel (a gifted landscape painter as well as Berlin's foremost architect). The Impressionist section, with its international "big guns" Manet, Monet, Renoir and Rodin, is worth the visit alone.

BODE-MUSEUM

Am Kupfergraben 1. Tues–Sun 10am–6pm (Thurs till 8pm). €12. MAP P.47, POCKET MAP D12

The stately Bode-Museum, with its recognizable dome, was originally called the Kaiser Friedrich Museum, and was renamed in 1956 after its inaugural curator Wilhelm van Bode. Opened after extensive refurbishments in 2006, the building is notable for its refined architectural details – the opulent staircases, monumental pilasters and demi-columns – as well as a wealth of art and artefacts from the Byzantine and Medieval periods. These are mainly from Germany but also come from major European art centres such as the Netherlands, Italy, France and Spain, and are culled from three major state museum collections: the sculpture collection, with highlights including the terracotta statues from Luca della Robbia, the Madonna from Donatello and the sculptures of Desiderio da Settignano; the Museum of Byzantine Art – the only one of its kind in Germany; and the Numismatic Collection, a vast and impressive collection of coins (and other forms of currency) that range from the seventh century BC to the twenty-first century.

On summer Sundays, the Bode Museum hosts popular outdoor classical concerts. Entry is free (donations welcome) and the setting, on the elegant Monbijou bridge, spectacular.

BODE MUSEUM

Unter den Linden and the government quarter

Berlin's grand boulevard, named for the Linden (lime) trees that line it, runs east–west from the site of the former royal palace to the Brandenburg Gate. The road originated as a bridle path for Duke Friedrich Wilhelm in the seventeenth century; by the nineteenth century it was a popular gathering place for many Berliners and Unter den Linden was furnished with new buildings, including the Neoclassical Neue Wache. Despite appearances, most of the buildings are reconstructions. Nonetheless it maintains its upscale aura, reflected in the fine-dining restaurants and expensive shops that predominate. Beyond the Brandenburg Gate lies the modern, yet no less authoritative Regierungsviertel ("government quarter"), a cluster of buildings starting with the Reichstag that stretch along the Spree. A stroll along the river past the striking Paul Löbe Haus and the Bundeskanzleramt, towards the Hauptbahnhof, is a pleasant and architecturally interesting way to pass a couple of hours.

DEUTSCHES HISTORISCHES MUSEUM

Unter den Linden 2 ⓤ/ⓢ Friedrichstr. ☏ 030 20 30 40, ⓦ www.dhm.de. Daily 10am–6pm. €8. MAP P.54–55, POCKET MAP D13

The German Historical Museum (Deutsches Historisches Museum) is spread across two buildings: the unique Baroque Zeughaus (armoury) and a modern

exhibition hall designed by Chinese-American architect I. M. Pei. The **Zeughaus** was first used as a museum for German history during the years of the GDR (1952–90), essentially to espouse the Marxist-Leninist concept of history. In 2006 a permanent exhibition "German history in images and artefacts" was inaugurated in the three hundred-year-old building (the oldest on Unter den Linden), which showcases two thousand years of German history via eight thousand objects from the museum's extensive collections. Supplementing this are special temporary exhibitions displayed on the four floors of the spacious **Pei building**, with its glass and steel lobby and winding staircase. There's also a very tasteful and little-known **cinema**, entered from the Spree side of the museum, with a historically protected interior, and a refined **café** serving great breakfasts, lunches and cakes.

NEUE WACHE

Unter den Linden 4 Ⓤ/Ⓢ Friedrichstr. ☎ 030 25 00 25. Daily 10am–6pm. MAP P.54–55, POCKET MAP D13

The Neue Wache (New Guard House) was Karl Friedrich Schinkel's first major commission in Berlin – he rose to the occasion by building a leading example of German Neoclassicism. Originally constructed as a guardhouse for the troops of the crown prince of Prussia, the building became a memorial to the Wars of Liberation (Napoleonic Wars) until 1918. From 1931 onwards it was a memorial for World War I, and the inner courtyard was covered over apart from a small opening in the roof letting through a slither of symbolic light. Post World War II, the GDR leadership turned it into the monument for the victims of fascism and militarism. An eternal flame was placed in a cube above the ashes of an unknown concentration camp prisoner and an unknown fallen soldier. After German reunification, the GDR memorial piece was removed and replaced by an enlarged version of Käthe Kollwitz's sculpture *Mother with her Dead Son* (*Pietá*). This sculpture is directly under the oculus, its exposure to the elements a metaphor for the suffering of civilians during World War II.

BEBELPLATZ

① Französische Str. MAP BELOW, POCKET MAP C13

This historical square on the south side of the Unter den Linden was constructed between 1741 and 1743 and was originally known as Opernplatz. Though framed by the opulent **Staatsoper** (see p.63), a library and the swanky *Hotel de Rome* (see p.153), it remains best known for the 1933 Nazi book burning that took place here, as instigated by propaganda minister Joseph Goebbels. The Nazis burned some twenty thousand books, including works by Thomas Mann, Erich Maria Remarque, Heinrich Heine and Karl Marx. At the centre of the square is a **memorial** of the burning by Micha Ullman, which consists of a glass-covered view into an underground chamber of empty bookshelves. Nearby,

an engraving of a line from Heinrich Heine translates as: "Where they burn books, they ultimately burn people".

DB KUNSTHALLE

Unter den Linden 13/15 **⑤** Französisches Str. **☎** 030 20 20 930, **ⓦ** www.deutsche-bank -kunsthalle.de. Daily 10am–8pm. €4, free on Mon. MAP BELOW, POCKET MAP C13

Located on the ground floor of the Deutsche Bank – where it replaced the highly successful Deutsche Guggenheim in 2013 – the DB Kunsthalle presents contemporary art from all corners of the globe (Asia, Africa, South America), running collaborations with local museums and galleries such as the Neue National-galerie and international institutions like London's Tate Modern. The Kunsthalle's opening exhibition in 2013 was a retrospective of Pakistani

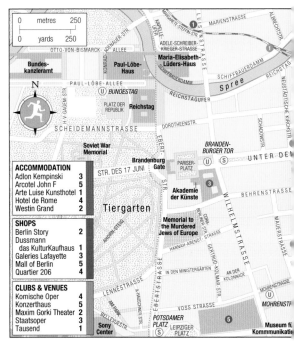

ACCOMMODATION
Adlon Kempinski	3
Arcotel John F	5
Arte Luise Kunsthotel	1
Hotel de Rome	4
Westin Grand	2

SHOPS
Berlin Story	2
Dussmann das KulturKaufhaus	1
Galeries Lafayette	3
Mall of Berlin	5
Quartier 206	4

CLUBS & VENUES
Komische Oper	4
Konzerthaus	5
Maxim Gorki Theater	2
Staatsoper	3
Tausend	1

artist Imran Qureshi, whom they proclaimed as "Artist of the Year", while other exhibitions have celebrated South American magical realism and the art of painting. The gallery café serves tapas

created by food artists and hosts weekly lunchtime lectures (Wed at 1pm): free guided tours through the current exhibition followed by a vegan lunch (not free) based on fresh farm produce.

CAFÉS & BARS

Café Einstein	3
Café Nö!	14
Lost in Grub Street	11
Newton Bar	15
Windhorst	1

RESTAURANTS

Bocca di Bacco	8
Borchardt	9
Chipps	12
Cookies Cream	5
Fischers Fritz	7
Ishin	2
Lutter & Wegner	13
Vau	10

Unter den Linden and the government quarter

3

UNTER DEN LINDEN AND THE GOVERNMENT QUARTER

GENDARMENMARKT

🚇 Hausvogteiplatz/Französische Str./ Stadtmitte. MAP P.54–55, POCKET MAP C14

The Gendarmenmarkt, one of Berlin's most beautiful squares, was created at the end of the seventeenth century as a market place (then called the Linden Markt) but its current name comes from the Regiment Gens d'Armes that had their stables here from 1736 to 1773. Despite its inherent grandness, it's a surprisingly quiet place defined by three landmark buildings: the Französischer Dom, Deutscher Dom and the **Konzerthaus** (Concert Hall, see p.63), which frame a central statue of Friedrich Schiller.
The **Französischer Dom** and **Deutscher Dom** are two seemingly identical churches facing each other across the square, poised in a stand off for visitor attention. The Französischer Dom (French Cathedral) is older, built between 1701 and 1705 by the Huguenot community, and contains a Huguenot museum, a restaurant on the top floor and a viewing platform. The pentagonal Deutscher Dom (German Cathedral), at the southern end of the square, was designed by Martin Grünberg,

GENDARMENMARKT

built in 1708 by Giovanni Simonetti and modified in 1785 after a design by Carl von Gontard, who added the domed tower. A popular Christmas market is held on the square during the holidays.

AKADEMIE DER KÜNSTE

Pariser Platz 4 (and Hanseatenweg 10, Tiergarten) 🚇/Ⓢ Brandenburger Tor ☎ 030 20 05 71 000, 🌐 www.adk.de. General visits daily 10am–7pm; exhibitions Tues–Sun 11am–7pm. Admission varies.
MAP P.54–55, POCKET MAP B14

Founded as the Prussian Academy of Arts in 1696 by Friedrich III, this public corporation continues its original mission to support and foster the arts. Its prestigious members have included Goethe,

AKADEMIE DER KÜNSTE

56

BRANDENBURG GATE

Mendelssohn-Bartholdy and Brecht; Max Liebermann headed the institution in the 1920s after the academy introduced a literature section. Under Hitler it was used as a headquarters for architect Albert Speer to redesign Berlin into "Germania", before being bombed almost to the ground (only the exhibition halls remained intact). During the GDR era it was turned into studios for Academy members like the sculptor Fritz Cremer and several master scholars such as Wieland Förster and Werner Stötzer. The glass-facade building, designed by Günter Behnisch, lies directly in front of what's left of the original academy, and its current members include German Nobel laureate Günter Grass, architects Daniel Libeskind and Sir Norman Foster and composer Sir Harrison Birtwistle. The venue holds a number of lectures, exhibits and workshops.

BRANDENBURG GATE

Pariser Platz Ⓤ/Ⓢ Brandenburger Tor
Ⓣ 030 25 00 23 33. MAP P.54-55, POCKET MAP A13
A former city gate (the only remaining of the period), the Brandenburg Gate (Branden-burger Tor) is one of the most recognizable icons of Berlin, if not Europe. Commissioned by Friedrich Wilhelm II of Prussia as a sign of peace, and

built by Carl Gotthard Langhans in 1788 from a design based upon the Propylaea (the gateway to the Acropolis in Athens), the gate has at various times been a symbol of victory, peace, division and unity. After the 1806 Prussian defeat at the Battle of Jena-Auerstedt, Napoleon took the Quadriga (added in 1793 by Johann Gottfried Schadow) to Paris. After Napoleon's defeat in 1814 and the Prussian occupation of Paris by General Ernst von Pfuel, the Quadriga was restored to Berlin. The Gate survived World War II and was one of the damaged structures still standing in the ruins of Pariser Platz in 1945. In December 2000, the Brandenburg Gate was closed for a €4 million private refurbishment by the Stiftung Denkmalschutz Berlin (Berlin Monument Conservation Foundation), reopening less than two years later. Today, it still draws punters by the busload. The best way to enjoy it is to stroll towards it via Unter den Linden, taking in the trees and run of shops, glamorous theatres and excellent museums along the way. It's a very touristy spot, so for a bit of peace and quiet pop in the Room of Silence on the north side, built specifically for visitors to rest and reflect.

MEMORIAL TO THE MURDERED JEWS OF EUROPE

Cora-Berliner-Str. 1 ⓤ/Ⓢ Brandenburger Tor
☎ 030 26 39 430, ⓦ www.holocaust
-mahnmal.de. Guided tours: ☎ 030 26 39 43
36, Memorial open 24hr; information centre
Tues–Sun: April–Sept 10am–8pm (last
entrance 7.15pm), Oct–March 10am–7pm (last
entrance 6.15pm). MAP P.54–55, POCKET MAP A14

Peter Eisenman's hugely controversial 2711 sombre concrete slabs (stelae) are arranged in a neat grid spread across 19,000 square metres of prime Berlin real estate near the Brandenburg Gate, the memorial's grand scale intended as a reminder of the magnitude of the Holocaust. The slabs are purposefully varying in height to give visitors walking among them a sense of disorientation and confusion, though from above the slabs appear to make a wave-like form. Soon after construction began in 2003, a Swiss newspaper reported that a subsidiary of the company hired to produce the anti-graffiti substance to cover the stelae, Degussa, had created the poison gas used to exterminate so many in the Nazi death camps of the Holocaust. Rather than spend an additional €2 million to undo the work and hire another company, work continued.

As impressive as the memorial is, it's really the 800-square-metre underground **information centre** (located in the southeastern corner) that leaves you reeling. The centre holds factual exhibits to balance the abstract memorial above, including personal information about many of the victims and a video archive ("Voices of Survival") where you can listen to Holocaust survivor testimonies in many languages, or even search for specific places, people or events in the database.

THE REICHSTAG

Platz der Republik 1 ⓤ Bundestag ☎ 030 22
73 21 52, ⓦ www.bundestag.de. Roof terrace
and dome accessible on pre-arranged guided
tours only (daily 8am–midnight; free) or with a
restaurant reservation (daily 9am–4.30pm &
6.30pm–midnight; ☎ 030 22 62 99 33).
MAP P.54–55, POCKET MAP A13

The Reichstag, the seat of the German Parliament, has played a crucial role in several of the city's most significant historic events. After the founding of the German Empire in 1872, German architect Paul Wallot was commissioned to create this imposing neo-Renaissance parliament building. It was constructed between 1884 and 1894 and mainly funded with wartime reparation money from France – following Prussia's defeat of France in 1871. The famous inscription "Dem Deutsche Volke" (To the German People) was added in 1916 by Wilhelm II. In 1933 a fire destroyed much of the Reichstag. Though it remains uncertain how the fire started, the Communists were blamed, giving a boost to Hitler and the Nazis, who would soon come

to power. The building was further damaged at the end of the War, when the Soviets entered Berlin. The picture of a Red Army soldier raising the Soviet flag on the Reichstag is one of the most famous twentieth-century images and symbolized Germany's defeat. The Reichstag was rebuilt between 1958 and 1972, but the central dome and most of the ornamentation were removed. During Berlin's division the West German parliament assembled here once a year as a way to indicate that Bonn was only a temporary capital – and indeed, after reunification, the Bundestag relocated here. The building was renovated again from 1995 to 1999, when the glass dome designed by Sir Norman Foster was added. At first the subject of much controversy, the dome has become one of the city's most recognized landmarks. Since April 1999, the Reichstag is once again the seat of the Bundestag – and also one of the city's largest attractions. Not all the building is open to the public: the most popular (and accessible) part is the glass dome, which features a roof terrace, restaurant and fantastic views over the city. It's currently only open to visitors with a restaurant reservation, who have registered to attend a sitting or lecture, or who sign up in advance for a guided tour. The audio guides (free) last twenty minutes and give all the facts about the building and the surroundings as you ascend and descend the 230m spiral staircase to the top.

ST HEDWIG'S CATHEDRAL

Hinter der Katholischen Kirsche 3
🚇 Französische Str. ☎ 030 20 34 810,
🌐 www.hedwigs-kathedrale.de. Visiting times (outside services) Mon–Sat 10am-5pm, Sun 1–5pm. Guided tours available on request. MAP P.54–55, POCKET MAP D14

The seat of the archbishop of Berlin, St Hedwig's Cathedral was the first Catholic church to be built in Germany after the Protestant Reformation. Consecrated in 1773, it was completely destroyed by Allied bombs in 1943, but reconstruction began in 1952 and was finally completed in 1963. The exterior is striking, but it's also worth popping inside to see the interior of the dome, composed of 84 reinforced concrete segments, and the impressive hanging organ (built in 1978 to replace one destroyed in the War), made by Klais of Bonn.

Shops

BERLIN STORY

Unter den Linden 40 ⓤ/Ⓢ Brandenburger Tor ☎ 030 20 45 38 42. Daily 10am–7pm. MAP P.54–55, POCKET MAP C13

The only bookshop in Berlin that is exclusively devoted to Berlin. Over ten thousand titles in twelve languages, including English, that cover everything from Prussian kings and the Third Reich to architecture and children's books. There's a café, theatre and bar and an associated history festival.

DUSSMANN DAS KULTURKAUFHAUS

Friedrichstr. 90 ⓤ/Ⓢ Friedrichstr. ☎ 030 20 25 11 11. Mon–Fri 9am–midnight, Sat 9am–11.30pm. MAP P.54–55, POCKET MAP C13

This giant store has five levels of books, CDs and…more books. A small shop at the back also features books about music and musical notation.

GALERIES LAFAYETTE

Friedrichstr. 76–78 ⓤ Stadtmitte ☎ 030 20 94 80. Mon–Sat 10am–8pm. MAP P.54–55, POCKET MAP C14

This elegant branch of the Parisian store opened in 1996. Housed in a glass temple

GALERIES LAFAYETTE

designed by Jean Nouvel, it stocks every super-exclusive brand you can think of, from Agent Provocateur to Yves Saint Laurent. There's also a vast variety of gourmet foods.

MALL OF BERLIN

Leipziger Pl. 12 Ⓢ Potsdamer Platz ☎ 030 20621770, ⓦ www.mallofberlin.de. Mon–Sat 10am–9pm. MAP P.54–55, POCKET MAP B15

Housed on the site of the city's former Wertheim Department Store (an architectural and retail highlight during the Weimar era), this is Germany's biggest shopping centre. Housing 270 stores, apartments and a hotel, it's a modern, elegant space with a mix of high street names (Zara, H&M), independent fashion boutiques and luxury outlets (Hugo Boss, Karl Lagerfeld). There's a third-floor food court.

QUARTIER 206

Friedrichstr. 71 ⓤ Stadtmitte ☎ 030 20 94 65 00, ⓦ www.q206berlin.de. Mon–Fri 10.30am–7.30pm, Sat 10am–6pm. MAP P.54–55, POCKET MAP C14

Unapologetically posh department store with flagships for the likes of Etro, Bally and Moschino, all set in a lavish, Art Deco-inspired interior.

Restaurants

BOCCA DI BACCO

Friedrichstr. 167–168 ⓤ Französische Str. ☎ 030 20 67 28 28, ⓦ www.boccadibacco.de. Mon–Sat noon–midnight, Sun 6pm–midnight. MAP P.54–55, POCKET MAP C14

Bocca di Bacco blends a down-to-earth atmosphere with high-quality cuisine, inspired by Tuscany and other parts of Italy. The menu includes pasta, game and fish and plenty of wonderful desserts. The three-course lunch is a pretty good deal.

BORCHARDT

Französische Str. 47 ⓤ Französiche Str.
☎ 030 81 88 62 62, ⓦ www.borchardt
-restaurant.de. Daily. 11.30am–midnight.
MAP P.54–55, POCKET MAP C14

A reincarnation of a
nineteenth-century meeting
place for high society,
Borchardt mark two is a tasteful
facsimile with marble columns,
plush seating and an Art
Nouveau mosaic that was
discovered during renovations.
The place draws politicians,
celebrities and tourists, and
cuisine is high-quality
French-German, though if
you're not a regular, service is
likely to be offhand at best.

CHIPPS

Jägerstr. 35 ⓤ Hausvogteiplatz ☎ 030 28 08
806, ⓦ www.chipps.eu. Mon–Fri 8am–late, Sat
& Sun 9am–late. MAP P.54–55, POCKET MAP D14

This venture from the owner
of *Cookies Cream* features
panoramic windows, a
light-filled, sleek interior and
terrace. The open kitchen
serves seasonal and regional
ingredients. You can mix and
match your dishes (meat and
fish are served as side orders –
evening dishes from €16),
while hearty breakfasts include
the "hangover".

COOKIES CREAM

Behrenstr. 55 ⓤ Französische Str. ☎ 030 27
49 29 40, ⓦ www.cookiescream.de. Tues–Sat
6–11pm. MAP P.54–55, POCKET MAP C13

Deliberately difficult to find (it's
behind the *Westin Grand* on
Friedrichstr; see website for
creative directions) this stylish
restaurant is worth seeking out.
Chef Stephan Hentschel has
made this one of the best
vegetarian restaurants in the
city. At €39 for a three-course
menu and €20 for a main, it's
pricey but far from prohibitive,
and the seasonal, inventive
food is worth it.

ISHIN

FISCHERS FRITZ

The Regent, Charlottenstr. 49
ⓤ Französische Str. ☎ 030 20 33 63 63,
ⓦ www.fischersfritzberlin.com. Daily
6.30–11.30am & 6.30–10.30pm. MAP P.54–55,
POCKET MAP C14

Fischers Fritz is the domain
of Christian Lohse, whose
way with fish and seafood
has earned him numerous
accolades (including two
Michelin stars). This is
imaginative stuff, bursting with
originality in terms
of presentation, flavours
and ideas. There's a price
for Lohse's expertise of
course, namely €130 for four
courses.

ISHIN

Mittelstr. 24 ⓤ/ⓢ Brandenburger Tor/
Friedrichstr. ☎ 030 20 67 48 29, ⓦ www
.ishin.de. Mon–Sat 11am–10pm (kitchen till
9.30pm). MAP P.54–55, POCKET MAP C13

There are four *Ishin* restaurants in Berlin. The interior of
this central one is slightly
functional but the decent,
fresh sushi, good prices (full
menus from €5) and quick
service make it very popular,
especially for lunch. There's a
happy hour all day Wednesday
and Saturday (plus Mon, Tues,
Thurs & Fri till 4pm), plenty
of veggie dishes and free
green tea.

LUTTER & WEGNER

Charlottenstr. 56 Ⓤ Französische Str. ☎ 030 20 29 540, 🖥 www.l-w-berlin.de. Daily 11am–1am, kitchen till midnight. MAP P.54-55, POCKET MAP C14

This refined, airy Austro-German restaurant is the finest of the *Lutter & Wagner* mini empire – it was here the wine merchant started (in 1811). Prices are high (set menus around €35, mains from €15.50) but that's what happens when the *New York Times* crowns your Wiener Schnitzel the best outside Vienna (though the Sauerbraten is the real highlight). There's a cheaper bistro with a shorter menu too.

VAU

Jägerstr. 54-55 Ⓤ Hausvogtplatz ☎ 030 20 29 730, 🖥 www.vau-berlin.de. Mon–Sat noon–2.30pm & 7–10.30pm. MAP P.54-55, POCKET MAP D14

An acclaimed, reservations-only restaurant run by Kolja Kleeberg, a famous TV chef who produces fantastic, modern takes on classic international cuisine. The six-course menu costs €130, three-course lunches are €65, and the wine list is incredible.

Cafés and bars

CAFÉ EINSTEIN

Unter den Linden 42 Ⓤ/Ⓢ Brandenburger Tor ☎ 030 20 43 632. Daily 7am–10pm. MAP P.54-55, POCKET MAP B13

The younger sibling to the famous *Einstein* (see p.142), this branch doesn't have the same panache, but it's popular with Berlin's cultural elite and serves excellent Austro-Hungarian specialities. Also good for a coffee and cake.

CAFÉ NÖ!

Glinkastr. 23 Ⓤ Französische Str. ☎ 030 20 10 871, 🖥 www.cafe-noe.de.

Mon–Fri noon–1am, Sat 7pm–1am, kitchen till midnight. MAP P.54-55, POCKET MAP B14

This wine bar-restaurant serves good food for good prices. The menu includes *Flammkuchen* (from €7.50) and the like, plus a huge mixed plate for two featuring almost everything on the menu is €25.

LOST IN GRUB STREET

Jägerstraße 34 Ⓤ Hausvogteiplatz ☎ 030 20 60 37 80, 🖥 www.lostingrubstreet.de. Daily from 6pm. MAP P.54-55, POCKET MAP D14

Surrounded by diplomatic residences, this new spot from the owners of *Beckett's Kopf* (see p.95) is cranking Berlin's burgeoning cocktail scene up a notch, combining a "gentleman's club" interior with an inventive bar menu. All cocktails – which arrive on a drinks trolley – are made with boutique spirits from small independent distilleries.

NEWTON BAR

Charlottenstr. 57 Ⓤ Stadtmitte ☎ 030 20 29 54 21, 🖥 www.newton-bar.de. Mon–Wed & Sun 10am–3am, Thurs–Sat 10am–4am. MAP P.54-55, POCKET MAP C14

Dedicated to photographer Helmut Newton, this classy cocktail bar, all leather chairs and oak furnishings, is popular with a mature, well-heeled crowd. The large windows look out onto Gendarmenmarkt, though since a huge Newton photograph called *Big Nudes* covers one wall, you won't be short on eye candy either way.

WINDHORST

Dorotheenstr. 65 Ⓤ/Ⓢ Friedrichstr. ☎ 030 20 45 00 70. Mon–Fri 6pm–late, Sat 9pm–late. MAP P.54–55, POCKET MAP C13

Though it's not in a residential area, this tucked-away cocktail haven feels like a neighbourhood spot. It's a smart, fairly simple place, but the cocktails are above average and go well with the jazz (on vinyl) that they love to play.

Clubs and venues

KOMISCHE OPER

Behrenstr. 55–57 Ⓤ Französische Str. ☎ 030 47 99 74 00, Ⓦ www.komische-oper -berlin.de. MAP P.54–55, POCKET MAP C13

Specializing in German opera and musicals, the Comic Opera – the smallest of Berlin's three opera houses – was built between 1891 and 1892. Since 2004 it has been operated by the Berliner Opernstiftung.

KONZERTHAUS

Gendarmenmarkt Ⓤ Französische Str. ☎ 030 20 30 92 101 (tickets) Ⓦ www .konzerthaus.de. MAP P.54–55, POCKET MAP C14

The concert house was built on the ruins of the national theatre by Schinkel in 1821. Since 1984 it has been the home of the Konzerthausorchester Berlin and is regarded to be amongst the best classical concert venues in the world. Daily tours are available (for example Sat 11am; 50min, €3).

MAXIM GORKI THEATER

Am Festungsgraben 2 Ⓤ/Ⓢ Friedrichstr. ☎ 030 20 22 10, Ⓦ www.gorki.de. MAP P.54–55, POCKET MAP D13

Named after the Russian socialist-realist author, this large theatre hosts classic dramas by him plus contemporary works by the likes of Fassbinder. All shows except premieres have English subtitles.

STAATSOPER

Unter den Linden 7 Ⓤ Unter Den Linden ☎ 030 20 35 45 55, Ⓦ www.staatsoper-berlin .de. MAP P.54–55, POCKET MAP D13

This is one of the world's leading opera houses, its history going back to the eighteenth century and including illustrious conductors like Richard Strauss. Closed for renovation until 2017, performances take place at the SchillerTheater (Bismarckstr. 110; Ⓤ Ernst-Reuter-Platz).

TAUSEND

Schiffbauerdamm 11, Albrechtstr. Ⓤ/Ⓢ Friedrichstr. ☎ 030 27 58 20 70, Ⓦ www.tausendberlin.com. Tues–Sat from 7.30pm. €10. MAP P.54–55, POCKET MAP B12

Decorated with an enormous eye that emits a golden glow over the tunnel-shaped space, this upmarket bar-club, anonymous from the outside, attracts a dapper crowd, so be to look the part. Inside you'll find a mix of upbeat disco, jazz and R&B. At the back of the club is a hidden, high-end Ibero-Asian fusion restaurant, *Cantina* – think foie gras risotto, black cod and sashimi salad. Reservations essential.

KOMISCHE OPER

Alexanderplatz and the Nikolaiviertel

Alexanderplatz – or Alex, as it's colloquially known – is one of Berlin's ugliest, bleakest and best-known squares. Named in honour of a visit from Russian Tsar Alexander I in 1805, by the start of the twentieth century it had become a commercial centre busy enough to rival Potsdamer Platz. Under the GDR it was a nondescript pedestrianized area and in 1989 was the site of the Peaceful Revolution, the largest demonstration in the history of East Germany. Today its grey, concrete GDR tower blocks, themselves towered over by the needle-like spire of the Fernsehturm (TV Tower), join more recent buildings like the Alexa shopping mall and the Saturn electronics store to create a thoroughly charmless transport hub. More scenic, though touristy, is the adjacent Nikolaiviertel, with its pretty old town feel and various museums, a reconstruction of the historical heart of the city that dates back to the thirteenth century.

FERNSEHTURM AT CHRISTMASTIME

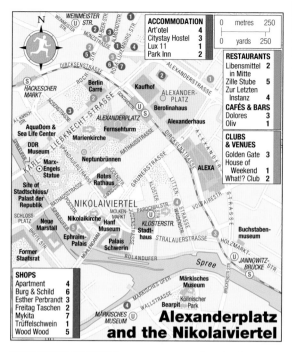

ACCOMMODATION
Art'otel	4
Citystay Hostel	3
Lux 11	1
Park Inn	2

RESTAURANTS
Libensmittel in Mitte	2
Zille Stube	5
Zur Letzten Instanz	4

CAFÉS & BARS
Dolores	3
Oliv	1

CLUBS & VENUES
Golden Gate	3
House of Weekend	1
What!? Club	2

SHOPS
Apartment	4
Burg & Schild	6
Esther Perbrandt	3
Freitag Taschen	2
Mykita	7
Trüffelschwein	1
Wood Wood	5

Alexanderplatz and the Nikolaiviertel

FERNSEHTURM (TV TOWER)

Panoramastr. 1a ⓤ/Ⓢ Alexanderplatz
☏ 030 24 75 75 875, ⓦ www.tv-turm.de.
Daily: March–Oct 9am–midnight; Nov–Feb
10am–midnight. €13. MAP ABOVE, POCKET MAP F12

The city's most ubiquitous structure, the 368m concrete spike known as the Fernsehturm (television tower), is the building most likely to crop up in all your photographs when you get home – whether you realized you'd been photographing it or not. Built in 1969 as a broadcasting system for East Berlin, and intended as a showpiece structure for the GDR, visible in West Berlin, it has a visitor platform at 200m – a lift zooms you up in forty seconds – and a small photographic exhibition in the lobby where you can see how the tower was built (it took four years). Above the visitor platform, there's also a rotating restaurant, the *Telecafé*, that serves coffee, snacks and meals while revolving once around the tower's axis every thirty minutes. The tower receives around a million visitors a year and the queues can be long whatever the weather. You don't need a reservation for the tower, but it can be handy for the restaurant (in high season). Another option is to get a VIP ticket (adults €23, under 16s €12, available on the website in advance), which enables you to dodge the queues and has an option for a table reservation.

If the sun's out when you're out and about, take a look up at the Fernsehturm and see if you can spot the cross that's reflected across the main steel sphere: the religious symbolism caused a great deal of embarrassment for the atheist GDR government.

DDR MUSEUM

Karl-Liebknecht-Str. 1 Ⓤ/Ⓢ Alexanderplatz
☎ 030 84 71 23 731 (tickets), Ⓦ www
.ddr-museum.de. Mon–Fri & Sun 10am–8pm,
Sat 10am–10pm. €7 (discounts sometimes
offered via website). MAP P.65, POCKET MAP E13

Located opposite the Berliner
Dom (see p.46), this collection
of memorabilia from the
Deutsche Demokratische
Republik (DDR/GDR) makes
for a fun, interactive and
informative visit. There are
screens to touch, buttons to
press, drawers to open – even a
Trabant to sit in and a bugged
apartment to listen in on. You
can inspect a reconstruction of
a GDR living room and ponder
the East German penchant for
public nudity – little wonder it's
one of the most visited
museums in Berlin. Though
many of the displays feed on
the current penchant for
Ostalgie, there is also an
emphasis on the darker side of
GDR life – party, state, prison
– making this a much more
rounded experience than it
used to be.

ROTES RATHAUS

Rathausstr. 15 Ⓤ Klosterstr.
Ⓢ/Ⓤ Alexanderplatz ☎ 030 90 260. Mon–Fri
9am–6pm. Free (ID required).
MAP P.65, POCKET MAP E13

This distinctive building gets
its name (which means red
town hall) from the red clinker
brick of its facade. The building,
inspired by Italian High
Renaissance architecture, was
erected in the 1860s. During
communist times, it was East
Berlin's town hall, when the
red in the name really came
into its own; today it's the
office of the city mayor, and
is the political centre of power
in Greater Berlin. Its neo-
Renaissance clock tower and
frieze depicting Berlin's history
until 1879 in 36 terracotta
plaques, each 6m long, are its
most impressive architectural
features. At the top of the grand
stairwell is a coat-of-arms hall
and some exhibits. The building
also has a cafeteria with
low-price lunches.

MARIENKIRCHE

Karl-Liebknecht-Str. 8 Ⓤ/Ⓢ Alexanderplatz
Ⓦ www.marienkirche-berlin.de. Daily
10am–6pm (no visits during services). Free.
MAP P.65, POCKET MAP E12

Standing somewhat incon-
gruously at the edge of
Alexanderplatz and the
Marx-Engels-Forum, the
Marienkirche (church of
St Mary) – one of Berlin's
oldest churches – is the last

remnant in the area of its time. Built some time in the thirteenth century, its oldest part is the granite base, upon which a hall church (Hallen-kirche) stands. The tower was added during the fifteenth century, and the steeple in 1790 by Carl Gotthard Langhan, architect of the Brandenburg Gate. The church escaped heavy damage during World War II and was later fully restored. Visitors today can see the *The Dance of Death* (*Totentanz*), a large fresco (2m high, 22m long), dating from about 1485, that was discovered in 1860 under layers of paint and depicts various classes of society dancing with death. Other notable artworks include a bronze baptismal font from 1437, *The Crucifixion* painted by Michael Ribestein in 1562 and an alabaster pulpit created by Andreas Schlüter in 1703, decorated with reliefs of John the Baptist and personifications of Faith, Hope and Love.

ROTES RATHAUS

BUCHSTABENMUSEUM

Holzmarktstr. 66 ⓤ/Ⓢ Jannowitzbrücke ☎ 0177 42 01 587, ⓦ www.buchstaben museum.de. Thurs–Sun 1–5pm. €6.50. MAP P.65, POCKET MAP J5

Buchstaben means "letter" (as in "alphabetical character"), and this unique museum – formerly located near Alexanderplatz before moving to this slightly larger location in 2013 – is dedicated solely to the preservation and protection of artisan-esque examples of lettering in the age of digitalization. Though the museum is still building its permanent collection, the assortment of old and new industrial signs is well worth navigating the slightly eccentric opening hours for. Though the museum collects lettering of any language, the ultimate goal is to honour "local colour", which museum founder Barbara Dechant feels is waning.

AQUADOM AND SEA LIFE CENTER

Spandauer Str. 3 ⓤ/Ⓢ Alexanderplatz ☎ 030 99 28 00, ⓦ www.sealifeeurope.com. Daily 10am–7pm. €17.95. MAP P.65, POCKET MAP E13

The Sea Life Center's chief claim to fame is the AquaDom – the world's largest cylindrical fish aquarium, a 25m-tall acrylic glass aquarium, with built-in transparent elevator, located right in the lobby of the adjacent *Radisson SAS* hotel. Filled with around 900,000 litres of seawater, the aquarium contains around 1500 fish, covering 56 species. The AquaDom can be visited separately, but visitors who want a broader overview of the underwater world can visit the Sea Life Center first, a succession of themed tunnels that illustrate marine life from various habitats including the Spree and the Pacific Ocean. It's insightful enough and a well laid-out exhibition, though it lacks the comprehensive scope and diversity – not to mention the manatees and sharks – of the Zoo Aquarium (see p.128).

EPHRAIM PALAIS

Poststr. 16, corner Mühlendamm
Ⓤ Klosterstr. or Ⓤ/Ⓢ Alexanderplatz ☎ 030
24 00 21 62, Ⓦ www.stadtmuseum.de. Tues &
Thurs–Sun 10am–6pm, Wed noon–8pm. €5.
MAP P.65, POCKET MAP E13

This attractive Rococo-style residential palace, located in the southern corner of Berlin's Nikolaiviertel, is a replica of a 1762 original built by Veitel Heine Ephraim, a court jeweller. His original building was torn down in 1935–36 when the Mühlendamm was widened, but a painstaking reconstruction has produced an exquisite place, with its elegantly curving, decorated facade (complete with cherubs), Tuscan columns, wrought-iron balconies and an oval staircase and ornate ceiling crafted by Schlüter. As well as special exhibitions on themes relating to the history and culture of Berlin, the "Salon Ephraim" and the Museum Laboratory offer family-friendly events and workshops.

MÄRKISCHES MUSEUM

Am Köllnischen Park 5 Ⓤ/
Ⓢ Jannowitzbrücke ☎ 030 24 00 21 62,
Ⓦ www.stadtmuseum.de. Tues & Thurs–Sun
10am–6pm, Wed noon–8pm. €5. MAP P.65,
POCKET MAP F14

The red-brick Märkisches Museum, built at the turn of the twentieth century, is the headquarters of Berlin's City Museum Foundation. The permanent exhibition "Here is Berlin" invites you to stroll through the city's streets and discover how Berlin has changed over the centuries. The museum also hosts a wide array of art-historic collections in its atmospheric rooms, with medieval sculptures, artefacts and paintings telling the story of Berlin from the first settlers

until now (German text only). Thoughtfully divided into sections of the city – Unter den Linden, Friedrichstrasse and so on – favourites include a working mechanical musical instrument that's shown off every Sunday (3pm), seven original graffitied segments of the Berlin Wall and a Kaiserpanorama: a stereoscope dating from around 1900 that produces a fascinating 3D show of images from nineteenth-century Berlin.

HANF MUSEUM

Mühlendamm 5 Ⓤ/Ⓢ Alexanderplatz or
Ⓤ Klosterstr. ☎ 030 24 24 827, Ⓦ www
.hanfmuseum.de. Tues–Fri 10am–8pm,
Sat & Sun noon–8pm. €4.50. MAP P.65,
POCKET MAP E13

The Hanf Museum is 250 square metres of space devoted exclusively to the agricultural, manufacturing, industrial and legal aspects of hemp – a plant most commonly associated with marijuana. This museum, while slightly dingy, isn't just for the stoners: the aim is to give a broader overview of this fascinating botanical treasure and its myriad applications, from textile and paper to medicine and cosmetics. Texts are in German only.

Shops

APARTMENT

Memhardstr. 8 ⓤ/Ⓢ Alexanderplatz ☎ 030 28 04 22 51. Mon–Sat noon–7pm. MAP P.65, POCKET MAP F12

You'll have to be careful not to walk right past what looks like an all-white art space: the goods lie downstairs (follow the spiral staircase), where you'll find jeans, jackets, shoes and accessories with a distinctly Berlin twist. For more retro styles, check out Cash around the corner.

BURG & SCHILD

Rosa-Luxemburg-Str. 3 ⓤ Rosa-Luxemburg-Platz ☎ 030 24 63 05 01. Mon–Fri 11am–8pm, Sat 11am–7pm. MAP P.65, POCKET MAP E12

Visit an America that's long vanished by way of brands like Stetson, Levi's, Filson and Buzz Rickson's, all on display in a store decorated with vintage motorbikes that generate an authentic odour of oil and tar.

ESTHER PERBANDT

Almstadtstr. 3 ⓤ Weinmeisterstr. ☎ 030 88 53 67 91. Mon–Fri 10am–7pm, Sat noon–6pm. MAP P.65, POCKET MAP E12

A relative veteran of the Berlin fashion scene, Esther Perbandt sells (pricey) rock and avant-garde styles with an audaciously gender-bending

slant. As well as clothing, expect bags, belts and jewellery.

FREITAG TASCHEN

Max-Beer-Str. 3 ⓤ/Ⓢ Alexanderplatz ☎ 030 24 63 69 61, ⓦ www.freitag.ch. Mon–Fri 10am–8pm, Sat 10am–6pm. MAP P.65, POCKET MAP E12

The Mitte flagship store features concrete, couches and catwalk lighting – all of which provides the perfect backdrop for Markus Freitag's creations: 1600 colourful, durable bags in every shape (tote, clutch, laptop, satchel etc) imaginable.

MYKITA

Rosa-Luxemburg-Str. 6 ⓤ/Ⓢ Alexanderplatz ☎ 030 67 30 87 15. Mon–Fri 11am–8pm, Sat 11am–6pm. MAP P.65, POCKET MAP E12

Sunglasses and spectacles with a stylish twist, sold in a hip, minimal space with large street-facing windows. Berlin-based Mykita opened in 2003, and has achieved international prominence.

TRÜFFELSCHWEIN

Rosa-Luxemburg-Str. 21 ⓤ Rosa-Luxemburg Platz ☎ 030 70 22 12 25. Mon–Sat noon–8pm. MAP P.65, POCKET MAP F11

This pleasant, airy store sells everything from sexy shoes and trendy jumpers to belts and dapper swimwear. Labels include Universal Works, Knowledge Cotton Apparel, Howlin' and Superga.

WOOD WOOD

Rochstr. 3–4 Ⓤ/Ⓢ Alexanderplatz ☎ 030 28 04 78 77, Ⓦ www.woodwood.dk. Mon–Fri noon–8pm, Sat noon–7pm. MAP P.65, POCKET MAP E12

One of the best stops in the area for all things streetwear, this long-serving Berlin branch of Copenhagen-based Wood Wood stocks an incredible sneaker collection plus contemporary fashion items.

Restaurants

LEBENSMITTEL IN MITTE

Rochstr. 2 Ⓤ Weinmeisterstr. ☎ 030 27 59 61 30. Mon–Fri noon–midnight, Sat 11am–midnight. MAP P.65, POCKET MAP E12

If you like "slow" home cooking this unassuming spot on Rochstrasse is a good choice. Specializing in German cuisine (mainly from the south), the menu features hearty soups, sausages, sauerkraut and *Spätzle* (a type of soft egg noodle), as well as a decent selection of German/Austrian wines and Bavarian beer, all served against a homely, elegant backdrop.

ZILLE STUBE

Spreeufer 3 Ⓤ Klosterstr. ☎ 030 24 25 247, Ⓦ www.zillestube-nikolaiviertel.de. Daily 11am–10pm; Heinrich Zille show Tues 3–5pm. MAP P.65, POCKET MAP E13

A great place to break up a stroll around the Nikolaiviertel, the menu here features Berlin specialities like *currywurst* and *Eisbein* (knuckle of pork), all served in cosy, timewarp surroundings. Named after the area's most famous caricaturist, Heinrich Zille, there's a two-hour show every Tuesday at 3pm that transports guests back to the artist's turn-of-the-century Berlin.

ZUR LETZTEN INSTANZ

Waisenstr. 14–16 Ⓤ Klosterstr. ☎ 030 24 25 528, Ⓦ www.zurletzteninstanz.de. Mon 6pm–1am, Tues–Sat noon–1am. MAP P.65, POCKET MAP F13

Yes it's the oldest restaurant in Berlin (the building goes right back to 1561), yes the interior is textbook Alt Berlin, and yes it's a tourist haunt, but the food here – traditional dishes like pork knuckle, dumplings and Berlin meatballs – is delicious and care is taken to source ingredients from local producers. Portions are hearty and there's Pilsner on draft to wash it all down.

Cafés and bars

DOLORES

Rosa-Luxemburg-Str. 7 Ⓢ/Ⓤ Alexanderplatz ☎ 030 28 09 95 97, Ⓦ www.dolores-online.de. Mon–Sat 11.30am–10pm, Sun 1–10pm. MAP P.65, POCKET MAP E12

Run by Germans who spent a considerable time in California, Berlin's first burrito shop is a basic but colourful spot that offers pre-prepared "classics", "make-your-own", customizable

burritos and also quesadillas, salads and soups. A good spot for a cheap, filling bite (burritos from €4.50) or takeaway.

OLIV

Münzstr. 8 ⓤ Weinmeisterstr./ Rosa-Luxemburg-Platz ☎ 030 89 20 65 40. ⓦ www.oliv-cafe.de. Mon–Fri 8.30am–7pm, Sat 9.30am–7pm, Sun 10am–6pm. MAP P.65, POCKET MAP E12

With a modern interior, great coffee and decent, unpretentious food (sandwiches, quiches, soups, cakes), *Oliv* is a pleasant spot for breakfast or lunch, and very conveniently located if you're seeking respite from boutique bashing. Cash only.

Clubs and venues

GOLDEN GATE

Dircksenstr. 77–78 ⓤ/Ⓢ Jannowitzbrücke ☎ 030 28 29 295. ⓦ www.goldengate-berlin .de. Wed from 10pm, Thurs–Sat from 11pm. MAP P.65, POCKET MAP J5

Lurking beneath the tracks near Jannowitzbrücke train station (close to the river Spree), this club consists of two wilfully shabby rooms kitted out in secondhand furniture and is dedicated to two- or three-day-long free-for-alls. The crowds here tend to be a dressed down, unpretentious lot who arrive well after midnight to try their luck with the difficult bouncers. Music policy is mostly house and techno but there are sometimes surprises.

HOUSE OF WEEKEND

Alexanderstr. 7 (15th floor and open rooftop) ⓤ/Ⓢ Alexanderplatz ☎ 030 25 89 93 66. Summer daily from 7pm; winter Thurs–Sun from 11pm. €10–12. MAP P.65, POCKET MAP F12

Accessed via a lift that shoots punters up to the top of a Communist-era tower block, this chic, spacious club has attained veteran status in the city thanks to its consistently good house and techno parties. International guests and high-profile residents play most weekends. The wonderful roof terrace – open from 7pm daily in summer – is a must.

WHAT!? CLUB

Karl-Liebknecht-Str. 11 ⓤ/Ⓢ Alexanderplatz ⓦ www.what-club.de. Fri & Sat from 11pm. Admission varies. MAP P.65, POCKET MAP E12

Hidden beneath the *McDonald's* at Alexanderplatz, the *What!?* club has a typically trashy Berlin interior, but the defiantly upbeat atmosphere and open-minded music policy make it apt for punters seeking something vaguely underground yet quietly commercial. The main room is just a black space with floor-to-ceiling mirrors and blasts of kaleidoscopic lighting, and the music is a mix of hip-hop, dancehall, darkwave and 90s pop.

Potsdamer Platz and Tiergarten

A major public transport hub and popular entertainment district, Potsdamer Platz was one of the liveliest squares in Europe during the 1920s. Reduced to rubble during the War, afterwards it became – literally – a no-man's-land, sandwiched between the different sectors. What little remained was levelled when the Berlin Wall went up in 1961. After the Wall fell, it became the largest construction site in Europe as an ambitious rebuilding programme started. Commercial, even futuristic in tone, the centrepiece today is the Sony Center, surrounded by a new U-Bahn station and a few slabs from the old Berlin Wall. Just to the west is the Kulturforum, a fine collection of cultural institutions, built in the 1960s as West Berlin's response to East Berlin's Museumsinsel, including the Gemäldegalerie, and its important collections of Old Masters. Adjacent to the Platz is Tiergarten, Berlin's oldest and most beautiful park.

SONY CENTER

Potsdamer Str. 4 ⓤ/ⓢ Potsdamer Platz ☎ 030 23 09 795, ⓦ www.sonycenter.de. Free. MAP P.74–75, POCKET MAP A15

The striking, eco-friendly, glass-and-steel Sony Center, by Helmut Jahn, opened in 2000 and cost a cool €750 million to build. The centre houses shops for everything from cosmetics and jewellery to, of course, Sony electronics, plus restaurants, a conference centre, art and film museums, cinemas, including an **IMAX**, and a **Legoland** (daily 10am–7pm; ⓦ www.legoland discoverycentre.de; €14–18.50,

SONY CENTER

THE VIEW FROM THE PANORAMAPUNKT

according to time slots). The "Forum", the semi-enclosed roofed space, is used for occasional cultural and entertainment events. There's plenty to do, although the experience is generally soulless and the shopping expensive (though there is free wi-fi).

FILM AND TELEVISION MUSEUM

Potsdamer Str. 2 Ⓤ/Ⓢ Potsdamer Platz
☎ 030 30 09 030, ⓌＷ www.deutsche
-kinemathek.de. Tues–Sun 10am–6pm, Thurs
till 8pm. €7; free Thurs 4–8pm. MAP P.74–75,
POCKET MAP A15

One of the must-sees in the Sony Center is the impressively slick **Deutsche Kinemathek** museum, which collects German cinema under one roof. This "journey through film history" explores the pioneering years, silent-film divas, films from the Weimar era, cinema under the Nazis and goes right up to contempo-rary cinema, with rooms that cover postwar German filmmakers (1946–80) and the present (from 1981). As well as a special exhibit on Germany's biggest star, Marlene Dietrich, there's memorabilia and model film sets from key directors including Fritz Lang and an exhibit that compares East and West German television

broadcasts. The museum also organizes the retrospective section of the Berlinale film festival, and hosts special film series, exhibitions and events.

KOLLHOFF TOWER

Potsdamer Platz 1 Ⓤ/Ⓢ Potsdamer Platz
☎ 030 25 93 70 80, ⓌＷ www.panoramapunkt
.de. Platform winter: daily 10am–6pm; summer:
daily 10am–8pm; last lift 30min before closing.
€6.50. MAP P.74–75, POCKET MAP A15

Located on the northern edge of Potsdamer Platz, the 25-storey (103m), dark, peat-fired brick Kollhoff Tower is named after architect Hans Kollhoff, a member of the international team of architects (headed by Renzo Piano) that designed many of the buildings for the new Platz. The ground floor houses a number of restaurants and shops, the upper floors are used for office space and – the real highlight – the **Panorama-punkt** on the top floors, offers an open-air viewing platform, reached via Europe's fastest elevator. From the top you can see the Reichstag, Brandenburg Gate, TV Tower, Sony Center, Tiergarten and Kulturforum. Admission includes entry to the viewing platform, an exhibition on the history of the area and there's also a café with an outdoor terrace.

DAIMLER CONTEMPORARY

Alte Potsdamer Str. 5, in Haus Huth
Ⓤ/Ⓢ Potsdamer Platz Ⓣ 030 25 94 14 20.
Ⓦ www.collection.daimler.com. Daily
11am–6pm. Free. MAP BELOW, POCKET MAP A15

The Daimler art collection
was set up in 1977 as a space
for twentieth-century art,
initially mainly focused on
German artists. The museum
expanded in the 1990s with
works by other European and
American artists, including
Andy Warhol and Jeff Koons,
and moved into the elaborately
renovated Haus Huth in 1999.
The collection includes
approximately 1800 works by
international artists,
showcased in rotating
exhibitions across this
attractive 600-square-metre
space, which used to be a
restaurant and storage area.
Much of the collection is
modernist in nature –
geometric, challenging and
abstract – so not one for
traditionalists. As well as
exhibiting its own collection,
the gallery regularly puts
on temporary exhibitions.

GEMÄLDEGALERIE

Matthäikirchplatz 4/6 Ⓤ/Ⓢ Potsdamer Platz
Ⓣ 030 26 62 951, Ⓦ www.smb.museum/gg.
Sat & Sun 10am–6pm. €10. MAP BELOW,
POCKET MAP E6

With a history that goes back
to 1830, the Gemäldegalerie
holds one of the world's most
renowned collections of
classical European painting.
Created from the treasures of
the Prussian royalty – including
that of Frederick the Great
– the collection used to be part
of Museum Island (see p.46).
The museum – and some of the
works – were damaged by
Allied bombing during World
War II, and the artworks were

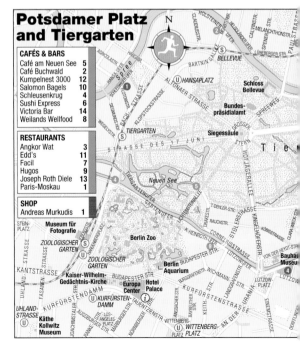

Potsdamer Platz and Tiergarten

CAFÉS & BARS
Café am Neuen See 5
Café Buchwald 2
Kumpelnest 3000 12
Salomon Bagels 10
Schleusenkrug 4
Sushi Express 6
Victoria Bar 14
Weilands Wellfood 8

RESTAURANTS
Angkor Wat 3
Edd's 11
Facil 7
Hugos 9
Joseph Roth Diele 13
Paris-Moskau 1

SHOP
Andreas Murkudis 1

then split between East and West during the Cold War. After the Wall fell the collection came together again here. Spread across 72 rooms, divided up by country, with sections on Italian, Flemish and Dutch works, the treasures include many highpoints of European art by including works by Bruegel, a particularly good selection by Cranach (pictured), Dürer, Raphael, Rubens, Vermeer and many others. The Rembrandt room and Caravaggio's exquisite Cupid, *Love Conquers All*, are both worth seeking out.

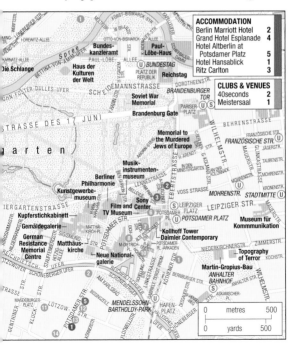

ACCOMMODATION	
Berlin Marriott Hotel	2
Grand Hotel Esplanade	4
Hotel Altberlin at Potsdamer Platz	5
Hotel Hansablick	1
Ritz Carlton	3

CLUBS & VENUES	
40seconds	2
Meistersaal	1

KUNSTGEWERBEMUSEUM

Matthäikirchplatz Ⓤ/Ⓢ Potsdamer Platz
☎ 030 26 64 24 242, Ⓦ www.smb.museum
/kgm. €8. MAP P.74–75, POCKET MAP E6

Following a major renovation, Berlin's Museum of Decorative Arts – one of the oldest in Germany – reopened in 2014 and provides a systematic overview of the key achievements in European design. Over 7000 square metres of white-walled space, the museum covers all major styles and periods, including jaw-dropping silks, tapestries, Renaissance bronzes, contemporary furniture, Rococo glassware, faïence work, porcelain, gold and silver. Newer areas include a Fashion Gallery – which houses around 130 costumes and accessories representing 150 years of fashion history – plus the departments of Design (think Bauhaus classics mixed with contemporary designers like Philippe Starck and Konstantin Grcic), Jugendstil and Art Deco. A second collection can be found at **Schloss Köpenick** (Schlossinsel 1 Ⓢ Köpenick; April–Sept Tues–Sun 11am–6pm; Oct–March Thurs–Sun 11am–5pm; €6), a Baroque palace located in a picturesque setting on an island in the river Dahme. Exhibited here are over five hundred items from the sixteenth to eighteenth centuries, as well as Renaissance, Baroque and Rococo furniture and interior decorations.

KUPFERSTICHKABINETT

Matthäikirchplatz Ⓤ/Ⓢ Potsdamer Platz
☎ 030 26 64 24 242, Ⓦ www.smb.museum
/kk. Tues–Fri 10am–6pm, Sat & Sun
11am–6pm; study room Tues–Fri 9am–4pm.
€6. MAP P.74–75, POCKET MAP E6

The Kupferstichkabinett, or "print room", is the largest collection of graphic art in

BERLINER PHILHARMONIE

Germany, and one of the four most important museums of its kind in the world. The museum houses over 500,000 prints and 110,000 drawings, watercolours, pastels and oil sketches from European artists from the Middle Ages to the present, all on paper. Major artists such as Sandro Botticelli, Albrecht Dürer, Rembrandt, Adolph von Menzel, Pablo Picasso and Andy Warhol are represented. Due to the size and sensitivity of the collection (being largely on paper), there's no permanent display – visitors must check for special exhibitions, or request to see specific art works via the study room.

BERLINER PHILHARMONIE

Herbert-von-Karajan-Str. 1 Ⓤ/Ⓢ Potsdamer
Platz ☎ 030 25 48 80, Ⓦ www.berliner
-philharmoniker.de. MAP P.74–75, POCKET MAP E6

Built by architect Hans Scharoun between 1960 and 1963, the Berliner Philharmonie is one of the most important concert halls in Berlin and home to the world-renowned Berlin Philharmonic. The asymmetrical, tent-like building has an equally distinctive pentagon-shaped concert hall (plus a smaller hall, Kammermusiksaal, which seats 1180) that enables great views from all sides. Guided tours of both the Philharmonic Hall and the Chamber Music Hall are offered daily from 1pm (☎030 25 48 81 34; €5/€3).

MUSIKINSTRUMENTEN-MUSEUM

Tiergartenstr. 1 (visitors' entrance Ben-Gurion-Str.) ⓤ/Ⓢ Potsdamer Platz ☎030 25 48 81 56, ⓦ www.mim-berlin.de. Tues, Wed & Fri 9am–5pm, Thurs 9am–8pm, Sat & Sun 10am–5pm. €6 including audioguide; guided tours Sat (11am) & Thurs (6pm) €3 extra. MAP P.74–75, POCKET MAP E6

The Musikinstrumenten-Museum embraces Germany's glorious musical history, with over three thousand instruments from the sixteenth to the twenty-first centuries, making it one of the country's largest collections. Many are on permanent display here, including a rare Stradivarius violin, Frederick the Great's flutes, a glass harmonica invented by Benjamin Franklin and – the flamboyant centrepiece – a massive Mighty Wurlitzer theatre organ once owned by the Siemens family, which is demonstrated every Saturday at noon. The museum also veers into electronic music with electric guitars, mixing stations and other experimental instruments, including the Mixtur-Trautonium on which composer Oskar Sala created sound effects for Hitchcock's film *The Birds*.

NEUE NATIONALGALERIE

Potsdamer Str. 50 ⓤ/Ⓢ Potsdamer Platz ☎030 26 64 23 040, ⓦ www.smb.museum /nng. Tues, Wed, & Fri 10am–6pm, Thurs 10am–8pm, Sat & Sun 11am–6pm. €10. MAP P.74–75, POCKET MAP E6

The "temple of light and glass" (as it modestly known) and its sculpture gardens were famously designed by Bauhaus affiliate Ludwig Mies van der Rohe. Opened in 1968, the museum

houses an extensive collection of twentieth-century European paintings and sculptures from the nineteenth century to the 1960s, including household names like Bacon, Picasso, Klee, Dix and plenty of German art (E.L. Kirchner, Beckmann). The museum displays portions of its permanent collection on a rotating basis, so each visit is different, and a number of special exhibitions also occur throughout the year, during which the permanent collection may not be on view. There's also a café on the ground floor (10.30am–5.45pm). Note, however, that the museum closed at the end of 2014 for refurbishments, with no reopening date specified.

MUSEUM FÜR KOMMUNIKATION

Leipziger Str. 16 ⓤ Stadtmitte ☎030 20 29 40, ⓦ www.mfk-berlin.de. Tues 9am–8pm, Wed–Fri 9am–5pm, Sat & Sun 10am–6pm. €4. MAP P.74–75, POCKET MAP C15

Founded in 1872 as the first postal museum of the world, the Museum for Communication experienced a rebirth in 2000, as evidenced by the blue neon writing on the neo-Baroque facade and three robots in the lobby. The permanent exhibition showcases the origins, development and future perspectives of the "information society", while the computer gallery on the second floor extends the exhibition into virtual space. Highlights of the permanent exhibition are wax seals, postcards and stamps (such as the famous Blue Mauritius), telephones (including some of the first), radios, film, telegraphs and computers. The museum's interactive and lively approach makes it an ideal destination for kids, but adults will appreciate the temporary exhibitions featuring cutting-edge artists.

THE GERMAN RESISTANCE MEMORIAL CENTRE

Stauffenbergstr. 13–14 (entrance through the commemorative courtyard)
ⓤ Mendelssohn-Bartholdy-Park ☎ 030 26 99 50 00, ⊛ www.gdw-berlin.de. Mon–Wed & Fri 9am–6pm, Thurs 9am–8pm, Sat & Sun 10am–6pm. Free. MAP P.74–75, POCKET MAP D6

Located in an historic section of the former headquarters of the Nazi army high command, the site of the assassination attempt on Adolf Hitler on July 20, 1944, the **Gedenkstätte Deutscher Widerstand** (German Resistance Memorial Centre) documents the action taken against the Nazis between 1933 and 1945. The permanent exhibition has over five thousand photographs and documents spread across eighteen topics that go beyond Nazi dissent to address the wider context of resistance, including the role of Christian beliefs in protest, opposition by young people specifically and general defiance of wartime environments in daily life. The memorial courtyard, meanwhile, is dedicated to the conspiring German army officers who were killed after the assassination attempt. The

exhibition is mostly in German but English audioguides (and related books) are available from reception.

BAUHAUS MUSEUM

Klingelhöferstr. 14 ⓤ Nollendorfplatz
☎ 030 25 40 020, ⊛ www.bauhaus.de. Daily except Tues 10am–5pm. Mon, Sat & Sun €8, Wed–Fri €7 (includes audio tour). MAP P.74–75, POCKET MAP D6

Germany's Bauhaus ("building house") design school may have only lasted from 1919 to 1933 but it went on to became one of the twentieth century's most influential movements – more famous outside the country than Goethe or Schiller. Founded by Walter Gropius, the movement explored the links between fine art and craftsmanship and – a bit later – art and mass production. The Bauhaus Archive and Museum, housed in a distinctive building designed by Gropius himself, is the best place to explore the breadth and depth of Bauhaus's expansive activities. Here are tubular steel furniture from Marcel Breuer, armchairs and desks from Mies van der Rohe, paintings from Itten, Schlemmer, Feininger, Albers and Klee… even dapper wallpaper and beautiful chess sets. The archive next door holds the largest Bauhaus resource in the world, while the museum shop stocks an impressive range of high-quality reproductions, and there's an adjoining café.

HAUS DER KULTUREN DER WELT

John-Foster-Dulles-Allee 10 ⓤ/ⓢ Bundestag
☎ 030 39 78 71 75, ⓦ www.hkw.de. Daily
10am–7pm. Exhibitions: Daily except Tues
11am–7pm; free entry Mon, varies at other
times. MAP P.74–75, POCKET MAP E5

Known as the "pregnant oyster" because of its distinctively curvaceous facade, the House of World Cultures hosts exhibitions with a focus on artistic and cultural movements in contemporary global societies. Formerly known as the Kongresshalle conference hall, the building, designed in 1957 by US architect Hugh Stubbins Jr, was a gift from the United States (John F. Kennedy spoke here during his 1963 visit to West Berlin). In 1980 the roof collapsed, injuring many people (and killing one) and

was rebuilt in its original style in 1987. The building's maze of rooms include an exhibition hall, auditorium for concerts and theatre and a congress hall, and it is an ideal location for the colourful variety of events held here throughout the year. The eclectic and globally minded spread of events range from educational programmes to exhibitions, music, performing arts, literature festivals and more. Note that the venue is closed from June 2016 to January 2017 for renovations.

THE TIERGARTEN

MAP P.74–75, POCKET MAP D5

Full of paths, forested areas, lakes and meadows, the luscious and vast Tiergarten park – bisected by Strasse. des 17 Juni – began its life as the preferred hunting ground for the electors of Brandenburg. Designed in its current form in 1830 by landscape architect Peter Joseph Lenne, it is now one of the most relaxing spots in Berlin, and is dotted with a couple of interesting attractions, with the Siegessäule (see p.80) its focal point.

THE SIEGESSÄULE

SIEGESSÄULE

Grosser Stern 1 ⓤ Hansaplatz. April–Oct Mon–Fri 9.30am–6.30pm, Sat & Sun 9.30am–7pm; Nov–March Mon–Fri 10am–5pm, Sat & Sun 10am–5.30pm. €3. MAP P.74–75, POCKET MAP D5

You can't miss the huge victory column at the centre of the "Grosser Stern" (great star) roundabout in the Tiergarten. The cocksure monument is otherwise known as the tricky to pronounce Siegessäule, built from 1864 to 1873 after a design by Johann Heinrich Stack to commemorate the Prussian victory in the Prusso-Danish war of 1864. It's 69m (25ft) tall, weighs 35 tons and features a *Goddess of Victory* on top, added later after further Prussian victories in wars against Austria and France. At the base you can see bas-reliefs of battles and at the top there's an observatory, which gives great views of the Reichstag, the Brandenburg Gate and the Fernsehturm, but you have to climb the 285 steps to access it. There's also a small café, souvenir shop and small exhibition connecting the column with the events in German history that it represents.

SCHLOSS BELLEVUE

Spreeweg 1 ⓤ Hansaplatz. Closed to the public. MAP P.74–75, POCKET MAP D5

Situated on an area of 20 hectares (about 50 acres) beside the river Spree, Schloss Bellevue was built for Prince August Ferdinand of Prussia, the younger brother of Frederick II of Prussia. The sparkling white home was designed by architect Philipp Daniel Boumann and has the distinction of being the first Neoclassical building constructed in Germany. It was uninhabited in the nineteenth century and used by various institutions such as a museum of ethnography in the 1930s. In 1938, the building was converted into a guesthouse of the government and the entrance to the palace was redesigned. Severely damaged in World War II, it was renovated during 1954–59 and set up as the official residence of the federal president in Berlin. The main sights include a ballroom designed by Carl Gotthard Langhans, the huge lawn behind the palace and the modern building to the south – known as the "presidential egg" due to its oval shape. The palace is currently closed to visitors.

JOSEPH ROTH DIELE

Shop

ANDREAS MURKUDIS

Potsdamer Str. 81E ⓤ Kurfürstenstr. ☎ 030 68 07 98 306, Ⓦ www.andreasmurkudis.com. Mon–Sat 10am–8pm. MAP P.74–75, POCKET MAP E7

Set in the former *Tagesspiegel* newspaper building, this vast, white, bright space designed by lead architects Gonzales Haase is almost all used to highlight the high end (and sometimes pointedly eccentric) products selected by Andreas Murkudis, the brother of fashion designer Kostas Murkudis. The latter's designs are here, as are Valextra briefcases and quality brands like Pringle and Céline.

Restaurants

ANGKOR WAT

Paulstr. 22 ⓤ/Ⓢ Hauptbahnhof ☎ 030 39 33 922, Ⓦ www.angkorwatrestaurant.de. Tues–Fri 6–11pm, Sat & Sun noon–11pm. MAP P.74–75, POCKET MAP D4

This cavernous restaurant serves a mean Cambodian fondue. The friendly service makes up for the exotic decor, and if you don't like frying your own meat, the menu extends to other Cambodian classics with plenty of spices and creamy coconut.

EDD'S

Lützowstr. 81 ⓤ Kurfürstenstr. ☎ 030 215 52 94, Ⓦ www.edds-thairestaurant.de. Mon–Fri 11.30am–3pm & 6pm–midnight, Sat 5pm–midnight, Sun 2pm–midnight. MAP P.74–75, POCKET MAP E7

Edd and his wife present well-balanced, spicy Thai food (the banana blossom salad is a signature dish) in an elegant – largely wood – space free of kitsch. It's expensive for Thai food (€15.50–25 mains) but popular, so make a reservation.

FACIL

The Mandala Hotel, Potsdamer Str. 3 ⓤ/Ⓢ Potsdamer Platz ☎ 030 59 005 ext. 1234, Ⓦ www.facil.de. Mon–Fri noon–3pm & 7–11pm, closed Sat & Sun. MAP P.74–75, POCKET MAP A15

Michael Kempf's restaurant in *The Mandala Hotel* not only offers amazing food but also splendid views from its fifth-floor dining room, surrounded by a lush bamboo garden. Popular with business types, politicos and serious foodies, Kempf's Michelin-starred, fish-heavy menu has become justly famous. Evening mains range from €26 to €68; try a lunch for something slightly cheaper (€19–45 per course; reservations required).

HUGOS

Hotel InterContinental, Budapester Str. 2 ⓤ Zoologischer Garten ☎ 030 26 02 12 63, Ⓦ www.hugos-restaurant.de. Tues–Sat 6.30–10.30pm, closed mid-July to mid-Aug. MAP P.74–75, POCKET MAP C6

In a gorgeously appointed room at the top of the *Hotel InterContinental*, superstar chef Thomas Kammeier creates Michelin-starred "New German–Mediterranean" food that you can sample – for a price – while enjoying the restaurant's panoramic views (menus €98–142).

JOSEPH ROTH DIELE

Potsdamer Str. 75 ⓤ Kurfürstenstr. ☎ 030 26 36 98 84, Ⓦ www.joseph-roth-diele.de. Mon–Fri 10am–midnight. MAP P.74–75, POCKET MAP E7

A splash of charm and colour on nondescript Potsdamer Strasse, this quirky restaurant pays homage to inter-war Jewish writer Joseph Roth. The daily specials are very reasonable (€4.95–9.95), though the food is far from high end. Popular with a wide range of people at lunchtimes.

PARIS-MOSKAU

Alt-Moabit 141 ⓤ/Ⓢ Hauptbahnhof ☎ 030
39 42 081, ⓦ www.paris-moskau.de. Daily
from 6pm. MAP P.74-75, POCKET MAP E4

This curious mix of old Berlin
and contemporary elegance is
set in a nineteenth-century rail
signalman's house (it's named
after the Paris-Moscow line)
and serves hearty dishes like
deer and rabbit, fish dishes
and vegetarian lasagne with
beetroot and chestnuts
(€39–65). It's all backed up by
a fine wine list and a great
summer garden with views of
the government quarter.

Cafés and bars

CAFÉ AM NEUEN SEE

Lichtensteinallee 2 ⓤ Zoologischer Garten
☎ 30 25 44 930, ⓦ www.cafeamneuensee.de.
Daily 9am-midnight. MAP P.74-75, POCKET MAP C6

A fine stop off on any tour of
the Tiergarten, this old-school
beer garden with modern
restaurant offers great coffee and
draught beers, and a menu
including pizza and pasta dishes
(€10). It's beautifully set on the
Neuen See lake, and there are
even rowing boats for rent.

CAFÉ BUCHWALD

CAFÉ BUCHWALD

Bartningallee 29 ⓤ Hansaplatz ☎ 030 39 15
931, ⓦ www.konditorei-buchwald.de. Daily
9am-6pm. MAP P.74-75, POCKET MAP C4

A short stroll down a pleasant
path from Schloss Bellevue, *Café
Buchwald* has been standing
here for over 160 years. Not just
standing but selling some of the
best cakes in town – former
suppliers to the court they still
make such delicious confections
as home-made *Baumkuchen*.
There are a few seats in the
charming little front garden.

KUMPELNEST 3000

Lützowstr. 23 ⓤ Kurfürstenstr. ☎ 030 26 16
918, ⓦ www.kumpelnest3000.com. Mon–Thurs
& Sun 7pm–5am, Fri & Sat 7pm–late. MAP
P.74-75, POCKET MAP E7

Hard to believe that this
charming den of iniquity is
only a few minutes' stroll from
Potsdamer Platz. With its
deliberately tacky decor, loyal
mixed/gay crowd and anything
goes atmosphere, especially at
weekends, it's a good place if
you're in the area and looking
for the lure of the mirrored
discoball rather than the
commercial glare of the Platz.

SALOMON BAGELS

Alte Potsdamer Str. 7, inside Potsdamer
Platz Arkaden ⓤ/Ⓢ Potsdamer Platz ☎ 030
25 29 76 26, ⓦ www.salomon-bagels.de.
Mon–Sat 9am–10pm. MAP P.74-75, POCKET MAP
A15

Bagels, bagels, bagels. And
sandwiches. And excellent
cakes, like their New York-style
cheesecake. Located in a mall,
this shop does takeaways, but
there are sofas too – a good
spot for a cheap snack (€6–13).

SCHLEUSENKRUG

Müller-Breslau-Str. corner Unterschleuse
ⓤ/Ⓢ Zoologischer Garten ☎ 030 31 39 909,
ⓦ www.schleusenkrug.de, Daily: summer
10am–midnight; winter 11am–6pm.

A classic Berlin beer garden, *Schleusenkrug* is a fine place to tuck into a glass of beer and an organic *Wurst*, enjoy a coffee while watching the boats cruise down the canal, or lap up the live music they have from time to time in the summer.

SUSHI EXPRESS

Potsdamer Platz 2 ⓤ/Ⓢ Potsdamer Platz ☎ 030 26 55 80 55, Ⓦ www.sushi-expressberlin.de. Mon–Fri 10.30am–8pm, Sat & Sun noon–8pm. MAP P.74–75, POCKET MAP A15

It's a bit of a hassle to find, but *Sushi Express* – located in the Sony Center courtyard in a passage to the S-Bahn – offers a decent range of conveyor-belt sushi, especially when half-price offers are on (daily 11.30am–9pm). Hot dishes and lunchboxes also available, though it's usually packed at lunchtimes. Main courses €5.

VICTORIA BAR

Potsdamer Str. 102 ⓤ Kurfürstenstr. ☎ 030 25 75 99 77, Ⓦ www.victoriabar.de. Mon–Thurs & Sun 6.30pm–3am, Fri & Sat 6.30pm–4am. MAP P.74–75, POCKET MAP E7

This much-loved cocktail bar is great for a low-key and decently mixed drink in the week or a livelier atmosphere at weekends. The long bar, subdued lighting and discreet but upbeat music create a decent buzz.

WEILANDS WELLFOOD

Marlene-Dietrich-Platz 1 ⓤ/Ⓢ Potsdamer Platz ☎ 030 25 89 97 17, Ⓦ weilands-wellfood.de. Mon–Fri 10.30am–8pm, Sat & Sun noon–8pm. MAP P.74–75, POCKET MAP A15

Right by a pond near bustling Potsdamer Platz, this health-conscious, fast-food style store sells food low in calories and high in vitamins: couscous, salads, curries and sandwiches stacked with fresh ingredients. Popular with local workers at lunchtimes.

BOATS BY CAFÉ AM NEUEN SEE

Clubs and venues

40SECONDS

Potsdamer Str. 58 ⓤ/Ⓢ Potsdamer Platz ☎ 030 89 06 420, Ⓦ www.40seconds.de. Fri & Sat 11pm–late. €10. MAP P.74–75, POCKET MAP E6

Named after the amount of time it takes for the elevator to whisk you up to the top floor, this part futurist, part 1980s throwback bar gives great views over Potsdamer Platz. There are three lounge areas, lit by Verner Panton lamps, and balconies for summer. The music is standard R'n'B, house and electronic, and the mood is glamorous.

MEISTERSAAL

Köthener Str. 38 ⓤ/Ⓢ Potsdamer Platz ☎ 030 32 59 99 710, Ⓦ www.meistersaal-berlin.de. MAP P.74–75, POCKET MAP F6

This one hundred-year-old music venue and recording studios has drawn major artists from Kurt Tucholsky and David Bowie to U2 and Herbert Grönemeyer. Built in 1913 in what was once Berlin's music quarter, the building fell into disrepair after World War II. Since then, though, the Meistersaal has become Berlin's version of London's Abbey Road, world-renowned for its excellent acoustics.

Prenzlauer Berg and Wedding

Built in the nineteenth century as a working-class district, Prenzlauer Berg was neglected by the GDR after World War II, becoming a crumbling ghetto for intellectuals, punks and bohemians. Following merciless post-Wall gentrification, wealthy creative types and middle-class families have gravitated here, drawn by the area's handsome, cobbled streets, leafy squares like Helmholtzplatz and Kollwitzplatz, and its distinctive Alt Berlin atmosphere, with lots of independent bars and cafés, Kastanienallee's boutiques and the buzzy Sunday flea market at Mauerpark. While Prenzlauer Berg's nightlife has been reduced to a few late-night bars, just over the famous Bösebrücke – where the Bornholmer Strasse border crossing was first officially breached in November 1989 – lies the former Western district of Wedding. Known for its large immigrant population and edgy charm, this up-and-coming borough is peppered with the kind of underground spaces that were once common in Prenzlauer Berg during the 1990s.

GEDENKSTÄTTE BERLINER MAUER

Bernauer Str. 111–119 ⊕ Bernauer Str./ ⓢ Nordbahnhof ☎ 030 46 79 86 666. ⓦ www.berliner-mauer-gedenkstaette.de. Open-air exhibition and memorial grounds daily 8am–10pm; visitor centre Tues–Sun 10am–6pm. Free. MAP P.86–87, POCKET MAP G2

Based slightly away from the tourist centre, so avoiding the crowds that throng Checkpoint Charlie, the Berlin Wall Memorial takes a more academic look at Germany's division. A section of the former border strip is

STALL AT MAUERPARK FLEA MARKET

the focus for the **memorial**, while an outdoor exhibition on the former death-strip shows the history of Bernauer Strasse and the Wall itself. Stretching 1.4km up to the Mauerpark, it includes traces of border obstacles that retain the appearance of the Wall as it would have been at the time.

The **museum** opposite, expanded in 2014, now hosts a permanent exhibition ("1961–1989: the Berlin Wall"), which documents the lives of those attempting to escape the dictatorship (the most successful escape tunnels were dug near here) and the resistance efforts – sometimes fatal – organized by those living nearby. There's also a separate exhibition on the division of the U-Bahn and S-Bahn lines displayed in the adjacent **Nordbahnhof** station (open during station opening hours). Prayer services for the victims of the Berlin Wall are held in the **chapel** on weekdays at noon.

MAUERPARK FLOHMARKT

Bernauer Str. 63–64 Ⓤ Bernauer Str. ☏ 030 29 77 24 86, Ⓦ www.mauerparkmarkt .de. Sun 9am–6pm. Free. MAP P.86–87, POCKET MAP H2

One of Berlin's best loved flea markets, Mauerpark is a city institution, popular every Sunday with hungover students, bargain hunters, families and shade-wearing clubbers who come to scan the international food stalls, clothes shops and nostalgic bric-a-brac that seems to extend forever. You can find everything here from bike parts, 1950s cutlery sets and faded jigsaws to new and vintage clothes, GDR memorabilia, record players and lots of vinyl and CDs. As with most flea markets, there's a decent amount of what might uncharitably be called "junk" but also some genuine antiques. Adjacent to the market you'll find the actual **Mauerpark**, a strip of landscaped green that was once the site of a stretch of Berlin Wall and the associated death-strip, loomed over by the Friedrich-Ludwig-Jahn-Sportpark and the Max-Schmeling-Halle. When the weather's warm check out the weekly karaoke session in the "bearpit", which attracts massive crowds from 2.30/3pm.

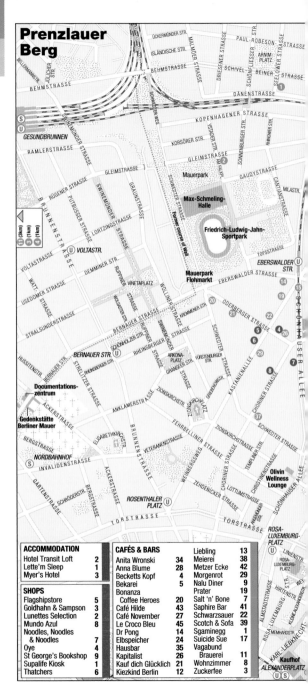

Prenzlauer Berg

ACCOMMODATION	
Hotel Transit Loft	2
Lette'm Sleep	1
Myer's Hotel	3

SHOPS	
Flagshipstore	5
Goldhahn & Sampson	3
Lunettes Selection	9
Mundo Azul	8
Noodles, Noodles & Noodles	7
Oye	4
St George's Bookshop	1
Supalife Kiosk	1
Thatchers	6

CAFÉS & BARS			
Anita Wronski	34	Liebling	13
Anna Blume	28	Meierei	38
Becketts Kopf	4	Metzer Ecke	42
Bekarei	5	Morgenrot	29
Bonanza Coffee Heroes	20	Nalu Diner	9
Café Hilde	43	Prater	19
Café November	27	Salt 'n' Bone	7
Le Croco Bleu	45	Saphire Bar	41
Dr Pong	14	Schwarzsauer	22
Elbspeicher	24	Scotch & Sofa	39
Hausbar	35	Sgaminegg	1
Kapitalist	26	Suicide Sue	17
Kauf dich Glücklich	21	Vagabund Brauerei	11
Kiezkind Berlin	12	Wohnzimmer	8
		Zuckerfee	3

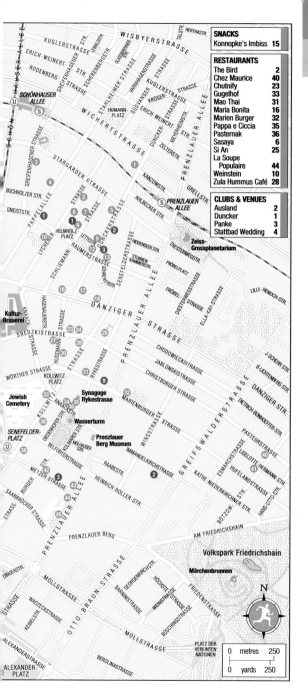

SNACKS
Konnopke's Imbiss **15**

RESTAURANTS
The Bird	**2**
Chez Maurice	**40**
Chutnify	**23**
Gugelhof	**33**
Mao Thai	**31**
Maria Bonita	**16**
Marien Burger	**32**
Pappa e Ciccia	**35**
Pasternak	**36**
Sasaya	**6**
Si An	**25**
La Soupe Populaire	**44**
Weinstein	**10**
Zula Hummus Café	**28**

CLUBS & VENUES
Ausland	**2**
Duncker	**1**
Panke	**3**
Stattbad Wedding	**4**

KOLLWITZPLATZ

Kollwitzplatz ⓤ Eberswalder Str./
Senefelderplatz. MAP P.86–87, POCKET MAP J2

Kollwitzplatz is one of
Prenzlauer Berg's best-known
and most attractive squares. It
was named after artist Käthe
Kollwitz (1867–1945), who
lived in the area at the turn of
the twentieth century (a simple
plaque commemorates her
former home on Kollwitzstr.)
and whose squat, serious-
looking **sculpture** is one of the
main features of the square.
From the appearance of the
lavishly restored facades it is
hard to tell that Kollwitzplatz
was once one of Berlin's poorest
areas, but Kollwitz's work
(see p.132) reveals the area to
have once been home to the
city's more impoverished and
downtrodden citizens. This
was one of the first areas to be
gentrified when the Wall fell
in 1989 and today symbolizes
Prenzlauer Berg's yuppie status
as well as its bias towards
families (some call this part of
the city Pramzlauerberg). It's
a lovely place to come for a
stroll – three **playgrounds** and
a leafy **park** lie within the
square and endless restaurants,
cafés and smart boutiques are
scattered around its perimeter.
Saturdays are especially
popular thanks to the extensive
farmers' market, offering
everything from organic meat
and fish, fruit and veg, sweets
and coffee and clothes. A
smaller (and less crowded)
organic market also takes place
on Thursdays. In summer
especially the fun carries on till
late at night.

JEWISH CEMETERY

Schönhauser Allee 23–25 ⓤ Senefelderplatz.
Mon–Thurs 8am–4pm, Fri 7.30am–1pm.
☏ 030 44 19 824. Free. MAP P.86–87,
POCKET MAP J2

A short hop from the
Senefelderplatz U-Bahn,
Prenzlauer Berg's small but
charming Jewish Cemetery
(Jüdischer Friedhof) was built
to cater for the overspill from
the one on Mitte's Grosse
Hamburger Strasse. It was
mostly used between 1827
and 1880, at a time when the
Jewish population in this area
was thriving, and holds
approximately 22,000 graves
and almost a thousand
hereditary family plots,
including the graves of painter
Max Liebermann, the
publisher Leopold Ullstein, the
composer Giacomo Meyerbeer
and German-Jewish banker
Joseph Mendelssohn (son of
the influential philosopher
Moses Mendelssohn). Sadly
many gravestones, the original
cemetery entrance and
mourning chapel were

destroyed during World War II and subsequent anti-Semitic vandalism – and many graves are still in a dilapidated state, some riddled with bullet holes. The cemetery was rebuilt in the 1960s, and the adjacent lapidarium – on the site of the former mourning hall – was opened in 2004 as a place to preserve and protect sixty of the most valuable stones, as well as to display panels on Jewish culture and Jewish mourning rituals. Note that men are obliged to cover their heads to visit the cemetery: hats can be borrowed from the lapidarium but visitors are urged to bring their own.

SYNAGOGE RYKESTRASSE

Rykestr. 53 Ⓤ Senefelderstr. ☎ 030 88 02 80, Ⓦ www.synagoge-rykestrasse.de. Open for services only. Fri 6pm (winter), 7pm (summer) & Sat 9.30am. MAP P.86–87, POCKET MAP J2

Built by Johann Hoeniger at the turn of the twentieth century, this gorgeous Neoclassical synagogue (inaugurated in 1904) is one of Germany's largest – and one of Berlin's loveliest. The building survived *Kristallnacht* in 1938 as it was located between "Aryan" apartment buildings, although precious Torah scrolls were damaged and rabbis and congregation members were deported to Sachsenhausen (see p.144). The synagogue was also used as stables during the war, but was finally restored to its former glory by architects Ruth Golan and Kay Zareh in 2007, who used black-and-white photographs and a €6-million budget to lavishly recreate the remarkable original. Outside of service times, the synagogue can only be visited via prior arrangement.

THE WASSERTURM

Corner of Knaackstr. & Rykestr. Ⓤ Eberswalder Str./Senefelderplatz. MAP P.86–87, POCKET MAP J2

Designed by Henry Gill, constructed by the English Waterworks Company and finished in 1877, the 30m-high cylindrical brick water tower, known as "Dicker Hermann", has become one of Prenzlauer Berg's unofficial symbols. Among the oldest of its kind in the city, it was one of the first places to provide running water in the country, and remained in use until the 1950s. Its engine house was used as an unofficial prison by the SA in 1933–45 – 28 bodies were later found in the underground pipe network, and a commemorative plaque stands outside on Knaackstrasse. During GDR times the tower was used to store canned fish, which could apparently be smelled across the whole neighbourhood. The building was then abandoned and became a "playground" for local kids. Today the refurbished tower is home to much-coveted cake-wedge shaped apartments (formerly belonging to the tower's operators), while the underground reservoir space hosts sporadic cultural events.

OLIVIN WELLNESS LOUNGE

Schönhauser Allee 177 Ⓤ Senefelderplatz ☎ 030 44 04 25 00, Ⓦ www.olivin-berlin.com. Daily: autumn/winter noon–midnight; summer 5pm–midnight. MAP P.86–87, POCKET MAP J3

With its exposed brick walls, saunas and an excellent bamboo garden, this Finnish sauna is a great way to unwind whatever the season. Special offers are available in winter and massages start at a very reasonable €48 an hour. No access to men on Thursdays. Cash only.

KULTURBRAUEREI

Schönhauser Allee 36 (entrance on Sredzkistr.) ⓤ Eberswalder Str. or trams #20, #50, #53. ☎ 030 24 70 50, ⓦ www .kulturbrauerei-berlin.de. Mon–Sat 9am–7pm. Free for main complex, price varies for specific venues. MAP P.86–87, POCKET MAP J2

This lovely, sprawling, red-and-yellow brick complex dates to 1842, when it was a small brewery and pub. It was expanded to its current size by famous brewer Schultheiss, who took it over in 1853. Since the late 1990s, it's been one of Prenzlauer Berg's major commercial hubs, with offices, bars, restaurants, clubs and an eight-theatre cinema (Kino in der KulturBrauerei; ☎ 018 05 11 88 11, ⓦ www .cinestar.de). It is, however, a fairly soulless place, out of synch with Prenzlauer Berg's more independent cultural scene – although the Scandinavian Christmas Market is worth a visit, as is the **Museum in der KulturBrauerei** (Knaackstr. 97; ☎ 030 46 77 77 911; free) – opened 2013 – whose permanent exhibition, "Everyday Life in the GDR", documents East German cultural history. The Kesselhaus concert hall hosts some decent indie rock and pop shows. You can also pick up guided cycle tours (March–Nov; ☎ 030 43 73 99 99, ⓦ www.berlinonbike.de).

MUSEUM PANKOW

Prenzlauer Allee 227–228 ⓢ Senefelderplatz. Mon–Fri 9am–7pm; Sat & Sun 10am–6pm. ☎ 030 90 29 53 917. Free. MAP P.86–87, POCKET MAP J3

Spread across the first floor of a former school, this small but lively museum documents the history of the district and its working-class inhabitants from the nineteenth century to today. The permanent exhibition consists mainly of photos and text (German only) displayed along corridors, though a couple of large rooms and a separate building across the courtyard occasionally host more modern, multimedia exhibitions on themes such as the evolution of lesbian, gay and transgender life in the area.

ZEISS-GROSSPLANETARIUM

Prenzlauer Allee 80 ⓢ Prenzlauer Allee. ☎ 030 42 18 450. For opening hours and prices see ⓦ www.sdtb.de. MAP P.86–87, POCKET MAP K1

A massive building set back from bustling Prenzlauer Allee, the Zeiss Planetarium was built in 1987. At the time, it was one of Europe's largest and most modern stellar theatres, with a giant, golf-ball-esque silver dome measuring 23m across. Reopened in early 2016, its auditorium still contains a digital projection of earth's starry skies into the roof, but the program of astronomical, science, film and music events are more cutting edge, as well as entertaining and educational. Many of the new shows are multi-lingual too (English, Spanish, Russian), and the planetarium often opens later on Friday and Saturday evenings for special events.

KULTURBRAUEREI

Shops

FLAGSHIPSTORE

Oderberger Str. 53 Ⓤ Eberswalder Str.
☎ 030 43 73 53 27, ⓦ www.flagshipstore
-berlin.de, Mon–Sat noon–8pm. MAP P.86–87,
POCKET MAP H2

Representing dozens of Berlin's
fashion labels and international
designers, Flagshipstore offers
a vast range of urban clothing
and accessories (for women
and men), plus shoes,
magazines and more.

GOLDHAHN UND SAMPSON

Dunckerstr. 9 Ⓤ Eberswalder Str. ⓦ www
.goldhahnundsampson.de. Mon–Fri 8am–8pm,
Sat 9am–8pm. MAP P.86–87, POCKET MAP J1

A foodies' paradise that houses
a vast spread of herbs, spices
and other tasty delicacies
from all over the world, plus
cookbooks and kitchen
utensils. It holds regular wine
tasting and cookery courses.

LUNETTES SELECTION

Dunckerstr. 18 Ⓤ Eberswalder Str. ☎ 030 44
71 80 50, ⓦ www.lunettes-selection.de,
Mon, Tues & Fri noon–8pm, Wed 10am–8pm.
Thurs & Sat noon–6pm. MAP P.86–87,
POCKET MAP K1

Vintage eyewear fanatics will
adore this small space, which
stocks original frames from
brands like Alain Mikli and
Christian Dior, as well as
in-house designs by Uta Geyer.

MUNDO AZUL

Choriner Str. 49 Ⓤ Senefelderplatz
☎ 030 49 85 38 34. Mon 10am–6pm, Tues–Fri
10am–7pm, Sat 10am–4pm. MAP P.86–87,
POCKET MAP J2

"Blue world" is a children's and
illustration bookstore that
stocks beautiful books in
French, Spanish, German and
English, and also runs events
and exhibitions. A must for
visiting parents.

MUNDO AZUL

NOODLES, NOODLES & NOODLES

Schönhauser Allee 156 Ⓤ Eberswalder Str.
☎ 030 44 04 54 93. Mon–Fri 10am–7pm,
Sat noon–4pm. MAP P.86–87, POCKET MAP J2

Despite its slightly under-the-
radar location, this distinctively
named store is worth seeking
out for its handsome furniture,
made using old-school
artisanal techniques and
high-quality materials and
built to last.

OYE

Oderberger Str. 4 Ⓤ Eberswalder Str.
☎ 030 66 64 78 21. Mon–Fri 1–8pm,
Sat noon–7pm. MAP P.86–87, POCKET MAP J2

Originally catering for
collectors of Latin, soul and
funk vinyl, Oye now covers an
impressive range of styles, from
Afrobeat and blip-hop to Berlin
club staples house and techno.

ST GEORGE'S BOOKSHOP

Wörther Str. 27 Ⓤ Eberswalder Str. ☎ 030
81 79 83 33. Mon–Fri 11am–8pm,
Sat 11am–7pm. MAP P.86–87, POCKET MAP J2

Founded in 2003 by British
twins Paul and Daniel, this
delightful bookstore sells a fine
selection of new and used
English-language books. There's
a sofa to chill on, free wi-fi and
they'll buy your used books.

SUPALIFE KIOSK

Raumerstr. 40 ⓤ Eberswalder Str. ☎ 030 44 67 88 26. Mon–Sat noon–7pm. MAP P.86–87, POCKET MAP J1

This small boutique sells the wares of Berlin urban artists, from comics and fanzines to silkscreen prints and paintings. They're well connected to some of the city's best-known artists so expect special one-offs too.

THATCHERS

Kastanienallee 21 ⓤ Eberswalder Str. ☎ 030 24 62 77 51. Mon–Fri 11am–7pm, Sat 11am–6pm. MAP P.86–87, POCKET MAP H2

Upmarket fashion store for women who like their dresses, skirts and shirts classy and sexy without ever being over the top. A perfect place to pick up sensual evening dresses or sophisticated club wear.

Restaurants

THE BIRD

Am Falkplatz 5 ⓤ/Ⓢ Schönhauser Allee ☎ 030 51 05 32 83, ⓦ www.thebirdinberlin .com. Mon–Fri 5pm–midnight. Sat & Sun noon–midnight. Cash only. MAP P.86–87, POCKET MAP H1

This no-nonsense New York-style steakhouse is famed for its large and tasty burgers, spicy chicken wings and casual ambience. With the neon bar, exposed brickwork and US accents it's a bit like being on the set of *Cheers*. A great place to fill up cheaply and sip on a cold beer. They now have a second place in Kreuzberg too (Kottbusser Damm 95; ☎ 030 61 65 67 77).

CHEZ MAURICE

Bötzowstr. 39 Ⓢ Greifswalder Str. ☎ 030 42 50 506, ⓦ www.chez-maurice.com. Daily from 6pm, Tues–Sat also noon–3.30pm. MAP P.86–87, POCKET MAP L3

One of the finer dining spots in the quietly upmarket Bötzowviertel, *Maurice* is an intimate, rustic place offering high-quality seasonal French dishes – they'll even take requests with enough notice - and an expansive wine list (over two hundred from France alone). The *plat du jour* specials (noon–3.30pm) are good value: two courses €11, three courses €16.

CHUTNIFY

Szredki Str. 43 ⓤ Eberswalderstr. ☎ 030 44 01 07 95, ⓦ www.chutnify.com. Tues–Sun noon–11pm. MAP P.86–87, POCKET MAP J2

Single-handedly challenging Berlin's dire reputation for mediocre, spice-avoiding Indian food, *Chutnify* specializes in South Indian street food with an emphasis on delicious *dosas*, crispy lentil crêpes and spicy *chai* teas. Designed by owner Aparna Aurora, it looks good too, with colourful furnishings and outside seating in summer.

GUGELHOF

Knaackstr. 37, cnr Kollwitzplatz ⓤ Senefelderplatz/Eberswalder Str. ☎ 030 44 29 229, ⓦ www.gugelhof.com. Mon–Fri from 7pm, Sat & Sun from 10am. MAP P.86–87, POCKET MAP J2

A Kollwitzplatz classic, *Gugelhof* has been serving

CHUTNIFY

GUGELHOF

consistently good Alsatian food since the Wall fell, and counts Bill Clinton among its many dignified diners. It's a surprisingly down-to-earth place, with friendly staff and robust yet refined cuisine that includes *Flammkuchen* (*tarte flambée*) and pork knuckle. Reservations recommended.

MAO THAI

Wörther Str. 30 Ⓤ Eberswalder Str. ☎ 030 44 19 261, Ⓦ www.maothai.de. Daily noon–11.30pm. MAP P.86–87, POCKET MAP J2

Don't be put off by the beaming Buddhas in the window – there's a refreshing lack of garish decoration inside this reliable neighbourhood Thai restaurant. Decent service and a tasty range of classics – *tom ka gai*, spring rolls, glass noodle salads – make this a popular place.

MARIA BONITA

Danziger Str. 33 Ⓤ Eberswalder Str. ☎ 030 20 25 53 38, Ⓦ www.maria-bonita .com. Tues–Sun noon–10pm. MAP P.86–87, POCKET MAP J2

Tucked away amidst the slew of *Imbisses* and kebab shops that make up much of this part of Danziger Strasse, *Maria Bonita* stands out for its above-average street-style Mexican food. You

couldn't swing an enchilada inside, but the burritos, tacos and quesadillas – and the guacamole for that matter – are well worth trying.

MARIEN BURGER

Marienburger Str. 47: tram M2 to Marienburger. ☎ 030 30 34 05 15, Ⓦ www .marienburger-berlin.de. Daily 11am–10pm. MAP P.86–87, POCKET MAP K2

This diminutive but buzzy burger hangout lures locals back again and again with huge, delicious beef, chicken, fish or vegetable burgers (the Marienburger is almost too big to eat in one sitting). Organic options also available.

PAPPA E CICCIA

Schwedter Str. 18 Ⓤ Senefelderplatz ☎ 030 61 62 08 01, Ⓦ www.pappaeciccia.de. Tues–Sat from noon, Sun from 11am. MAP P.86–87, POCKET MAP H2

Bored of the usual Berlin brunch formula? Check out Sundays at this smart-casual Italian restaurant, where chefs dole out freshly made antipasti and other scrumptious dishes, and diners gather on the long communal tables outside. It's all organic and there are decent vegetarian and vegan options. Ice cream, cakes and more on offer at the adjacent organic deli.

PASTERNAK

Knaackstr. 22–24 Ⓤ Senefelderplatz ☎ 030 44 13 399, Ⓦ www.restaurant-pasternak.de. Daily 9am–1am. MAP P.86–87, POCKET MAP J2

This long-standing Russian/ Jewish restaurant, named after the author of *Doctor Zhivago*, is best known for its incredible Sunday brunch (9am–3pm, €12.90): a regal spread of blini, caviar, fish and much more; it's so popular you'll need to get there early (no reservations). Evenings feature live piano music and fixed-price menus.

SASAYA

Lychener Str. 50 Ⓢ/Ⓤ Schönhauser Allee
Ⓣ 030 44 71 77 21, Mon & Thurs–Sun noon–
3pm & 6–11.30pm. MAP P.86–87, POCKET MAP J1

Bucking the trend for catch-all
pan-Asian menus, *Sasaya*
focuses on serving traditional
and innovative Japanese food.
The quality and freshness of the
ingredients is high, the food is
delicious and service is swift –
a serious contender for best
sushi spot in the city.

LA SOUPE POPULAIRE

Prenzlauer Allee 242 Ⓤ Rosa-Luxemburg-
Platz Ⓣ 030 44 31 96 80, Ⓦ www
.lasoupepopulaire.com. Thurs–Sat
noon–3pm and from 6pm. MAP P.86–87, POCKET
MAP J3

Next door to *Le Croco Bleu* (see
opposite), the equally hip *La
Soupe Populaire* restaurant is
run by star chef Tim Raue, and
serves up pricey but tasty,
Berlin-themed cuisine.

WEINSTEIN

Lychener Str. 33 Ⓤ Eberswalder Str. Ⓣ 030
44 11 842, Ⓦ www.weinstein.eu, Mon–Sat
5pm–2am, Sun 6pm–2am; kitchen
6–11.30pm. MAP P.86–87, POCKET MAP J1

This intimate wine bar and
restaurant, all sturdy wooden
tables and wine barrel
decoration, is a bit of a local
secret. The food has a strong
emphasis on local produce and
German wines, as well as
imported high-quality products
like Allgäu cheese and Iberian
ham. Mains start at €8.50, and
from Monday to Wednesday
you can get a selection of eight
small courses for €48.

ZULA HUMMUS CAFE

Husemann Str. 10 Ⓢ Senefelderplatz Ⓣ 030
41 71 51 00, Ⓦ www.zulaberlin.com. Daily
from noon. MAP P.86–87, POCKET MAP J2

The humble chickpea dish
reaches superlative status at
this cosy, Israeli-run hummus

spot. Visitors can stick with a
traditional hummus plate or try
out the *chilli con hummus* and
even *hummus goulasch* – all of
it is delicious. Home-made
pitta bread and a nice wine list
seal the deal.

Snacks

KONNOPKE'S IMBISS

Below Ⓤ Eberswalder Str. Ⓣ 030 44 27 765,
Ⓦ www.konnopke-imbiss.de. Mon–Fri 10am–
8pm, Sat noon–8pm. MAP P.86–87, POCKET MAP J1

This legendary stand has been
serving up Berlin street snacks
– *Currywurst, pommes frites,
Bockwurst* – since 1930.
Incredibly it's been run by the
same family all that time and
remains one of the best places
in the area for a quick bite.

Cafés and bars

ANITA WRONSKI

Knaackstr. 26–28 Ⓤ Senefelderplatz
Ⓣ 030 44 28 483. Daily 9am–1am. MAP P.86–87,
POCKET MAP J2

Located opposite the
Wasserturm, *Anita Wronski*
has two levels of wooden tables
and chairs and a welcoming,
established feel. It serves very
good breakfasts and brunches,
and while busy at weekends is
usually quiet enough through
the week to enjoy a good
newspaper or book in peace.

ANNA BLUME

Kollwitzstr. 83 Ⓤ Eberswalder Str. Ⓣ 030 44
04 87 49, Ⓦ www.cafe-anna-blume.de.
Daily 8am–2am. MAP P.86–87, POCKET MAP J2

Part flower shop, part café and
part bakery, this Art Deco
classic – named after a Kurt
Schwitters poem, whose lines
are elegantly inscribed on the
walls inside – is one of the
area's best known cafés. Slide
into one of the red leather

banquets and sample one of their superb cakes, or come early at the weekend and try a refined tiered breakfast platter.

BECKETTS KOPF

Pappelallee 64 ⒰/Ⓢ Schönhauser Allee ☎ 016 22 37 94 18. Mon & Sun 8pm–2am, Tues–Thurs 8pm–3am, Fri & Sat 8pm–4am. MAP P.86–87, POCKET MAP J1

It's easy to walk straight past this deliberately clandestine cocktail bar – but you'd be missing out. Look out for the glowering head of Mr Beckett staring at you from the darkness, and enter to find a sophisticated and intimate space with one of the best cocktail lists in town.

BEKAREI

Dunker Str. 23 Ⓢ Prenzlauer Allee ☎ 030 34 62 22 30, Ⓦ bekarei.com. Daily 7.30am–6.30pm. MAP P.86–87, POCKET MAP J1

This Greek-Portuguese bakery is a firm local favourite thanks to its freshly baked breads, pretzels, cakes and pastries. The interior is colourfully retro, the staff are friendlier than usual and menu items of note include pancakes, flakey *tiropitakia* and *pastel de nata*.

BONANZA COFFEE HEROES

Oderberger Str. 35 ⒰ Bernauer Str./ Eberswalder Str. ☎ 017 66 16 94 96, Ⓦ www .bonanzacoffee.de. Mon–Fri 8.30am–7pm, Sat & Sun 10am–7pm. MAP P.86–87, POCKET MAP H2

Coffee connoisseurs flock to *Bonanza* to sample the wares of their famed baristas: perfect lattes and flat whites knocked up on a fancy Strada machine. Staff are cool but friendly.

CAFÉ HILDE

Metzer Str. 22 ⒰ Senefelderplatz ☎ 030 04 05 04 172, Ⓦ www.hilde-berlin.com. Daily 9am–7pm. MAP P.86–87, POCKET MAP J3

This sizeable café on the corner of busy Prenzlauer Allee is a lovely spot to

unwind, with books and magazines to read during the day, home-made cakes and lunches, plus film screenings and book readings in the evenings. They also serve up Irish breakfasts and a mean eggs Benedict at weekends.

CAFÉ NOVEMBER

Husemannstr. 15 ⒰ Senefelderplatz/ Eberswalder Str. ☎ 030 44 28 425, Ⓦ www .cafe-november.de. Mon–Fri from 6pm, Sat & Sun from 11am. MAP P.86–87, POCKET MAP J2

Café November is an appealing, gay-friendly but mixed café that sells good cakes and *schnitzels*. There's a breakfast buffet until 3pm on Saturdays and 4pm on Sundays, free wi-fi and the outside patio is great in the summer.

LE CROCO BLEU

Prenzlauer Allee 242 ⒰ Rosa-Luxemburg-Platz ☎ 01774432359, Ⓦ www.lecrocobleu .com. Thurs–Sat from 6pm. MAP P.86–87, POCKET MAP J3

Hidden deep inside the revitalised Bötzow Brewery complex, this cocktail bar offers a glamorous, industrial-chic interior and cocktails innovative enough to warrant the occasional injection of smoke.

BRUNCH AT ANNA BLUME

DR PONG

Eberswalder Str. 21 ⓊEberswalder Str.
ⓌWww.drpong.net. Mon–Sat 7pm–late, Sun
6pm–late. MAP P.86–87, POCKET MAP J2

Like table tennis? Love beer?
Then *Dr Pong* is for you. The
action here revolves – literally
– around the central ping-pong
table. Rent a bat and join the
crowd as they move slowly
around the table, bats in one
hand, beer bottles in the other,
playing a communal game. Be
warned, though: the bar is on
the tourist beer crawl route.

ELBSPEICHER

Sredzkistr. 41 ⓊEberswalder Str.
☎030 52 68 26 02, ⓌWww.elbspeicherb.de.
Mon–Fri 8am–7pm, Sat & Sun 10am–7pm.
MAP P.86–87, POCKET MAP J2

Specializing in Hamburg
"Elbgold" roasts, this coffee hub
has a battleship grey espresso
bar downstairs and elegant,
spacious rooms and areas
upstairs in which you can
sample the world-class beans
and try the home-made
cookies, cakes and *ciabattas*.

HAUSBAR

Rykestr. 54 ⓊSenefelderplatz ☎0176 78
23 11 19. Daily 7pm–3am. MAP P.86–87,
POCKET MAP J2

This small, unpretentious,
dimly lit bar, right across from
the Wasserturm and a couple
of doors down from the
synagogue, is a great deal of
fun on the right nights – and
a great spot if you're seeking
some late-night drinking action
in the area.

KAPITALIST

Oderberger Str. 2 ⓊEberswalder Str.
☎0176 38 64 42 89. Mon–Fri noon–open end,
Sat & Sun 11am–open end. MAP P.86–87,
POCKET MAP J2

Kapitalist is a much less
anti-establishment place than
its beaten-up facade suggests

– in fact it's completely
harmless, drawing a friendly,
bubbly crowd of locals who
come for coffees and people
watching in the day and beer
and wine at night.

KAUF DICH GLÜCKLICH

Oderberger Str. 44 ⓊBernauer Str./
Eberswalder Str. ☎030 44 35 21 82,
ⓌWww.kaufdichgluecklich.de. Mon–Fri
noon–1am, Sat & Sun 10am–1am. MAP P.86–87,
POCKET MAP H2

Come here for waffles, ice
cream – and a spot of cutely
kitsch capitalism. "buy yourself
happy" is an irrepressibly
cheerful place where you can
not only get great coffee and
sweet treats, but also Buy any of
the second-hand furniture –
tables, chairs, lamps, sunglasses
– you see around you.

KIEZKIND BERLIN

Helmholtzplatz ⓊEberswalderstr. ☎030 40
05 78 50, ⓌWww.mein-kiezkind.de. Daily:
summer 9am–7pm; winter noon–6pm.
MAP P.86–87, POCKET MAP J1

Located right on leafy
Helmholtzplatz, this large,
family-orientated café is an
ideal place to take a break with
the little ones. Inside, they can
play with the abundant toys or
in the sandpit, or ride around
on the tricycles outside while
you enjoy a well-made latte and
slice of cake from the counter.

LIEBLING

Raumerstr. 36 ⓈPrenzlauer Allee/
ⓊEberswalder Str. ☎030 41 19 82 09,
ⓌWww.cafe-liebling.de. Mon–Fri 9am–2am,
Sat & Sun 10am till late. MAP P.86–87,
POCKET MAP J1

There's no sign on this café/bar,
but you'll find it right on the
corner of Dunckerstrasse and
Raumerstrasse. Inside is a subtly
cool interior, great cakes and
decent lunch options (paninis,
soups, quiches). The good wine
and beer, and the *au courant*

music on the system, makes it popular in the evenings too.

MEIEREI

Kollwitz Str. 42 Ⓤ Senefelderplatz ☎ 030 92 12 95 73, Ⓦ www.meierei.net. Mon–Fri 7.30am–6pm, Sat 9am–6pm, Sun 10am–6pm. MAP P.86–87, POCKET MAP J2

This itsy café-cum-deli in leafy Kollwitzstrasse offers a taste of the high life. Styled around a mountain hut interior, with alpine landscapes painted on the walls, the organic Swiss and Austrian cuisine – from *Weisswürst* (veal sausage) to apple *strudel* – is best enjoyed at one of the large outdoor tables.

METZER ECKE

Metzer Str. 33 Ⓤ Eberswalder Str. ☎ 030 44 27 656, Ⓦ www.metzer-ecke.de. Mon–Fri 4pm–1am, Sat 6pm–1am. MAP P.86–87, POCKET MAP F10

The oldest inn in Prenzlauer Berg (1913) inevitably packs plenty of old-school charm. It's faded slightly since its days as a major meeting point for Prenzlauer Berg's more bohemian contingent in the GDR, but still serves a decent Pilsner and *Lecker Bolettes* (meatballs) and *Bockwurst*.

KAPITALIST

MORGENROT

Kastanienallee 85 Ⓤ Eberswalder Str. ☎ 030 44 31 78 44, Ⓦ www.cafe-morgenrot .de. Tues–Thurs noon–1am, Fri & Sat 11am–3am, Sun 11am–1am. MAP P.86–87, POCKET MAP H2

Kastanienallee's best-known alternative café is located right next to an immense squat (one of the last in the area). Despite the anti-capitalist slogans and punk aura, it's a friendly, open place that serves up a good weekend breakfast (vegetarian) for which you pay between €4 and €7, depending on your income.

NALU DINER

Dunckerstr. 80A Ⓤ Eberswalder Str./ Ⓢ Prenzlauer Allee ☎ 030 89 75 86 33, Ⓦ www.nalu-diner.com. Mon, Wed & Fri 9am–10pm, Sat & Sun 9am–9pm. MAP P.86–87, POCKET MAP J1

Since opening in 2012, *Nalu's* pancakes (€4–5) have become renowned citywide, though the small menu also extends to other breakfasts (French toast, griddle combos), lunches and evening meals (burgers, steak-cheese sandwiches; €8–12). Free coffee refills and a continuous soundtrack of 1970s pop seal the deal.

PRATER

Kastanienallee 7–9 Ⓤ Eberswalder Str. ☎ 030 44 85 688, Ⓦ www.pratergarten.de. Beer garden April–Sept daily from noon; restaurant year-round Mon–Sat 6–11pm, Sun noon–11pm. MAP P.86–87, POCKET MAP J2

Dating back to 1837, *Prater* is the city's oldest beer garden and remains a fantastic place for a taste of traditional Berlin boozing, especially during summer when people swarm around the long tables and snack kiosks. During winter, it's all about feasting on home-made Berlin cuisine inside the classic interior.

SUICIDE SUE

Berlin-esque atmosphere that makes it decidedly popular.

SCOTCH & SOFA

Kollwitzstr. 18 ⓤ Senefelderplatz ☎ 030 44 04 23 71, ⓦ www.scotchandsofa.net. Daily 7pm–open end. MAP P.86–87, POCKET MAP F10

This quietly hip neighbourhood bar is a fine spot for sinking into a granny-style sofa, sipping on a cocktail and having a *tête-à-tête*. They always play interesting music – everything from Elvis to rap – and smokers and ping-pong fans can indulge their passions downstairs.

SGAMINEGG

Seelower Str. 2 ⓤ/Ⓢ Schönhauser Allee ☎ 030 44 73 15 25, ⓦ www.sgaminegg.de. Tues–Fri 8.30am–6pm, Sat 9.30am–6pm. MAP P.86–87, POCKET MAP J1

There are a dearth of decent cafés north of Stargarderstrasse, but *Sgaminegg* is an absolute treasure thanks to delicious coffees, home-made lunches – couscous, lentil and south German dishes – and a little shop that sells local produce.

SALT 'N' BONE

Schliemannstrasse 3 Ⓢ Schönhauser Allee ☎ 030 91 44 88 85, ⓦ www.saltnbone.de. Tues–Sun from 5pm. MAP P.86–87, POCKET MAP J1

The gastropub scene has well and truly arrived in Berlin with this place, where Sunday roasts and modern bar food are served up alongside local craft beers in a smart designer interior. Friendly staff and a largely expat clientele.

SAPHIRE BAR

Bötzowstr. 31 Ⓢ Greifswalder Str. ☎ 030 25 56 21 58, ⓦ www.saphirebar.de. Mon–Thurs & Sun 8pm–2am, Fri & Sat 8pm–4am. MAP P.86–87, POCKET MAP L3

The *Saphire Bar* mixes together its whisky and cocktail bar credentials as well as it mixes its drinks, with two elegant lounges to enjoy a cultivated yet unpretentious evening in. Now also has a sister bar, *Saphire Martini Lounge* (Sredzkistr. 62).

SCHWARZSAUER

Kastanienallee 13 ⓤ Eberswalder Str. ☎ 030 44 85 633, ⓦ www.schwarzsauer.com. Daily 9am–6am. MAP P.86–87, POCKET MAP J2

"Black and Sour" lives up to its name with its moody service, average food and smoky, plain interior. Still, it has a certain

SUICIDE SUE

Dunckerstr. 2 ⓤ Eberswalder Str. ☎ 030 64 83 47 45, ⓦ www.suicidesue.com. Mon–Fri 8am–6pm, Sat 9am–7pm, Sun 10am–7pm. MAP P.86–87, POCKET MAP J2

This local fave features crumpled leather armchairs, chunky wooden tables and a street-facing espresso bar. The food is tasty too: breakfast spans croissants and scrambled eggs (served in a tiny frying pan), but the real speciality is the *Stullen* – thick slices of home-made bread with toppings you mix and match yourself.

VAGABUND BRAUEREI

Antwerpener Straße 3 Ⓢ Seestrasse ☎ 030 52 66 76 68, ⓦ www.vagabundbrauerei.com. Daily from 7pm. POCKET MAP C1

One of Europe's first crowd-sourced breweries, *Vagabund* is run by three American friends with a highly infectious passion for craft beer. As well as their own excellent brews, they sell classic Belgian ales and lager from family breweries in Southern Germany, all in a welcoming, unpretentious atmosphere that draws locals and expats alike.

WOHNZIMMER

Lettestr. 6 ⓤ Eberswalder Str. ☎ 030 44 55 458, ⓦ www.wohnzimmer-bar.de. Daily 10am–late. MAP P.86–87, POCKET MAP J1

This retro, elegant "living room" is a local institution. One of the first spots to champion flea-market chic, it serves as both a daytime café and amiable bar later on. At weekends a cocktail bar magically pops up between its two rooms.

ZUCKERFEE

Greifenhagener Str. 15 ⓤ/ⓢ Schönhauser Allee ☎ 030 52 68 61 44, ⓦ www .zuckerfee-berlin.de. Tues–Sun 10am–6pm. MAP P.86–87, POCKET MAP J1

"Sugar Plum Fairy" is an apt name for this delightful place, tucked down a quiet street. The interior is dotted with tasteful ornamentation, while the menu features delicious waffles, cakes and uniquely presented breakfasts and lunches (book ahead at weekends).

Clubs and venues

AUSLAND

Lychener Str. 60 ⓢ Prenzlauer Allee ☎ 030 44 77 008, ⓦ www.ausland-berlin.de. MAP P.86–87, POCKET MAP J1

One for the experimentalists, *Ausland* is a non-profit club committed to promoting music, performance and related events. You can find anything from free jazz and sound art gigs to movies and installations, all of which take place in an undecorated bunker in front of an apartment block. Door fees go directly to the artists.

DUNCKER

Dunckerstr. 64 ⓢ Prenzlauer Allee ☎ 030 44 59 509, ⓦ www.dunckerclub.de. Mon–Thurs 10pm–late, Fri & Sat 11pm–late. Entry fee varies but free Thurs. MAP P.86–87, POCKET MAP K1

Duncker touches the musical parts other Prenzlauer Berg clubs don't reach, thanks to a mix of new wave and indie nights and particularly its weekly "Dark Mondays" – one of the city's few goth/industrial nights. Aptly enough it's located in a striking neo-Gothic church.

PANKE

Gerichtstr. 23 ⓢ Wedding ☎ 0163 831 4755, ⓦ www.pankeculture.com. Wed–Sat from 6pm. Admission varies. POCKET MAP E1

This alternative cultural hub, run by a group of Lithuanian friends, is hidden away in a network of run-down industrial courtyards. Expect underground DJ nights, which veer from hip-hop and soul to world and funk (never techno), plus film and art nights and a decent bar and café.

STATTBAD WEDDING

Gerichtstr. 65 ⓢ Wedding ☎ 030 46 79 73 50, ⓦ www.stattbad.net. Opening times vary. Admission €10–12 for club nights. POCKET MAP E1

This underground club occupies a former public swimming pool that dates back to 1907. The pool has been transformed into a dancefloor, complete with original sloping gradient, while other spaces (such as the former changing rooms) now serve as part of the club's infrastructure. Exposed pipework, a consistently good DJ line-up and occasional art exhibitions seal the deal.

Friedrichshain

Though part of an ensemble of former East inner-city areas, Friedrichshain has developed a slightly differently mien than that of neighbouring Mitte and Prenzlauer Berg. A magnet for lefties, anarchists and students, it has managed to resist the same levels of gentrification thanks to an organized squatter scene, activist demos and the occasional car-burning frenzy. That said, its defiantly unkempt environs have succumbed to an invasion of bars and cafés around Boxhagener Platz, and an encroaching media presence along the river. It's most popular for bar-hopping, clubbing and cheap midnight snacking, but the area does offer some heavyweight public monuments, the world-famous East Side Gallery and the imposing Karl-Marx-Allee among them. It's also home to – indeed named after – the lovely, sprawling Volkspark Friedrichshain.

VOLKSPARK FRIEDRICHSHAIN

Ⓤ Strausberger Platz/Weberwiese.
MAP P.182–183, POCKET MAP K3

Established 150 years ago to commemorate the centenary of Frederick the Great's accession to the throne, Volkspark Friedrichshain is one of Berlin's oldest parks. Casually straddling the boroughs of Prenzlauer Berg and Friedrichshain, it's a sprawling place featuring lots of recreational opportunities (tennis courts, volleyball nets and climbing walls) and a wealth of impressive monuments. Highlights include the **Märchenbrunnen**, a neo-Baroque fountain built at the turn of the twentieth century, memorials to Frederick the Great, the German anti-fascist groups of World War II and a **peace bell** given to East Berlin by Japan. The park's two main hills (the 78m Grosse Bunkerberg and the 48m Kleine Bunkerberg) were constructed with rubble from the war. The park is also home to a café, *Café Schönbrunn,* and an open-air cinema (summer only).

EAST SIDE GALLERY

Mühlenstr. 1 Ⓤ Warschauer Str. ☎ 030 25 17 159, ⓦ www.eastsidegallery-berlin.com. Open 24hr. MAP P.182–183, POCKET MAP L6
This 1.3km-long section of the Berlin Wall by the Spree is purportedly the largest open-air gallery in the world and one of the city's best-known landmarks.

CAFÉ SYBILLE ON KARL-MARX-ALLEE

Painted in 1990 (on the east side) when the Wall fell, the gallery features works from over a hundred artists from all over the world. Over the years it has fallen victim to vandalism and erosion, hence a controversial decision to repaint it in time for the twentieth-anniversary celebrations in 2009. The East Side Gallery made the news again in 2013 when a section was removed to make way for some luxury apartments; the resulting outcry drew ten thousand protesters and an impromptu appearance by David Hasselhoff.

KARL-MARX-ALLEE

Ⓤ Frankfurter Tor/Strausberger Platz. MAP P.102–103, POCKET MAP L5

The monumental Karl-Marx-Allee, as the name suggests, is a thoroughly Communist phenomenon. Built between 1952 and 1960, the imposing 89m-wide, 2km-long street – book-ended by German architect Hermann Henselmann's tiered "wedding cake" towers at Frankfurter Tor and Strausberger Platz – was originally named Grosse Frankfurter Strasse. and later Stalinallee. The idea was to build luxurious apartments for workers (they were inevitably doled out to party officials) as well as a leisure area featuring shops, restaurants, cafés and the still-standing Kino International. On June 17, 1953, the street was the focus of worker demonstrations; at least 125 people died in the brutal suppression by Soviet forces that followed. Since reunification most of the buildings have been restored and the apartments converted into upmarket flats and offices. The vast dimensions of the street and its run of blocky Soviet

EAST SIDE GALLERY

architecture make it a fantastic place for a stroll. Stop off at *Café Sybille* (see p.105), which hosts a small but insightful museum on the street's history.

COMPUTERSPIELEMUSEUM

Karl-Marx-Allee 93a Ⓤ Weberwiese ☎ 030 60 98 85 77, Ⓦ www.computerspielemuseum.de. Daily 10am–8pm. €8. MAP P.102–103, POCKET MAP L5

The world's first ever Computer Games museum is a fun and highly interactive tribute to gaming, featuring pretty much every kind of arcade machine and games console ever made, from the pioneering Nimrod (1951) and legendary PONG (1972), right up to contemporary classics like Tomb Raider. There are plenty of opportunities to punch keyboards and waggle joysticks – and even get a jolly old electric shock via the two-player "Pain Station".

BOXHAGENER PLATZ MARKET

Boxhagener Platz Ⓤ Samariterstr. Ⓦ www.boxhagenerplatz.org. Farmers' market: Sat 9.30am–3.30pm. Flea market: Sun 10am–6pm. MAP P.102–103, POCKET MAP A17

The flea market at Boxhagener Platz is a popular place for locals and tourists alike to spend a Sunday. While not as large as Mauerpark (see p.85), you can find vinyl, vintage fashion, old crockery and more.

OBERBAUMBRÜCKE

ⓤ Warschauer Str. MAP BELOW, POCKET MAP M7

This attractive, Spree-spanning landmark connects the districts of Friedrichshain and Kreuzberg, today officially part of the same borough but previously divided by the Berlin Wall. The double-decker bridge (and its name) dates back to the eighteenth century when it was originally constructed – from wood – and acted as a gateway to the city. A new version opened in 1896, designed by architect Otto Stahn in brick gothic style. In 1945 the bridge was partly destroyed by the Wehrmacht to stop the Red Army crossing it, and afterwards ended up straddling the American and Soviet sectors. When the Berlin Wall went up in 1961, the bridge became part of East Berlin's border with West Berlin; when it fell in 1989, the bridge was restored to its former appearance with a new steel middle section designed by Spanish architect Santiago Calatrava. Today the bridge stands as a symbol of unity between Friedrichshain and Kreuzberg (and is the site of a friendly "water battle" in summer). Look out for the neon *Stone Paper Scissors* installation by Thorsten Goldberg – a political statement about the apparent arbitrariness of decisions to grant immigration or asylum status.

STASI MUSEUM

Ruschestr. 103, Haus 1, Lichtenberg
ⓤ Magdalenenstr. ☎ 030 55 36 854.
ⓦ www.stasimuseum.de. Mon–Fri 10am–6pm,
Sat & Sun noon–6pm. €6 (reductions for groups). MAP BELOW, POCKET MAP M5

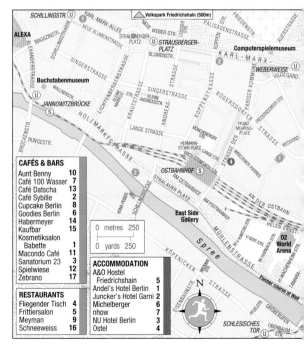

CAFÉS & BARS

Aunt Benny	10
Café 100 Wasser	7
Café Datscha	13
Café Sybille	2
Cupcake Berlin	8
Goodies Berlin	6
Habermeyer	14
Kaufbar	15
Kosmetiksalon Babette	1
Macondo Café	11
Sanatorium 23	3
Spielwiese	12
Zebrano	17

RESTAURANTS

Fliegender Tisch	4
Frittiersalon	5
Meyman	9
Schneeweiss	16

ACCOMMODATION

A&O Hostel Friedrichshain	5
Andel's Hotel Berlin	1
Juncker's Hotel Garni	2
Michelberger	6
nhow	7
NU Hotel Berlin	3
Ostel	4

East Germany's State Security Service – Stasi – struck terror into East Germans, using dark and dastardly spying methods to unveil any potential signs of rebellion. This museum – in Lichtenberg, just east of Friedrichshain – used to be the Stasi headquarters: it was stormed and taken over when the Wall fell by an indignant group of people, many of whose lives had been affected by years of abuse, and members of this group still run the museum today. Following extensive renovations, the main building of the campus (Haus 1, which housed the Minister of State Security among others) reopened in 2012 and the exhibition "State Security in the SED Dictatorship" has been on permanent display since 2015. Visitors can see Stasi chief Erich Mielke's

OBERBAUMBRÜCKE

ridiculously immense desk (and equally large number of telephones) and the complex filing system that includes samples of body odours. Tours in English, German and Swedish are available if requested in advance.

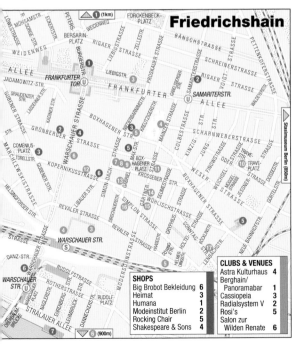

Friedrichshain

SHOPS
Big Brobot Bekleidung	6
Heimat	3
Humana	1
Modeinstitut Berlin	2
Rocking Chair	5
Shakespeare & Sons	4

CLUBS & VENUES
Astra Kulturhaus	4
Berghain/ Panoramabar	3
Cassiopeia	3
Radialsystem V	2
Rosi's	5
Salon zur Wilden Renate	6

BIG BROBOT BEKLEIDUNG

Shops

BIG BROBOT BEKLEIDUNG

Kopernikusstr. 19 ⓤ Frankfurter Tor ☎ 030 74 07 83 88. Mon–Fri 11am–8pm, Sat 11am–6pm. MAP P.102-103, POCKET MAP A16

Friendly and vaguely trashy store where you can browse rare toys, art books and streetwear.

HEIMAT

Niederbarnimstr. 17 ⓤ Samariterstr. ☎ 030 74 69 99 14. Mon–Fri noon–7pm, Sat noon–6pm. MAP P.102-103, POCKET MAP A16

Specializes in stylish T-shirts, bags and accessories. Robots, bicycles, strange animals and other hipster designs appear on almost every item.

HUMANA

Frankfurter Tor 3 ⓤ Frankfurter Tor ☎ 030 42 30 73 39. Mon–Sat 10am–8pm. MAP P.102-103, POCKET MAP A16

This immense five-storey warehouse, part of a grand Soviet palace, brims with secondhand clothes. The top floor has the best vintage gear.

MODEINSTITUT BERLIN

Samariterstr. 8 ⓤ Samariterstr. ☎ 030 42 01 90 88. Mon–Fri 10am–7pm, Sat 10am–6pm. MAP P.102-103, POCKET MAP B16

An Aladdin's cave of vintage clothes, accessories, bags, colourful shoes, disco lamps, leather jackets, rare magazines and old books.

ROCKING CHAIR

Gabriel-Max-Str. 13 ⓤ Samariterstr./ Frankfurter Tor ☎ 030 29 36 42 91. Mon–Fri noon–7pm, Sat 11am–4pm. MAP P.102-103, POCKET MAP A17

This charming vintage store is a great place for anything from a Hawaiian shirt to a retro handbag. Also open sunny Sundays.

SHAKESPEARE & SONS

Warschauerstr. 74 Ⓢ/ⓤ Warschauerstr. ⓦ shakesbooks.de. Mon–Sat 9am–8pm, Sun 10am–8pm. MAP P.102-103, POCKET MAP A16

One of the city's best English-language bookshops, this is a welcoming space filled with literary, sci-fi and academic classics, as well as a great selection of kids' books, French-language titles and Berlin-themed tomes. Inside, *Fine Bagels* serves up some of the best bagels in town.

Restaurants

FLIEGENDER TISCH

Mainzer Str. 10 ⓤ Samariterstr. ☎ 030 29 77 64 89, ⓦ www.fliegender-tisch.de. Daily from 5pm. MAP P.102-103, POCKET MAP B16

"The flying table" is a small, cosy place with just a few wooden tables. It's justly popular thanks to tasty Italian staples like thin-crust pizza and risotto for decent prices (€7–8).

FRITTIERSALON

Boxhagener Str. 104 ⓤ Samariterstr. ☎ 030 25 93 39 06, ⓦ www.frittiersalon.de. Daily 1pm–midnight. MAP P.102-103, POCKET MAP A16

With a name that won't appeal to healthy eaters, the "deep fried salon" actually serves delicious organic burgers and *Bratwurst*. There's always a burger-of-the-week deal, plus vegetarian and vegan options.

MEYMAN

Warschauer Str. 80 Ⓤ Frankfurter Tor ☎ 030 64 49 68 80. Mon–Thurs & Sun noon–2am, Fri & Sat noon–3am. MAP P.102–103, POCKET MAP A17

This unassuming restaurant is great for late-night cravings or for a break between bar hops. They specialize in tasty Moroccan and Arabic dishes along with pizza. Ingredients are fresh, prices are reasonable (€5.50–7.90 for a main), and there's usually a table free.

SCHNEEWEISS

Simplonstr. 16 Ⓤ Warschauer Str. ☎ 030 29 04 97 04, Ⓦ www.schneeweiss-berlin.de. Daily from 6pm. MAP P.102–103, POCKET MAP A17

One of Friedrichshain's few upmarket restaurants, "Snow White" is an understated place with a minimalist design and a menu that it describes as "Alpine" – Italian, Austrian and south German recipes such as *schnitzel* and pasta. There's a decent weekend brunch (from 10am), a fireplace lounge and a low-key bar vibe come evening.

Cafés and bars

AUNT BENNY

Oderstr. 7 (entrance on Jessnerstr.) Ⓤ Frankfurter Allee ☎ 030 66 40 53 00, Ⓦ auntbenny.com. Tues–Fri 9am–8pm, Sat & Sun 10am–8pm. MAP P.102–103, POCKET MAP B17

Canadian-run *Aunt Benny* is a welcoming, modern café. The range of teas and coffees is good, there's bagels, daily soups and other breakfast and lunch options available, plus free wi-fi and home-made baked treats.

CAFÉ 100 WASSER

Simon-Dach-Str. 39 Ⓤ Frankfurter Tor ☎ 030 29 00 13 56, Ⓦ www.cafe-100-wasser.de.

Mon–Thurs & Sun 9am–2am, Fri & Sat 9am–3am. MAP P.102–103, POCKET MAP A17

Named after the Austrian artist Hundertwasser, *100 Wasser* has a fittingly colourful interior of yellow walls and a red-brick bar. It's an unpretentious place, with a hearty menu of burgers, pizza and flans. The weekend all-you-can-eat brunch buffet (€10.50; 9am–4pm) is deservedly popular.

CAFÉ DATSCHA

Gabriel-Max-Str. 1 Ⓤ Samariterstr. ☎ 030 70 08 67 35, Ⓦ www.cafe-datscha.de. Daily from 10am. MAP P.102–103, POCKET MAP A17

Built in the style of a traditional Russian home – wood furniture, tall ceilings – albeit a fairly smart one, *Datscha* offers a rich spread of Russian and Ukrainian dishes like *borscht*, *blini* and *solyanka* (a spicy, sour soup). There's a daily changing lunch menu (€7.50) and Sunday brunch (10am–4pm; €12.40).

CAFÉ SYBILLE

Karl-Marx-Allee 72 Ⓤ Strausberger Platz ☎ 030 29 35 22 03, Ⓦ www.cafe-sibylle.de. Daily 10am–8pm. MAP P.102–103, POCKET MAP L5

It's worth a stop at *Café Sybille* not just for the ice cream, cakes and coffee, but because it also hosts a small museum about the history of Karl-Marx-Allee, with propaganda posters, socialist statues and other exhibits to browse while your drinks are made.

CUPCAKE BERLIN

Krossener Str. 12 Ⓤ Samariterstr. ☎ 030 25 76 86 87, Ⓦ www.cupcakeberlin.de. Daily noon–8pm. MAP P.102–103, POCKET MAP A17

The city's first outlet dedicated to cupcakes, all home-made by American owner, Dawn, for sale in a café that's every bit as sweet and retro as her cakes. Brownies, fantastic New York cheesecake and pecan pie are also available (all around €2.50).

GOODIES BERLIN

Warschauer Str. 69 ⊕ Frankfurter Tor
☎ 030 89 65 49 73, ⓦ www.goodies-berlin
.de. Mon–Fri 7am–8pm, Sat & Sun 9am–8pm.
MAP P.102–103, POCKET MAP A17

Goodies is a tiny but wholesome
café that serves home-made
baked goods, sandwiches and
bagels. The organic soup
changes daily and there's a small
but varied selection of salads
and vegan options. Free wi-fi,
and a children's area. Cash only.

HABERMEYER

Gärtnerstr. 6 ⊕ Samariterstr. ☎ 030 29 77 18
87. Daily 7pm–late. MAP P.102–103, POCKET MAP A17

This low-key, dive-style hangout
is a Friedrichshain classic.
Slightly off the main path, it
features dark lighting, table
football and pinball machines,
a miscellany of seating and DJs
playing Northern soul, rock and
techno. Best late on weekends.

KAUFBAR

Gärtnerstr. 4 ⊕ Samariterstr. ☎ 030 23 90
94 70, ⓦ www.kaufbar-berlin.de. Daily 10am–
midnight. MAP P.102–103, POCKET MAP A17

This neighbourhood favourite
enjoys a unique charm that
goes beyond its gimmick – that
everything from the chairs to
the artwork is for sale. Its
appeal lies in its breezy café
ambience; it's a great spot to
play games, read a book or
drink tea or wine. Light snacks
(salads, soups) are available
and a garden opens in summer.

KOSMETIKSALON BABETTE

Karl-Marx-Allee 36 ⊕ Schillingstr. ☎ 017 63
83 88 943, ⓦ www.barbabette.com. Daily from
6pm. MAP P.102–103, POCKET MAP K4

This glass box of a building was
once a cosmetics shop. At night,
the only identifying marker is
the warm glow of the cube's
interior lights. The ground floor
is sparsely furnished, while the
former treatment rooms

upstairs occasionally have book
readings and performances.

MACONDO CAFÉ

Gärtnerstr. 14 ⊕ Samariterstr. ☎ 030 54
73 59 43. Mon–Fri 3pm–late, Sat & Sun
10am–late. MAP P.102–103, POCKET MAP A17

Kitted out with fraying vintage
furniture, this local chill-out
spot offers a good selection of
books and board games and a
great atmosphere for lounging.
Serves brunch at weekends.

SANATORIUM 23

Frankfurter Allee 23 ⊕ Frankfurter Tor
☎ 030 42 02 11 93, ⓦ www.sanatorium23.de.
Daily from 6pm. MAP P.102–103, POCKET MAP A16

Set in a Soviet-style building,
Sanatorium is a fun hangout
with red-and-white leather
beds separated by see-through
curtains, Swiss red crosses
hanging on the ceilings, DJ sets
(electro and techno mainly)
and the odd art exhibition.

SPIELWIESE

Kopernikusstr. 24 ⊕ Warschauer Str. ☎ 030
28 03 40 88, ⓦ www.spielwiese-berlin
.de. Mon & Fri 4pm–midnight, Thurs 7pm–
midnight, Sat 2pm–midnight, Sun 2–8pm. MAP
P.102–103, POCKET MAP A17

Advertising itself as a "game
library", this café stocks over
1800 games, from chess to Risk.

GOODIES BERLIN

For a small fee (€1–3), you can play games in the café or rent them (€1–3 per day) to take home. A great place to lose yourself for a couple of hours.

ZEBRANO

Sonntagstr. 8 Ⓤ Samariterstr. ☎ 030 61 10 13 13, Ⓦ www.zebranobar.de. Daily 10am–late. MAP P.102–103, POCKET MAP B17

Located on the lovely "Sunday Street", *Zebrano* is a fairly hip neighbourhood bar with a good selection of draught beers, a great cocktail menu (happy hour daily 7–9pm) and decent breakfasts (till 4pm; €2.20–6.90).

Clubs and venues

ASTRA KULTURHAUS

Revaler Str. 99 Ⓤ/Ⓢ Warschauer Str. ☎ 030 20 05 67 67, Ⓦ www.astra-berlin.de. MAP P.102–103, POCKET MAP A17

Owned by *Lido* (see p.122), *Astra* is a force to be reckoned with on Berlin's live music scene with shows from local and international artists like La Roux and Ben Harper.

BERGHAIN/PANORAMABAR

Am Wriezener Bahnhof Ⓢ Ostbahnhof ☎ 030 29 36 02 10, Ⓦ www.berghain.de. Fri & Sat midnight–late. €10–15. MAP P.102–103, POCKET MAP L6

A strong contender for best club in the city, if not the world, this former power station attracts techno fans from all over the globe for its fantastic sound system, purist music policy and awe-inspiring industrial interior. The best time to arrive is after 5am on Saturday morning; the club runs till Sunday evening.

CASSIOPEIA

Revaler Str. 99 Ⓤ Warschauer Str. ☎ 030 47 38 59 49, Ⓦ www.cassiopeia-berlin.de. MAP P.102–103, POCKET MAP A17

Renovated from an urban dump into a fun concrete playground, this sprawling space has several club areas, an exhibition venue, huge indoor skate park, beer garden and the highest climbing tower in Berlin. Music veers from hip-hop and techno DJ sets to live funk and reggae and there's an open-air cinema in summer.

RADIALSYSTEM V

Holzmarktstr. 33 Ⓢ Ostbahnhof ☎ 030 28 87 88 588, Ⓦ www.radialsystem.de, MAP P.102–103, POCKET MAP K6

This sprawling space, housed in a former pumping station on the Spree, was retrofitted and reopened as a space for the arts in 2006, with a glass extension added. As well as visual and performing arts exhibitions, it hosts events ranging from opera concerts to relaxed jam sessions, which are often geared towards children and families.

ROSI'S

Revaler Str. 29 Ⓤ Warschauer Str. Ⓦ www.rosis-berlin.de. Thurs–Sat from 11pm. MAP P.102–103, POCKET MAP B17

Nothing more – or less – than a derelict industrial shack, decorated with secondhand furniture, graffiti and ping pong tables, *Rosi's* puts on some very decent indie, punk and electronic nights. Best in summer when the yard is open for barbecues.

SALON ZUR WILDEN RENATE

Alt-Stralau 70 Ⓢ Treptower Park Ⓦ www.renate.cc. MAP P.102–103, POCKET MAP M7

Located near the train tracks that run towards Treptower Park, *Renate* is an artist-run event space in a semi-derelict house with three floors, a cocktail bar and flamboyant decor that changes with each party. The music is good and the crowd is mixed. Open-air sister club, *Else*, is just across the bridge.

West Kreuzberg

The western section of Kreuzberg is centred on the main streets of Gneisenaustrasse and Bergmannstrasse, and pretty Viktoriapark. Once one of the poorest areas in Berlin, it's now one of its most bourgeois and bohemian and lies in sharp contrast to the more scruffy, multicultural part of the district to the east. Indeed, walking along café and boutique-lined streets like Bergmannstrasse you're reminded of the gentrified environs of Prenzlauer Berg. At the end of this street is Viktoriapark, whose iron cross monument gives the district its name, and nearby is Chamissoplatz, which hosts a popular organic farmers' market every Saturday morning.

CHECKPOINT CHARLIE/HAUS AM CHECKPOINT CHARLIE

Friedrichstr. 43–45 ⓤ Kochstr. ☎ 030 25 37 250, ⓦ www.mauermuseum.de. Daily 9am–10pm. €12.50. MAP OPPOSITE, POCKET MAP C15

"Checkpoint C" (or "Checkpoint Charlie" as it was called by the Western Allies) was the best-known Berlin Wall crossing point between East Berlin and West Berlin during the Cold War. Today it's one of the key places to learn about life in Berlin during the division. The museum – founded in 1962 by Dr Rainer Hildebrandt – is marked by the well-known "YOU ARE NOW LEAVING THE AMERICAN SECTOR" sign that remains outside the building alongside stone-faced (mock) guards, and a replica of the checkpoint (the original is in the Allied Museum in Dahlem). One of the most visited museums in Berlin, its exhibitions are focused mostly on the creative ways East Berliners tried to escape – hot-air balloons, vehicles with special compartments, even a one-man submarine. There are also related exhibits on the concept of freedom and non-violent protest in general, including the Charter 77 typewriter and Mahatma Gandhi's diary.

CHECKPOINT CHARLIE

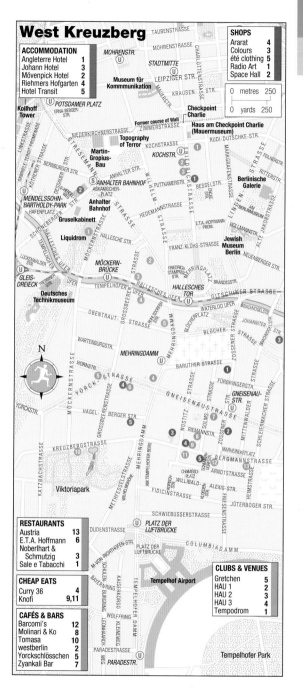

West Kreuzberg

ACCOMMODATION

Angleterre Hotel	1
Johann Hotel	3
Mövenpick Hotel	2
Riehmers Hofgarten	4
Hotel Transit	5

SHOPS

Ararat	4
Colours	3
été clothing	5
Radio Art	1
Space Hall	2

0 — metres — 250

0 — yards — 250

RESTAURANTS

Austria	13
E.T.A. Hoffmann	6
Noberlhart & Schmutzig	3
Sale e Tabacchi	1

CHEAP EATS

Curry 36	4
Knofi	9,11

CAFÉS & BARS

Barcomi's	12
Molinari & Ko	8
Tomasa	10
westberlin	2
Yorckschlösschen	5
Zyankali Bar	7

CLUBS & VENUES

Gretchen	5
HAU 1	2
HAU 2	3
HAU 3	4
Tempodrom	1

TOPOGRAPHY OF TERROR

Niederkirchnerstr. 8 ⓤ/ⓢ Potsdamer Platz
☏ 030 25 45 09 50, ⓦ www.topographie.de.
Daily 10am–8pm. Free. MAP P.109, POCKET MAP F6

From 1933–1945, the headquarters of the Gestapo, their "house prison" and the Reich Security main office stood on this site, making it one of the most notorious locations of Nazi brutality. It's now called the Topography of Terror (Topographie des Terrors) documentation centre, and though many of the buildings were destroyed in World War II, visitors can walk around the largely open-air museum, where exhibits display the history of the site, and explore the events of the Holocaust. A documentation centre focuses on the central institutions of the SS and police in the Third Reich and their crimes. The displays are graphic, so families with children should exercise caution. An audio-guide is available.

MARTIN-GROPIUS-BAU

Niederkirchnerstr. 7 ⓤ/ⓢ Potsdamer Platz
☏ 030 25 48 60, ⓦ www.gropiusbau.de. Free.
MAP P.109, POCKET MAP F6

Envisioned as an applied arts museum, the stunning Martin-Gropius-Bau has evolved into one of Berlin's major contemporary art venues. The ornate, Renaissance-style building was badly damaged during World War II, and rebuilt 1978–81. It draws big-name international displays on art and history, such as retrospectives of Frida Kahlo and Méret Oppenheim and exhibitions of Anish Kapoor and Ai Weiwei.

ANHALTER BAHNHOF

Askanischer Platz 6 ⓤ Mendelssohn-Bartholdy-Park ☏ 030 50 58 68 30. Free.
MAP P.109, POCKET MAP F7

This haunting landmark is a remnant of the Anhalter Bahnhof, once one of Berlin's busiest railway stations. The terminus opened in 1841, but its notoriety stems from World War II when it was one of the three stations used to deport Jews to Theresienstadt (or Terezín), and from there to the death camps. Nearly ten thousand Jews were deported from here, usually in groups of fifty to a hundred; the last train left on March 27, 1945. Though badly damaged in World War II, it was only closed in 1952. Today, all that remains is a portion of the entrance facade and a commemorative plaque, though an S-Bahn station shares its name.

DEUTSCHES TECHNIKMUSEUM

DEUTSCHES TECHNIKMUSEUM

Trebbiner Str. 9 ⓤ Gleisdreieck ☎ 030 90 25 40, ⓦ www.sdtb.de. Tues–Fri 9am–5.30pm, Sat & Sun 10am–6pm. €8. MAP P.109, POCKET MAP F7

Opened in 1982 in the former goods depot of the Anhalter Bahnhof, the German Technology Museum presents a comprehensive – some might say overwhelming – overview of technology created in Germany. The vast collection includes trains and planes, as well as computers, radios, cameras and more. There's a strong emphasis on rail, with trains from 1835 to the present day, but there are also maritime and aviation halls and exhibits on technology from the industrial revolution to the computer and space age, and on the development of the pharmaceutical and chemical industry. A new exhibition on information and communication networks and the history of mobility is housed in the annexe on Ladestrasse. Though much of the museum is based on viewing life-sized reproductions and actual machines, the Science Center Spectrum annexe at Möckernstrasse 26 is more interactive.

JEWISH MUSEUM BERLIN

Lindenstr. 9–14 ⓤ Hallesches Tor/Kochstr. ☎ 030 25 99 33 00, ⓦ www.jmberlin.de. Mon 10am–10pm, Tues–Sun 10am –8pm. €8. MAP P.109, POCKET MAP G7

Daniel Libeskind's Jewish Museum (Jüdisches Museum) is a must-see in Berlin, both historically and architecturally. The stark, zinc-covered building has been thoughtfully designed, with each element symbolizing various aspects of the historical Jewish experience over some two thousand years. The process of moving through the building – which really is a work of art – is an experience in itself, not least thanks to its

'MEMORY VOID' - JEWISH MUSEUM BERLIN

five vertical voids and walls of dark concrete. Guided tours are available and the restaurant serving traditional Jewish cuisine (though not kosher) is very good.

BERLINISCHE GALERIE

Alte Jakobstr. 124–128 ⓤ Hallesches Tor/Kochstr. ☎ 030 78 90 26 00, ⓦ www .berlinischegalerie.de. Daily except Tues 10am–6pm. €8, €4 first Mon of the month; special exhibitions prices vary; combined ticket with Jewish Museum available. Guided tours in English first Mon of month at 3pm. MAP P.109, POCKET MAP H7

Founded in 1975 as a private institution, the Berlinische Galerie was once part of the Martin-Gropius-Bau before moving to its current premises in 2004. Its mission is to showcase art made in Berlin, bringing together fine art, photography and architecture. The permanent exhibition includes works from 1870 to the present day, spanning major movements such as the Secessionists, Fluxus, Dada and the Expressionists, with works by Max Liebermann, Otto Dix, Georg Grosz and Hannah Höch. A spacious hall also hosts temporary exhibitions and there are tours, occasional lectures and film screenings.

BERLIN STORY MUSEUM & BUNKER

Schöneberger Str. 23A 🚇 Mendelssohn-Bartholdy-Park ☎ 030 20 45 46 73, 🌐 www .berlinstory-museum.de/English. Tues–Fri 10am–7pm (last admission 6pm), Sat & Sun noon–8pm (last admission 7pm). €5 (museum), €9.50 (bunker). MAP P.109, POCKET MAP F7

Formerly known as the Gruselkabinett ("horror cabinet"), this attraction now features the Berlin Story Museum and the Berlin Story Bunker. In the former, notorious scenes from Berlin's history are vividly recreated. There's also a scale model of the city and an authentic Trabi car to keep visitors entertained. In the adjacent bunker, visitors are taken through haunted scenes filled with ghouls and the supernatural.

VIKTORIAPARK

Between Kreuzbergstr., Dudenstr., Katzbachstr. and Methfesselstr. 🚇 Yorckstr./Mehringdamm. Open 24hr. MAP P.109, POCKET MAP F9

Famous for hosting Berlin's highest peak, "Vikky Park" is one of the most popular in the city. A multitude of pathways winds around and up the hill to give visitors stunning panoramic views, and there are playgrounds, landscaped rose gardens, a tumbling waterfall and even vineyards to enjoy and explore; the well-known *Golgatha* beer garden provides shade and sustenance.

TEMPELHOFER PARK

Columbiadamm 192 🚇 Südstern 🌐 tempelhoferfreiheit.de. Park daily sunrise to sunset (see website for exact times); free. Airport tours Mon–Thurs 4pm, Fri 1 & 4pm, Sat & Sun 11am & 2pm; 2hr; €12; book on ☎ 030 88 62 67 055. MAP P.109, POCKET MAP G9

The largest park in continental Europe, Tempelhofer Park is the site of the now defunct Tempelhof airport, an immense building created by the Nazis (the terminal was designed to resemble an eagle) which became famous for the 1948–49 Berlin Airlift. Tours of the airport building, which stages events through the year, relate the story. The huge space surrounding the airport doesn't boast any actual attractions but is still a great place to go cycling, walking, roller-skating – or to enjoy a picnic (which can be purchased on site).

LIQUIDROM

Möckernstr. 10 🚇 Möckernbrücke ☎ 030 25 80 07 820, 🌐 www.liquidrom-berlin.de. Mon–Thurs & Sun 9am–midnight, Fri & Sat 9am–1am. MAP P.109, POCKET MAP F7

This designer spa features saunas, slightly cramped chill-out areas and a large, domed flotation pool where you can drift and listen to soft electronic music, sometimes mixed live by DJs, as well as readings and live concerts. A range of massage treatments are also available.

CYCLISTS IN TEMPELHOFER PARK

Shops

ARARAT

Bergmannstr. 9 ⓤ Gneisenaustr. ☎ 030 69 49 532. Mon–Sat 10am–8pm. MAP P.109, POCKET MAP G9

It's easy to lose yourself in here, surrounded by prints and picture frames; over the road at no. 99, another branch sells postcards and gifts.

COLOURS

Bergmannstr. 102 ⓤ Mehringdamm ☎ 030 69 43 348. Mon–Sat 11am–7pm. MAP P.109, POCKET MAP G9

A retro fan's paradise with secondhand clothes spanning the 1960s to 1980s, but particularly good on the 1970s.

ÉTÉ CLOTHING

Bergmannstr. 18 ⓤ Gneisenaustr. ☎ 030 32 89 55 43. Mon–Sat 11am–8pm. MAP P.109, POCKET MAP G9

With shirts and hoodies from trusted brands like Cheap Monday, RVLT, Volcom and Iriedaily, and a decent range of sneakers, this is a good stop for streetwear in Kreuzberg.

RADIO ART

Zossener Str. 2 ⓤ Mehringdamm ☎ 030 69 39 435. Thurs & Fri noon–6pm, Sat 10am–1pm. MAP P.109, POCKET MAP G8

A fantastic and visually satisfying shop for radio lovers, with shelves brimming with vintage (and some modern) radio sets and record players.

SPACE HALL

Zossener Str. 33 ⓤ Gneisenaustr. ☎ 030 69 47 664. Mon–Wed & Sat 11am–8pm, Thurs & Fri 11am–10pm. MAP P.109, POCKET MAP G8

This two-store, multi-roomed record shop is one of the best stocked in the city, with a large CD collection at no. 33 (rock, pop, electronic, rap) and DJ-friendly vinyl at no. 35.

RADIO ART

Restaurants

AUSTRIA

Bergmannstr. 30, on Marheineke Platz ⓤ Gneisenaustr. ☎ 030 69 44 440. Daily 6pm–late (kitchen till 10.30pm). MAP P.109, POCKET MAP G9

In a hunting lodge-style interior, *Austria* serves classic Austrian dishes made with organic ingredients. The huge *schnitzel* is justly famous (mains €13.50–17.50).

E.T.A HOFFMANN

Yorckstr. 83 ⓤ Mehringdamm ☎ 030 78 09 88 09, ⓦ www.restaurant-e-t-a-hoffmann.de. Daily except Tues 5–11pm. MAP P.109, POCKET MAP G8

An upmarket bistro overseen by Thomas Kurt, who serves rich European dishes like entrecote with red wine shallots and scallops with foie gras, or set menus from €45. The interior is classic, and there's a lovely courtyard.

NOBELHART & SCHMUTZIG

Friedrichstr. 218 ⓤ Kochstr./Checkpoint Charlie ☎ 030 25 94 06 10, ⓦ www .nobelhartundschmutzig.com. Tues–Sat 6.30–10.30pm. MAP P.109, POCKET MAP G6

Founded by sommelier Billy Wagner, formerly of *Weinbar Rutz* (see p.40) and chef Micha Schäfer, this chic spot opened in 2015 with delicious, imaginative food, fiercely committed to a local and seasonal ethos.

SALE E TABACCHI

Rudi-Dutschke-Str. 23 Ⓤ Kochstr.
☎ 030 25 21 155, Ⓦ www.sale-e-tabacchi.de.
Daily 10am–11.30pm. MAP P.109, POCKET MAP G6

Located towards the Mitte end of Kreuzberg, "Salt and Tobacco" has a more classic feel than most restaurants in the area. It's known for its excellent seafood dishes (tuna €24, sea bass €22.50) Italian wines. The interior is large and airy and there's a garden out back.

Cheap eats

CURRY 36

Mehringdamm 36 Ⓤ Mehringdamm ☎ 030 25 17 368. Daily 9am–5pm. MAP P.109, POCKET MAP G8

Everyone in Berlin has a favourite place to eat *Currywurst* – sausage doused in curry sauce – but *Curry 36* is cited more often than most (along with *Konnopke's*, see p.94); its popularity alone guarantees it's a buzzy place to grab a snack (around €1.50).

KNOFI

Bergmannstr. 11 & 98 Ⓤ Gneisenaustr.
☎ 030 69 56 43 59 (no. 11), ☎ 030 69 45 807 (no. 98). Daily 8am–midnight (no. 11); daily 9am–midnight (no. 98). MAP P.109, POCKET MAP G9

There are two *Knofis* opposite each other. At no. 11 you'll find a small deli-style restaurant serving tasty Turkish food. Over the road is a Turkish deli.

Cafés and bars

BARCOMI'S

Bergmannstr. 21 Ⓤ Gneisenaustr. ☎ 030 69 48 138, Ⓦ www.barcomis.de. Mon–Fri 8am–9pm, Sat & Sun 9am–9pm. MAP P.109, POCKET MAP G9

Not quite as cosy as its Mitte branch (see p.41), but you can find excellent quality coffee – *Barcomi's* roasts its thirteen coffee varieties here, hence the decorative coffee sacks and delicious odour – as well as handmade breads, pastries, soups and sandwiches.

MOLINARI & KO

Riemannstr. 13 Ⓤ Gneisenaustr. ☎ 030 69 13 903. Mon–Fri 8am–midnight, Sat & Sun 9am–midnight. MAP P.109, POCKET MAP G9

This welcoming Italian café/ bar/restaurant, hidden away on a residential street, offers a menu of breakfast and snacks, pasta and pizza. A decent wine and beer selection make it good for evenings too.

TOMASA

Kreuzbergstr. 62 Ⓤ Mehringdamm
☎ 030 81 00 98 85, Ⓦ www.tomasa.de.
Mon–Thurs & Sun 9am–1am, Fri & Sat 9am–2am. MAP P.109, POCKET MAP F9

This old-school villa, on the edge of Viktoriapark, is a particularly pleasant place for a relaxed breakfast or lunch. The classic interior, good, seasonal menu (from tapas to pasta and Asian dishes) and friendly service attract a mixed clientele, families included. Sunday brunch (€16.50) is very popular.

WESTBERLIN

Friedrichstr. 215 Ⓤ Kochstr. ☎ 030 25 92 27 45, Ⓦ westberlin-bar-shop.de. Mon–Fri 8.30am–7pm, Sat & Sun 10am–7pm. MAP P.109, POCKET MAP G6

CURRY 36

has an incredible range of strange and surprising cocktails (often with home-made ingredients), acoustic concerts every Tuesday and Wednesday, a "play area" with football and pinball, and a beer garden with plenty of seating.

Clubs and venues

GRETCHEN

Obentrautstr. 19-21 ⬤ Hallesches Tor ☎ 030 25 92 27 02, ⬤ www.gretchen-club.de. Opening times and admission varies. MAP P.109, POCKET MAP G8

Named after a murderous character in Goethe's *Faust*, this alternative club space offers a handsome interior that's all columns and vaulted ceilings, and a mix of electronic sounds (drum and bass, dubstep, trip hop). A refreshing alternative to the usual Berlin "techno-shack" formulas.

HEBBEL AM UFER

HAU 1 Stresemannstr. 29; HAU 2 Hallesches Ufer 32; HAU 3 Tempelhofer Ufer 10 ⬤ Hallesches Tor ☎ 030 25 90 04 27, ⬤ www.hebbel-am-ufer.de. MAP P.109, POCKET MAP G7

Three neighbouring venues – Hebbel-Theater (HAU 1), Theater am Halleschen Ufer (HAU 2) and the small Theater am Ufer (HAU 3) – are the places for groundbreaking theatre, the occasional concert and more.

TEMPODROM

Möckernstr. 10 ⬤ Möckernbrücke ☎ 030 74 73 70, ⬤ www.tempodrom.de. MAP P.109, POCKET MAP F7

A giant tent-like arena in the heart of Berlin, Tempodrom puts on concerts, shows, plays, galas, conferences, fashion shows – you name it, Tempodrom's hosted it.

This handsome haven is part chic media hangout and part café. Occupying a grittier part of Friedrichstrasse that's only just starting to come to life, you can sip on a locally roasted flat white while working away on your laptop or browsing the broad selection of nice architecture, fashion and lifestyle magazines. They also have a decent selection of Berlin guides and information.

YORCKSCHLÖSSCHEN

Yorckstr. 15 ⬤ Mehringdamm ☎ 030 21 58 070, ⬤ www.yorckschloesschen.de. Mon-Sat 5pm-3am, Sun 10am-3am. MAP P.109, POCKET MAP F8

This place has been a Kreuzberg institution for over a hundred years, though it doesn't seem to have been updated since the 1970s. The menu is mostly basic and local – meatballs and *Leberkäse* (meatloaf) – and the service gruff, but the tree-shaded garden is a very pleasant place to eat. Live jazz, blues and country bands play most days (Wed-Sat 9pm, Sun 2pm).

ZYANKALI BAR

Gneisenaustr. 17 ⬤ Gneisenaustr. ☎ 030 83 01 70, ⬤ www.zyankali.de. Daily from 4pm. MAP P.109, POCKET MAP G8

This unique "herbal clinic" bar

East Kreuzberg

An isolated section of West Berlin throughout the Cold War, Kreuzberg has since grown into one of Berlin's most colourful districts – a magnet for left-wing anarchists, gays, Turkish immigrants (it's sometimes called Little Istanbul) and, increasingly, hipsters and tourists. Despite being a coherent borough (nowadays part of Kreuzberg-Friedrichshain), Kreuzberg is still largely considered two distinct halves roughly coterminous with the former postal codes: SO 36 and SW 61 in the eastern and western sides respectively. Much of the eastern part of Kreuzberg abutted the wall on the West side and was strongly associated with Berlin's squatter and anarchist scenes. Though the area has gentrified somewhat since those heady days, it maintains a grungy, vibrant feel that spreads out from Schlesisches Tor down to Kottbusser Tor and beyond, fuelled by an ever-expanding series of excellent independent bars, clubs and restaurants.

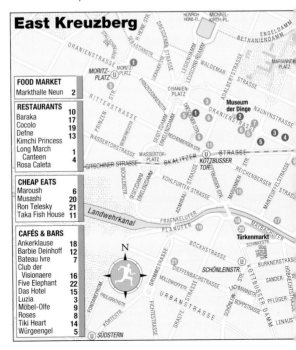

East Kreuzberg

FOOD MARKET	
Markthalle Neun	2

RESTAURANTS	
Baraka	10
Cocolo	17
Defne	19
Kimchi Princess	13
Long March Canteen	1
Rosa Caleta	4

CHEAP EATS	
Maroush	6
Musashi	20
Ron Telesky	21
Taka Fish House	11

CAFÉS & BARS	
Ankerklause	18
Barbie Deinhoff	12
Bateau Ivre	7
Club der Visionaere	16
Five Elephant	22
Das Hotel	15
Luzia	3
Möbel-Olfe	9
Roses	8
Tiki Heart	14
Würgeengel	5

MUSEUM DER DINGE

Oranienstr. 25 ① Kottbusser Tor ☎ 030 92 10 63 11. ⓦ www.museumderdinge.de. Mon & Fri–Sun noon–7pm. €5. MAP BELOW, POCKET MAP J7

A museum dedicated to the somewhat ambiguous culture of "things" could have gone either way. In fact it succeeds by presenting an interesting array of implements – around 25,000 to be precise. Everyday houseware, furniture and knick-knacks are mixed with the unusual, spanning the nineteenth century to the present day. Located on the top floor of a Kreuzberg apartment block, the museum is a design-fiend's dream, with exhibits including Manoli ashtrays, Art Deco fondue sets and World War II memorabilia, all inside a room that's modern and well organized. One of the latest attractions is

DISPLAY IN THE MUSEUM DER DINGE

the modular "Frankfurt Kitchen" designed by Viennese architect Margarete Schütte-Lihotzky in 1926 – the model for the fitted kitchen of today. The exhibition texts are in German and English, and you'll also find a colourful and nicely curated giftshop near the entrance.

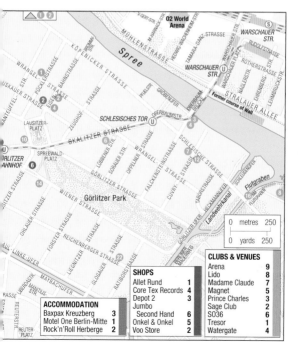

SHOPS

Allet Rund	1
Core Tex Records	4
Depot 2	3
Jumbo Second Hand	6
Onkel & Onkel	5
Voo Store	2

CLUBS & VENUES

Arena	9
Lido	8
Madame Claude	7
Magnet	5
Prince Charles	3
Sage Club	2
SO36	6
Tresor	1
Watergate	4

ACCOMMODATION

Baxpax Kreuzberg	3
Motel One Berlin-Mitte	1
Rock'n'Roll Herberge	2

Shops

ALLET RUND

Dresdener Str. 16 Ⓤ Kottbusser Tor
☎ 030 27 01 48 36. Mon–Fri noon–7pm, Sat
noon–5pm. MAP P.116–117, POCKET MAP J7

Joachin Semrau offers
fair-trade, Kreuzberg-made
designs for sizes 42 to 60, using
European fabrics.

CORE TEX RECORDS

Oranienstr. 3 Ⓤ Görlitzer Bahnhof ☎ 030 61
28 00 50. Mon–Sat 11am–8pm. MAP P.116–117,
POCKET MAP K7

The best place for punk or
hardcore music, as well as
related T-shirts, accessories,
books and concert tickets.

DEPOT 2

Oranienstr. 9 Ⓤ Görlitzer Bahnhof
☎ 030 61 14 655, Ⓦ www.depot2.de. Mon–Sat
11am–8pm. MAP P.116–117, POCKET MAP K7

An ice-cool assortment of
street-oriented fashions,
including Vans and other
stylish footwear.

JUMBO SECOND HAND

Wiener Str. 63 Ⓤ Görlitzer Bahnhof. Mon–Sat
11am–7.30pm. MAP P.116–117, POCKET MAP K7

It's all about quantity over
quality at this secondhand
clothes and accessories store.
It's worth trying to bargain.

ONKEL & ONKEL

Oranienstr. 195 Ⓤ Kottbusser Tor ☎ 030 56
79 47 50. Mon–Sat 10am–6pm. MAP P.116–117,
POCKET MAP K7

A magazine shop that
specializes in graphic design,
photography and street-art
books, Onkel & Onkel also
publishes its own titles, all in a
library-esque atmosphere.

VOO STORE

Oranienstr. 24 Ⓤ Kottbusser Tor ☎ 030 69 57
97 27 10, Ⓦ www.vooberlin.com. Mon–Sat
11am–8pm. MAP P.116–117, POCKET MAP J7

A former locksmiths turned
pop-culture concept shop, Voo
Store's gorgeous interior was
created by Danish designer and
architect Sigurd Larsen, while
its highly curated stock
specializes in both big names
and little-known designers.

Food market

MARKTHALLE NEUN

Eisenbahnstr. 42/43 Ⓤ Görlitzer Bahnhof.
Ⓦ markthalleneun.com. Market Thurs & Fri
noon–8pm; Kantine & Café Mon–Sat
noon–4pm. MAP P.116–117, POCKET MAP K7

This revitalized nineteenth-
century market hall has become
Berlin's foodie destination,
thanks to a weekly farmers'
market (Thurs and Fri), a host
of street-food stalls and events
focusing on sustainable and
local produce. The weekly Street
Food Thursday event (5–10pm)
is especially popular.

Restaurants

BARAKA

Lausitzer Platz 6 Ⓤ Görlitzer Bahnhof ☎ 030
61 26 330, Ⓦ www.baraka-berlin.de.
Mon–Thurs & Sun 11am–midnight, Fri & Sat
11am–1am. MAP P.116–117, POCKET MAP K7

North African food fans will
adore *Baraka*. The decor is

CORE TEX RECORDS

authentic without slipping into kitsch (although the back room comes close) and the food – *tagines*, chicken skewers, *schwarma* – is some of the best in town, and at decent prices (mains €5–12). The mixed plate for two is immense.

COCOLO

Paul-Lincke-Ufer 39 ⓤ Kottbusser Tor
☎ 030 98 33 90 73. Mon–Sat noon–11pm,
Sun 6–11pm. MAP P.116–117, POCKET MAP K8

Unarguably Berlin's best dedicated *ramen* spot, *Cocolo* started life with its Mitte branch (Gipstr. 3), expanding to this larger Kreuzberg location in 2014. Enjoy their slurp-a-licious dishes (including sweet pork belly and Kimchi *ramen*) at a shared table inside, or on the canal-facing terrace. Soups start at €9.

DEFNE

Planufer 92C ⓤ Kottbusser Tor/Schönleinstr.
☎ 030 81 79 71 11, ⓦ www.defne-restaurant
.de. Daily: April–Sept 4pm–1am; Oct–March
5pm–1am (kitchen till midnight all year).
MAP P.116–117, POCKET MAP J8

Defne serves up Turkish and Mediterranean food from fresh ingredients. Classics include *imam bayildi* (aubergines with pine nuts, peppers and tomato sauce, €9.90) or lamb skewers (€14.50). The interior is simple and spacious; the terrace, overlooking the Landwehr-kanal, is lovely in summer.

KIMCHI PRINCESS

Skalitzer Str. 36 ⓤ 0163 45 80 203, ⓦ www
.kimchiprincess.com. Daily noon–1am. MAP
P.116–117, POCKET MAP K7

Part of a trend for cool Korean eateries in Berlin, *Kimchi Princess* offers simple wooden pallets as seating, a spacious interior and staff as cool as the clientele. There's *bibimbap* and more on the menu, but the Korean barbecue is the

KIMCHI PRINCESS

thing to go for (from €16.90). The owners also run the nearby *Angry Chicken* (Oranienstr. 16), a must for spice fans.

LONG MARCH CANTEEN

Wrangelstr. 20 ⓤ Görlitzer Bahnhof ☎ 0178
884 9899, ⓦ longmarchcanteen.com. Daily
6pm–midnight. MAP P.116–117, POCKET MAP K7

Although folk justifiably flock here for the dim sum (€6–10), this trendy Chinese restaurant also serves up excellent, tapas-sized portions of other dishes like pak choi salad and marinated chicken skewers with water chestnuts. John Malkovich is just one of the A-listers who has been spotted here.

ROSA CALETA

Muskauer Str. 9 ⓤ Görlitzer Bahnhof
☎ 030 69 53 78 59, ⓦ www.rosacaleta.com.
Tues–Sat 6pm–1am, Sun 2pm–1am
MAP P.116–117, POCKET MAP K7

This Jamaican/European fusion restaurant has created quite a buzz in a city hopelessly devoid of Caribbean cuisine. There's plenty of jerk-style food on the menu, but also dishes like oven-roast pork fillet, mango-ginger lentil salad and tofu and vegetable stew (mains from €10). It also functions as an art space and hosts DJ parties.

Cheap eats

MAROUSH

Adalbertstr. 93 Ⓤ Kottbusser Tor ☎ 030 69
53 61 71, Ⓦ www.maroush-berlin.de. Daily
11am–2am. MAP P.116–117, POCKET MAP J7

With a cosy dining area,
authentically Middle Eastern
decor and tasty sandwiches,
kebabs, falafels and fresh
salads, this small Lebanese
restaurant is one of the better
of its type. Vegetarian options
also available.

MUSASHI

Kottbusser Damm 102 Ⓤ Schönleinstr.
☎ 030 69 32 042. Mon–Sat noon–10.30pm,
Sun 2–8pm. MAP P.116–117, POCKET MAP J8

This tiny spot serves up
decent sushi in a refreshingly
designer-free space, decorated
with posters of sumo wrestlers
and populated with just a few
bar tables. The Japanese chefs
prepare fresh, tasty *makis* and
inside-out rolls for very good
prices (€6.50 for a set menu).

RON TELESKY

Dieffenbachstr. 62 Ⓤ Schönleinstr. ☎ 030 61
62 11 11. Mon–Fri 12.30–10pm, Sat & Sun
1.30–10pm. MAP P.116–117, POCKET MAP J8

Canadian pizza served from a
canoe – how can you say no?

Especially when the pizza
toppings include sweet potato,
mango, feta and maple syrup.
Aside from the canoe
(outside) the interior features
national emblems like a
moose head. Vegan options
available.

TAKA FISH HOUSE

Adalbertstr. 97 Ⓤ Kottbusser Tor ☎ 0157 74
24 62 19. Mon–Thurs 9am–11pm, Fri–Sun
9am–2am. MAP P.116–117, POCKET MAP J7

Tucked away on bustling
Kottbusser Tor and
surrounded by kebab and
falafel shops, this unassuming
Turkish *imbiss* has just a
handful of tables inside and
out, but serves up some of the
most delicious, freshly grilled
fish sandwiches in the city.

Cafés and bars

ANKERKLAUSE

Kottbusser Damm 104 Ⓤ Kottbusser Tor
☎ 030 69 35 649, Ⓦ www.ankerklause.de.
Mon 4pm–4am, Tues–Sun 10am–4am.
MAP P.116–117, POCKET MAP J8

Situated by Maybachufer,
next to the Turkish market
(Tues & Fri; see p.125),
Ankerklause is a popular
café during the day, with a
decent range of snacks (and
seats out front and a terrace
overlooking the water out
back). Later, there's something
of the alternative scene about it
when the jukebox plays
rock'n'roll classics.

BARBIE DEINHOFF

Schlesische Str. 16 Ⓤ Schlesisches Tor
Ⓦ www.barbiedeinhoff.de. Daily 7pm–late.
MAP P.116–117, POCKET MAP L7

This colourful dive bar is a lot
of fun, attracting a heady mix
of transvestites, gay men and
curious onlookers. The decor
runs from deliberately kitsch to
the colourfully futuristic and

MAROUSH

there are regular DJs and happenings. A fun place to get comprehensively trashed (two-for-one happy hour Tues 7pm–midnight), though there are also often cultural events early evening.

BATEAU IVRE

Oranienstr. 18 ⓤ Görlitzer Bahnhof ☎ 030 61 40 36 59. Daily 9am–3am, kitchen till 4pm (except tapas). MAP P.116-117, POCKET MAP K7

Probably the best café/bar on lively Oranienstrasse, *Bateau Ivre* feels like it's been there forever, eschewing the trends for something much more timeless. The classic long bar puts out macchiatos, soups and tapas during the day and wines, beer and cocktails at night. You're lucky if you get a seat outside; head to the raised back area for more intimacy.

CLUB DER VISIONAERE

Am Flutgraben 1 ⓤ Schlesisches Tor ☎ 030 69 51 89 42 ⓦ www.clubdervisionaere .com. May–Sept Mon–Fri 2pm–late, Sat & Sun noon–late. Food served daily 6pm–1am. Admission €1–5. MAP P.116-117, POCKET MAP M8

Just beyond the Kreuzberg/ Treptow border, this legendary summer-only techno bar enjoys a unique setting on the intersection of the Spree and Flutgraben canal. The bar and DJ booth is in an old ceramic-tiled boathouse, and punters stand (and dance) on the floating docks outside. It's minimal techno all the way and a fantastically upbeat place.

FIVE ELEPHANT

Reichenberger Stra. 101 ⓤ Görlitzer Bahnhof ☎ 030 96 08 15 27, ⓦ www.fiveelephant.com. Mon–Fri 8.30am–7pm, Sat & Sun 10am–7pm. MAP P.116-117, POCKET MAP L8

Opened by American and Austrian team Kris Shackman and Sophie Weigensamer in 2010, this highly regarded café not only brews (and roasts) some of the best "third wave" coffee in town, but also has a much talked about cheesecake selection.

DAS HOTEL

Mariannstr. 26a ⓤ Kottbusser Tor ☎ 030 84 11 84 33. Daily noon–open end. MAP P.116-117, POCKET MAP J8

Located on a residential street near the Paul-Linke-Ufer, *Das Hotel* is a combination bar, club and bistro that serves burritos and coffee. The candlelit bar is charming but get there early at weekends or you won't get a seat. The downstairs club plays music from the 1940s onwards, with a "no hits and no techno" policy.

LUZIA

Oranienstr. 34 ⓤ Kottbusser Tor ☎ 030 81 79 99 58, ⓦ www.luzia.tc. Daily noon–5am. MAP P.116-117, POCKET MAP J7

Oranienstrasse's key hipster hangout, *Luzia* is styled in the manner of an industrial loft, with exposed brickwork, velvet armchairs, wall paintings by street artists, rough wallpaper and a bizarre upstairs space that you have to climb a ladder to get to. Decent drinks and cocktails mean it's buzzing most nights.

MÖBEL-OLFE

Reichenberger Str. 177 ⓤ Kottbusser Tor ☎ 030 23 27 46 90, ⓦ www.moebel-olfe.de. Tues–Sun 6pm–late. MAP P.116-117, POCKET MAP J7

Sandwiched between a string of Turkish snack bars in a run-down building behind Kottbusser Tor, this unusual, smoky, local bar attracts gays, hipsters, ageing drunks and more. There are regular DJ nights but it's more about experiencing the diversity of the Kreuzberg crowds.

ROSES

Oranienstr. 187 ⓤ Kottbusser Tor/Görlitzer Bahnhof ☎ 030 61 56 570. Daily 9.30pm–6am. MAP P.116–117, POCKET MAP K7

A legendary gay hangout, *Roses* provides a welcoming bosom for all manner of sexual orientations to crowd around. The kitsch decor mirrors the clientele and the fun vibe well. Sunday is the main day – and the "gayest" – but women are welcome anytime.

TIKI HEART

Wiener Str. 20 ⓤ Görlitzer Bahnhof ☎ 030 61 07 47 03, ⓦ www.tikiheart.de. Daily 10am–late. MAP P.116–117, POCKET MAP K8

Berlin's only Hawaiian-rockabilly themed joint is renowned for its unapologetically kitsch interior and innovative menu. The breakfasts, served till 5pm, feature items like the "Oi-Fast" – a heady mix of scrambled eggs and chorizo. There are veggie burgers and – one for the serious rockers – a Lemmy burger grilled in whisky. Strong cocktails are served and the *Wild at Heart* club next door (ⓦ www.wildatheartberlin.de) roars into action with regular rock, punk, metal and surf nights.

WÜRGEENGEL

Dresdener Str. 122 ⓤ Kottbusser Tor ☎ 030 61 55 560. Daily 7pm–late. MAP P.116–117, POCKET MAP J7

One of the best bars in Kreuzberg, "the exterminating angel" has red walls, great tapas, decadent decor and an extensive cocktail and wine list. The feel is timeless, though with a trendy clientele.

Clubs and venues

ARENA

Eichenstr. 4 ⓤ Treptower Park ☎ 030 53 32 030, ⓦ www.arena-berlin.de. Around €10. MAP P.116–117, POCKET MAP M8

This huge area next to the Spree encompasses the *Arena Club*, *Glashaus*, the actual Arena, the *Badeschiff* and the *Hoppetosse*. There are frequent electronic dance parties at *Arena Club*, sometimes the *Hoppetosse* café (on a boat) can turn into a club and at Arena itself you can catch rock and metal shows, as well as events and festivals.

LIDO

Cuvrystr. 7 ⓤ Schlesisches Tor ☎ 030 69 56 68 40, ⓦ www.lido-berlin.de. Times and prices vary according to event. MAP P.116–117, POCKET MAP L7

An old-school club in a former theatre that's been going for nearly ten years, *Lido* is known for championing new music, and is home to a younger indie crowd, with the occasional techno or house event. The club also has a courtyard with canopy that makes it suitable for winter throw-downs.

MADAME CLAUDE

Lübbener Str.19 ⓤ Görlitzer Bahnhof ☎ 030 84 11 08 59, ⓦ www.madameclaude.de. Daily 7pm–late. MAP P.116–117, POCKET MAP L7

This quirky hangout has live music six days a week, ranging

ROSES

from indie-rock and experimental to folk. Be prepared to feel slightly unsettled by the decor, which is upside down and on the ceiling. Pay what you want for entrance.

MAGNET

Falckensteinstr. 48 Ⓤ/Ⓢ Schlesisches Tor/ Warschauerstr. Ⓦ www.magnet-club.de, Daily 10pm–late. MAP P.116–117, POCKET MAP L7

Formerly a Prenzlauer Berg rock'n'roll mainstay, *Magnet* moved to more suitably grungy Kreuzberg in 2010. It hosts regular DJ parties and live shows, ranging from pop to rock and from metal to hip-hop.

PRINCE CHARLES

Prinzenstr. 85f Ⓤ Moritzplatz ☎ 030 200 950 933, Ⓦ www.princecharlesberlin.com. Thurs–Sat 7pm–open end. Admission varies. MAP P.116–117, POCKET MAP K7

Hidden away a basement near Moritzplatz that once housed a swimming pool, this square-shaped, fairly upscale club has a penchant for bass-heavy parties that transcend techno tropes in favour of house, jazzy beats and hip hop spun by a mix of local and international DJs.

SAGE CLUB

Köpenicker Str. 76, accessed via the north entrance to Ⓤ Heinrich-Heine-Str. ☎ 030 27 89 830, Ⓦ www.sage-club.de, Thurs 8pm–late (admission free till 10pm; €6 after), Fri & Sat 10/11pm–late (admission €10). POCKET MAP J6

A sprawling maze of dancefloors, *Sage Club* attracts a youthful, exuberant, rock-oriented crowd on Thursdays (Rock at Sage), a fetish crowd on Fridays and progressive house and trance audiences most other times. The complex also has a restaurant and cocktail bar, with a Spree-side location popular for open-air parties in summertime.

SO36

Oranienstr. 190 Ⓤ Görlitzer Bahnhof ☎ 030 61 40 13 06, Ⓦ www.so36.de. Opening times and admission vary. MAP P.116–117, POCKET MAP K7

One of the city's most legendary clubs, *SO36* has its roots in punk, post-punk and alternative music – musical heroes who've played here include Iggy Pop, David Bowie and Einstürzende Neubauten. Nowadays it hosts alternative and electronic shows, including monthly parties like Gayhane, a Turkish "homoriental" party, and "Ich bin ein Berliner", where you can catch an array of Berlin-based artists playing everything from garage to synth-pop.

TRESOR

Köpenicker Str. 70 Ⓤ/Ⓢ Ostbahnhof/ Jannowitzbrücke. Mon & Wed–Sat midnight–late. Admission varies. POCKET MAP J6

Housed in what was the main central-heating power station for East Berlin, the colossal location of the third incarnation of this ground-breaking club is breathtaking. Only a tiny portion of its 28,000 square metres is in use, but the club is sizeable enough with three different rooms dedicated to cutting-edge, muscular techno played by a rotating roster of international DJs.

WATERGATE

Falckensteinstr. 49 Ⓤ Schlesisches Tor ☎ 030 61 28 03 94. Wed, Fri & Sat 11pm–late, occasional Tues & Thurs events. €6–15. MAP P.116–117, POCKET MAP L7

This slick, split-level club right on the Spree enjoys a killer combination of panoramic windows, excellent sound system and constant flow of renowned DJs. Music is electro, house and minimal techno. Expect to see Berlin residents like Richie Hawtin and Booka Shade too.

Neukölln

Neukölln, with its strings of bars, galleries, shops and cafés, is one of the city's most overtly hip districts. Once upon a time it was Rixdorf, a tiny village outside Berlin studded with windmills and boasting fantastic views from its impressive hillsides. In came the Industrial Revolution and away went the hills (used for buildings as the city expanded), and Rixdorf developed into a district of entertainment and revelry – so much so that in 1912 it was renamed Neukölln in an effort to change its riotous image. Postwar Neukölln became home to many Turkish, Aran and Kurdish communities, who still give the area its character, along with the more recent influx of expats and artists priced out of Berlin's other inner-city districts. Indeed, the resultant clash of working-class residents and middle-class creatives – reflected in intensely rising rents and odd juxtapositions of gaudy video arcades and hipster hangouts around Weserstrasse and bustling Hermannplatz – forms the heart of Berlin's gentrification debate and lends Neukölln its somewhat edgy reputation.

ALT-RIXDORF

Ⓤ Karl-Marx-Str. MAP OPPOSITE

The most obvious reminders of Neukölln's medieval origins lie between the main arteries of Karl-Marx-Strasse and Sonnenallee, an area known as Alt-Rixdorf. A wander around the cobbled streets – centred on historical **Richardplatz** – reveals a centuries-old blacksmith's business, attractive churches and the remains of the district's eighteenth-century Bohemian village – founded for Protestant refugees fleeing persecution – with its cute houses and attractive gardens.

KÖRNERPARK

Schierker Str. 8 Ⓢ Berlin-Neukölln ☎ 030 90 23 92 876, ⓦ www.koernerpark.de. Park Tues–Sun 10am–6pm; café till 8pm. Free. MAP OPPOSITE

Refined Körnerpark might not be the biggest park in Neukölln,

but it is easily the prettiest – a stark contrast to the vast, featureless expanse of nearby Tempelhofer Park (see p.112). With its manicured hedges, elegant promenades and marble fountains, it provides an ideal setting for wedding photos

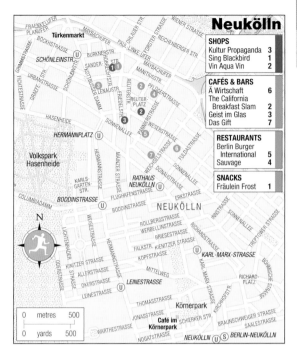

Neukölln

and summertime events such as galas, fairs and concerts. The charming, ivy-covered **Orangerie** – unique among Berlin's parks – is a highlight, and contains the elegant covered *Café im Körnerpark*, which has a popular outdoor terrace in the warmer months.

VOLKSPARK HASENHEIDE

Entrances on Hasenheide, Columbiadamm and Karlsgartenstr. ⓤ Hermannplatz. Open 24hr. MAP ABOVE, POCKET MAP J9

Originally used as a hunting ground for the Grand Elector in the seventeenth century, then as parade grounds for the Prussian military, this green expanse in the heart of Neukölln is today the domain of local sun-worshippers and picnickers. The long rows of trees are reminders of the former shooting ranges but little else of the park's past

remains; instead, the main draws are a popular petting zoo, restaurant and a (summer-only) open-air stage for music, films and theatre. A popular funfair is also held in the southern part of the park each May.

TÜRKENMARKT

Maybachufer Str. ⓤ Schönleinstr. ⓦ www .tuerkenmarkt.de. Tues & Fri 11am–6.30pm. MAP ABOVE, POCKET MAP K8

Located on the border between Neukölln and Kreuzberg (Kreuzkölln as it's widely known), the twice-weekly Turkish Market has become an institution for Berlin's significant Turkish population as well as families, hipsters and tourists. It's colourfully chaotic, complete with yelling vendors peddling the usual arrays of fruit and vegetables, fabric and shoe stalls, stands selling tasty snacks and, occasionally, live music.

Shops

KULTUR PROPAGANDA

Reuterstr. 62 ⓤ Hermannplatz ☎ 030 98 29
61 90, ⓦ www.kultur-propaganda.de. Tues–Fri
2–7pm, Sat noon–5pm. MAP P.125, POCKET MAP K9

Founded in 2008 (and formerly
known as *arm und sexy*), this
atmospheric little vintage and
knick-knack shop sells a range
of hand-picked items, from
gimmicky gifts for tourists to
quality goods from the 1950s
through to the 1980s, such as a
line of lovely vintage typewriters.

SING BLACKBIRD

Sanderstr. 11 ⓤ Schönleinstr. ☎ 030 54 84
50 51, ⓦ www.singblackbird.tumblr.com. Daily
1–7pm. MAP P.125, POCKET MAP K8

Housed in a former phone-sex
HQ, Sing Blackbird has the
edge over other secondhand
clothes stores thanks to a savvy
selection that favours vintage
garments from the 1970s, 1980s
and 1990s, an adjacent café that
serves smoothies and
cold-pressed juices. They also
host occasional flea markets.

VIN AQUA VIN

Weserstr. 204 ⓤ Hermannplatz ☎ 030 94 05
28 86, ⓦ www.vinaquavin.de. Mon–Wed
5–9pm, Thurs & Fri 3–9pm, Sat 1–9pm.
MAP P.125, POCKET MAP K9

This sophisticated wine shop
and bar has introduced a new
level of sophistication to this
famously hipster street. In
addition to a fine selection of
international wines (many
available by the glass), there's
a roaring fireplace for the
colder months, chesterfield
armchairs and a dining table
out back for tastings and
private dinner events.

Restaurants

BERLIN BURGER INTERNATIONAL

Pannierstr. 5 ⓤ Hermannplatz ☎ 016 04 82
65 05, ⓦ www.berlinburgerinternational.com.
Mon–Thurs noon–midnight, Fri & Sat noon–
1am, Sun noon–10pm. MAP P.125, POCKET MAP K9

There can never be enough
burger joints in Berlin, it
seems. This tiny space – just a
long food bar and a smattering
of outdoor picnic tables – lures
punters in with fresh
ingredients and generous
portions: the BBI burger is
enormous. Burgers from €4.90.

SAUVAGE

Pflügerstr. 25 ⓤ Hermannplatz ☎ 030 53 16
75 47, ⓦ www.sauvageberlin.com. Tues–Sun
6pm–midnight. MAP P.125, POCKET MAP K9

Housed in a former brothel,
Sauvage may appear at first

SAUVAGE

glance something of a novelty restaurant, the concept being to celebrate the "caveman" diet of the Paleolithic era. While it sounds gimmicky – not to mention heavy – on paper, the presentation is surprisingly light and modern, the ambience intimate and cool and the ingredients are mostly organic – no grains, no processed sugar and no dairy. Mains from €10.

Snacks

FRÄULEIN FROST

Friedelstr. 39 ⑪ Schönleinstr. ☎ 030 95 59 55 21. Mon–Fri 1–7pm, Sat & Sun noon–7pm. MAP P.125, POCKET MAP K6

One of the district's best-loved ice-cream shops, the Frosty Fräulein serves up delicious cones and tubs of *bio-eis*, as well as sweet and savoury waffles. In summer, the outdoor patio provides a meeting point for hipsters, romantic couples and local families alike.

Cafés and bars

Ä WIRTSCHAFT

Weserstr. 40 ⑪ Rathaus Neukölln ☎ 030 30 64 87 51, ⓦ www.ae-neukoelln.de. Daily 5pm–late. MAP P.125, POCKET MAP L9

One of the first of many informal bars to open up on boho Weserstrasse, the *Ä Bar* still holds its own as a meeting point for young creative types, expats and locals. Flea-market decor, dim lighting and table football give it a classic Berlin dive-bar atmosphere, matched to a soundtrack of indie and electro and occasional acoustic gigs from interna-tional bands.

THE CALIFORNIA BREAKFAST SLAM

Innstr. 47 ⑪ Rathaus Neukölln ☎ 030 68 69 624 Daily 10am–midnight. MAP P.125, POCKET MAP K8

Created by a Californian musician longing for an escape from the typical German breakfast of cold cuts and *Brötchen* (rolls), this Neukölln hipster haven is big on portions as well as flavour, with fluffy pancakes and dozens of different egg dishes, such as spicy *huevos rancheros*, all prepared from scratch with fresh ingredients. Breakfast served till 4pm.

GEIST IM GLAS

Lenaustr. 27 ⑪ Hermannplatz ☎ 017 655 330 450, ⓦ www.geistimglas.com. Mon–Thurs & Sun 7pm–2am, Fri & Sat 7pm–4am. MAP P.125, POCKET MAP K9

This trendy bar prides itself on serving drinks and dishes not so common elsewhere in the city. The cocktail menu features dozens of house-made "spirits", and "Calexican" tacos are served from noon. It usually buzzes with a young, clued-up crowd.

DAS GIFT

Donaustr. 19 ⑪ Hermannplatz ⓦ www .dasgift.tumblr.com. Mon–Wed 7pm–1am, Thurs–Sat 7pm–late. MAP P.125, POCKET MAP L9

Founded by Barry Burns, of Scottish post-rock band Mogwai, and his wife Rachel, this corner pub has quickly become a local in-spot. Its charm lies in its simplicity: just a regular wood interior with a long bar and an artisan drink menu that includes Scottish ales, German brews and lots of whisky and cocktails. There's Irn-Bru and imported British crisps, and also an exhibition space (the *Giftraum*) that occasionally hosts pop-up events.

Charlottenburg

Part of the four boroughs that make up City West (along with Wilmersdorf, Schöneberg and Tiergarten) Charlottenburg has long been the beating heart of West Berlin and remains so today. Known for its wealthy residents and expensive shops, it's generally dismissed by the more boho east, and has much more in common with cities like London, Paris or Milan. The area's main artery, Kurfürstendamm (Ku'damm as it's colloquially known), which takes its name from the former Kurfürsten (Electors) of the Holy Roman Empire, is one of the most famous avenues in the city. It's often described as the city's Champs-Élysées, but the abundance of shops and relative dearth of impressive architecture makes it feel more like London's Oxford Street. However, many of the streets that run between Ku'damm and Kantstrasse have a charm of their own, with a wealth of independent cafés, bars, restaurants, bookstores and boutiques. The area is also home to some of the city's major sights such as Berlin's zoo and aquarium, Schloss Charlottenburg, the Kaiser Wilhelm Memorial Church and the Käthe Kollwitz Museum.

BERLIN ZOO

Hardenbergplatz 8 ⓤ/Ⓢ Zoologischer Garten ☎ 030 25 40 10, ⓦ www.zoo-berlin.de. Daily: mid- to late March 9am–5.30pm; late March to early Sept 9am–7pm; early Sept to late Oct 9am–6.30pm; late Oct to mid-March 9am–5pm. €13, zoo & aquarium €20. Family tickets available. MAP P.130–131, POCKET MAP B6

Berlin's zoo is Germany's oldest and one of the world's most popular, attracting (along with the adjacent aquarium) more than three million visitors in 2014. It opened in 1844 with animals donated by the royal family but was decimated during World War II, leaving only 91 surviving animals. It now houses over seventeen thousand animals spanning 1400 species. The hippo house is a highlight, while famous residents include the world's second-oldest gorilla: 58-year-old Fatou.

BERLIN AQUARIUM

Budapester Str. 32 ⓤ/Ⓢ Zoologischer Garten ☎ 030 25 401, ⓦ www.zoo-berlin.de. Daily 9am–6pm. €13. MAP P.130–131, POCKET MAP C6

BERLIN AQUARIUM

Situated next to the zoo, the city's impressive aquarium holds the title for world's most biodiverse collection. From jellyfish to crocodiles and other reptiles and tropical fish, the aquarium has over fourteen thousand creatures on three floors. Built in 1913, the aquarium has retained its old-fashioned appearance albeit incorporating modern elements. Take a walk on the bridge spanning the reptile pit and check out the new glass-roofed "Hippoquarium".

MUSEUM FÜR FOTOGRAFIE

Jebensstr. 2 Ⓤ/Ⓢ Zoologischer Garten ☏ 030 26 64 24 242, Ⓦ www.smb.museum /mf. Tues, Wed & Fri 10am–6pm, Thurs 10am–8pm, Sat & Sun 11am–6pm. €10. MAP P.130–131, POCKET MAP Bo

The Museum of Photography opened in 2004 in a former casino building, and has quickly risen in popularity, drawing about 120,000 visitors a year. The city's largest museum dedicated to the art form, it covers 2000 square metres and houses a thousand images by famous *Vogue* photographer Helmut Newton, whose provocative black-and-white photographs made him famous in the world of fashion photography and beyond; his work is shown on a rotating basis in addition to exhibits of other photographers. In the large Kaisersaal, on the second floor, you'll find the Kunstbibliothek's collection, which explores all kinds of photography ranging from the nineteenth to twenty-first centuries.

C/O BERLIN (AMERIKA HAUS)

Hardenbergstr. 22–24 Ⓤ Zoologischer Garten ☏ 030 28 44 41 60, Ⓦ co-berlin.org. Daily 11am–8pm. €10. MAP P.130–131, POCKET MAP B6

Since its foundation back in 2000, C/O Berlin has hosted some of the city's best photography exhibitions, with shows featuring international heavyweights such as Martin Parr, Annie Leibovitz, Rene Burri and Karl Lagerfeld. The gallery moved in 2013 from Mitte to West Berlin's Amerika Haus, where it hosted open-air exhibitions until the venue's reopening in 2014. Visitors can expect a high standard of curation and big-name retrospectives, as well as continued promotion of young and new local talent.

Charlottenburg

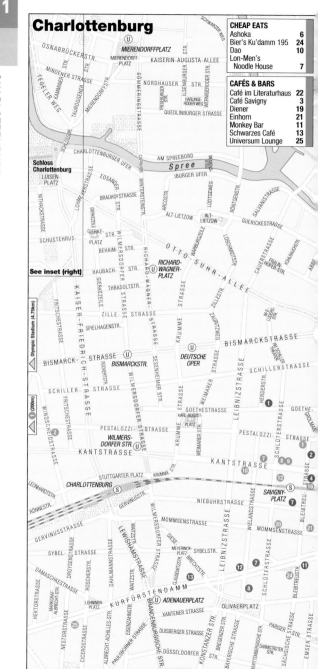

CHEAP EATS	
Ashoka	6
Bier's Ku'damm 195	24
Dao	10
Lon-Men's Noodle House	7

CAFÉS & BARS	
Café im Literaturhaus	22
Café Savigny	3
Diener	19
Einhorn	21
Monkey Bar	11
Schwarzes Café	13
Universum Lounge	25

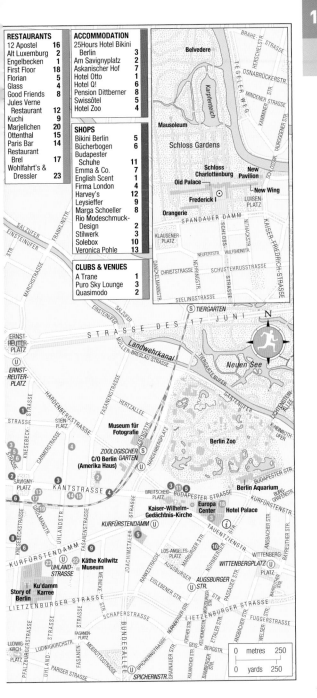

RESTAURANTS
12 Apostel	16
Alt Luxemburg	2
Engelbecken	1
First Floor	18
Florian	5
Glass	4
Good Friends	8
Jules Verne Restaurant	12
Kuchi	9
Marjellchen	20
Ottenthal	15
Paris Bar	14
Restaurant Brel	17
Wohlfahrt's & Dressler	23

ACCOMMODATION
25Hours Hotel Bikini Berlin	3
Am Savignyplatz	2
Askanischer Hof	7
Hotel Otto	1
Hotel Q!	6
Pension Dittberner	8
Swissôtel	5
Hotel Zoo	4

SHOPS
Bikini Berlin	5
Bücherbogen	6
Budapester Schuhe	11
Emma & Co.	7
English Scent	1
Firma London	4
Harvey's	12
Leysieffer	9
Marga Schoeller	8
Rio Modeschmuck-Design	2
Stilwerk	3
Solebox	10
Veronica Pohle	13

CLUBS & VENUES
A Trane	1
Puro Sky Lounge	3
Quasimodo	2

KAISER-WILHELM-GEDÄCHTNIS-KIRCHE

KAISER-WILHELM-GEDÄCHTNIS-KIRCHE

Breitscheidplatz ⓤ Kurfürstendamm
☎ 030 21 85 023, ⓦ www.gedaechtniskirche
-berlin.de. Church: daily 9am–7pm. Hall of
Remembrance: Mon–Fri 10am–6pm, Sat
10am–5.30pm, Sun noon–5.20pm. Guided
tours: daily 1.15pm, 2pm & 3pm, Mon, Fri &
Sat also 10.15am, 11am & noon. Church and
tours free. MAP P.130–131, POCKET MAP B7

The Kaiser Wilhelm Memorial
Church, built between 1891
and 1895 in neo-Romanesque
style by architect Franz
Schwechten, was commissioned
by Kaiser Wilhelm II and
served as a symbol of Prussian
unity. Nearly destroyed during
a World War II air raid, all that
remains are the ruins of the
spire and entrance hall. A new
structure was built in 1961, and
the stunning, blue stained-glass
windows fitted in concrete
bricks contrast memorably with
the haunting skeleton of the
old. The base of the old spire
and entrance hall is now a
memorial hall, with exhibits
documenting the old church
through photos and artefacts
that survived the bombing.

KÄTHE KOLLWITZ MUSEUM

Fasanenstr. 24 ⓤ Uhlandstr. ☎ 030 88 25 210,
ⓦ www.kaethe-kollwitz.de. Daily 11am–6pm.
€6. MAP P.130–131, POCKET MAP B7

German artist Käthe Kollwitz's
work was greatly influenced by
the loss of her son in World
War I and her grandson in
World War II. She was a
pacifist who lived in Berlin for
fifty years, and was the first
woman elected to the Prussian
Academy of the Arts but
resigned her post in 1933 in
protest at Hitler's rise to power.
Kollwitz's works were banned
by the Nazis. Many of her
pieces are powerful reminders
of some of the most painful
aspects of her life. Works on
display here include dour
self-portraits, plaintively titled
sketches, woodcuts, litho-
graphs, war protest posters and
sculptures. The building itself is
the oldest private home on
Fasanenstrasse, built in 1871
and restored in the 1980s.

STORY OF BERLIN

Kurfürstendamm 207–208 ⓤ Uhlandstr.
☎ 030 88 72 01 00, ⓦ www.story-of-berlin.de.
Daily 10am–8pm, last admission 6pm; bunker
tours in English at noon, 2pm, 4pm & 6pm
€12. MAP P.130–131, POCKET MAP A7

The Story of Berlin aims to
transport visitors to each of
the eight centuries of Berlin's
history through multimedia
displays that include photos,
films and interactive exhibits.
It follows the history of the city
from its founding in 1237,
to the Thirty Years' War,
Frederick the Great's reign, the
1920s, World War II, the Cold
War and the fall of the Wall.
Also included is a guided tour
of an atomic bomb shelter on
the site.

SCHLOSS CHARLOTTENBURG

Spandauer Damm 10–22 ⓤ Sophie-Charlotte-
Platz/Richard-Wagner-Platz ☎ 033 19 69 40,
ⓦ www.spsg.de. Old Palace Tues–Sun:
Jan–March noon–4pm; April–Oct 10am–6pm;
€12. New Wing daily except Tues: April–Oct
10am–6pm; Nov–March 10am–5pm; €8.

Belvedere April–Oct Tues–Sun 10am–6pm; closed Nov–March; €3. Mausoleum April–Oct Tues–Sun 10am–6pm; €2. New Pavilion Tues–Sun: April–Oct 10am–6pm; Nov–March 10am–5pm; €4. Combined ticket €17. MAP P.130–131, POCKET MAP A4

As you walk through Schloss Charlottenburg, you'll be in no doubt as to why its builder, Frederick I, was known as an extravagant spender who nearly bankrupted the state. The former Elector of Brandenburg, who named himself king of Prussia in 1701, had this ornate Baroque palace built as a summer home for his wife, Sophie Charlotte, in 1695. It started as a relatively modest dwelling but ballooned to its present palatial status with additions throughout the 1700s. Majestic rooms, art and plenty of porcelain characterize the interiors. In fact, the art in the palace constitutes the largest collection of eighteenth-century French paintings outside of France. There's a separate entrance fee for each of the three main buildings; The **Old Palace** features Baroque rooms, royal apartments, Chinese and Japanese porcelain and silverware chambers; the **New Wing** is more Rococo with an array of refined furniture in apartments built by Frederick the Great; and the

Schinkel-built **New Pavilion** features a collection of arts and crafts. Visitors can also visit the **Mausoleum**, which contains the graves of, and memorials to, members of the Hohenzollern family, and the **Belvedere**, which displays a collection of Berlin porcelain. The reconstructed **Orangerie** is also open for concerts and the gardens are open and free. Guided tours are offered of the historic apartments and chapel.

OLYMPIC STADIUM

Olympischer Platz 3 ○ Olympiastadion
○ 030 30 68 81 00, ○ www.olympiastadion
-berlin.de. Daily: April–Oct 9am–7pm; Nov–March 10am–4pm; Aug 9am–8pm. €7. Guided tours available. MAP P.130–131, POCKET MAP A5

Berlin's Olympic stadium, built for the 1936 Summer Olympics (immortalized in the film *Olympia* by Leni Riefenstahl), is one of the last surviving remnants of Nazi architecture in Berlin. Occupied by the British military following the war and used by them until 1994, the stadium is now used for concerts and events and also as the official ground of Hertha BSC, Berlin's most famous football club. It was renovated for the 2006 World Cup and now has the highest all-seated capacity in Germany (74,228). The stadium remains an impressive place to visit.

Shops

BIKINI BERLIN

Budapester Str. 38–50 Ⓤ/Ⓢ Zoologischer
Garten ☎ 030 55 49 64 54, Ⓦ www.bikiniberlin
.de. Mon–Sat 10am–8pm. MAP P.130–131, POCKET
MAP B6

This trendy concept mall in a
1950s building place was –
arguably – the place that put
West Berlin back on the map.
Spanning offices and a cinema,
as well as the *25hours* hotel and
bar (see p.156 and p.139), the
lower three floors offer chic
retail and gastronomy.

BÜCHERBOGEN

Stadtbahnbogen 593 Ⓢ Savignyplatz
☎ 030 31 86 59 11. Mon–Fri 10am–8pm,
Sat 10am–7pm. MAP P.130–131, POCKET MAP A7

You could spend hours in this
famed art book store, located
beneath Savignyplatz S-Bahn.
You'll find plenty of English-
language books in the design,
photography, art and theatre
sections, though nothing in the
literature section, sadly.

BUDAPESTER SCHUHE

Kurfürstendamm 199 Ⓤ Uhlandstr.
☎ 030 88 11 707. Mon–Fri 10am–7pm, Sat
10am–6pm. MAP P.130–131, POCKET MAP A7

A spacious and well-stocked
shoe shop whose wares run the
gamut from reasonably priced
leather classics to designer
models from Prada and Tod's.

EMMA & CO

Niebuhrstr. 2 Ⓢ Savignyplatz ☎ 030 88 67
67 87. Mon–Fri 11am–7pm, Sat 11am–4pm.
MAP P.130–131, POCKET MAP A7

Lovingly decorated store with
attentive staff. They carry
alternative wooden toys, as well
as the classic brands for
children, and babywear.

ENGLISH SCENT

Goethestr. 15 Ⓢ Deutsche Oper ☎ 030 32
44 655. Mon, Tues, Thurs & Fri 10am–2pm &
3–6.30pm, Wed 2–6.30pm, Sat 10am–3pm.
MAP P.130–131, POCKET MAP A6

Located in a suitably evocative
old building, English Scent
offers a range of fragrances,
skincare products, shaving
supplies, and even toothpastes.

FIRMA LONDON

Bleibtreustr. 50 Ⓢ Savignyplatz ☎ 030 83 21
08 93. Tues–Fri noon–7pm, Sat noon–5pm.
MAP P.130–131, POCKET MAP A6

Run by former Stella McCartney
designer Sandra Tietje and
gallerist Florian von Holstein,
this is not for the financially
faint-hearted, but it does stock
some gorgeous vintage furniture
and accessories.

HARVEY'S

Kurfürstendamm 56 Ⓤ Adenauerplatz ☎ 030
88 33 803. Mon–Sat 11am–8pm. MAP P.130–131,
POCKET MAP A7

A wonderland of men's
designer clothes from designers
such as Comme des Garçons
and Yohji Yamamoto.

LEYSIEFFER

Kurfürstendamm 218 Ⓤ Uhlandstr. ☎ 030 88
57 480. Mon–Sat 9am–7pm, Sun 10am–5pm
(closed Sun from June–Aug). MAP P.130–131,
POCKET MAP B7

This Ku'damm branch of the
famed German chocolateria

BÜCHERBOGEN

STILWERK

Kantstr. 17 ⓢ Savignyplatz ☏ 030 31 51 50.
Mon–Sat 10am–7pm. MAP P.130–131, POCKET MAP A6

Swanky designer mall, located near Zoologischer Garten, comprising shops dedicated to home decoration, jewellery and fashion. Expect high-end stores like Bang & Olufsen, with one or two cheaper options as well. There's a café and even a babysitting service for those who want to dump the kids.

SOLEBOX

Nürnbergerstr. 16 ⓤ Wittenbergplatz
☏ 030 91 20 66 90. Mon–Sat 11am–8pm.
MAP P.130–131, POCKET MAP C7

A spacious shrine to streetwear, stocking Reebok, Converse, Ellesse and Adidas sneakers plus T-shirts and hoodies.

VERONICA POHLE

Kurfürstendamm 64 ⓤ Adenauerplatz ☏ 030 88 33 731. Mon–Fri 10.30am–7.30pm, Sat 11am–6.30pm. MAP P.130–131, POCKET MAP A7

Over 200 square metres filled with designer garments from Alexander McQueen to Zinga Cashmere. Besides basics, bags and jewellery there's a wide array of dresses.

does a brisk trade. Aside from the usual sweet goodies, there's also a small coffee bar, useful if you're looking for a break from all the shopping.

MARGA SCHOELLER

Knesebeckstr. 33 ⓤ Uhlandstr. ☏ 030 88 11 112. Mon–Wed 9.30am–7pm, Thurs & Fri 9.30am–8pm, Sat 9.30am–6pm. MAP P.130–131, POCKET MAP A7

Opened in 1929 by the eponymous Frau Schoeller, this bookstore, one of the longest running in Europe, was a focal point for West Berlin's postwar literary scene. Schoeller's son now runs it, continuing to sell a fantastic range of German- and English-language books on poetry, theatre and philosophy as well as fiction, history and plenty of tomes about Berlin and Germany.

RIO MODESCHMUCK-DESIGN

Bleibtreustr. 52 ⓢ Savignyplatz ☏ 030 31 33 152. Mon–Wed & Fri 11am–6.30pm, Thurs 11am–7pm, Sat 11am–6pm. MAP P.130–131, POCKET MAP A6

Designer Barbara Kranz opened her jewellery store back in 1984 – she calls her creations "after 5pm" jewellery due to their natural evening-wear flamboyance and glamour.

Restaurants

12 APOSTEL

Bleibtreustr. 49 ⓢ Savignyplatz ☏ 030 31 21 433, Ⓦ www.12-apostel.de. Daily 11am–1am.
MAP P.130–131, POCKET MAP A6

A smart, Baroque-style interior (check the kitsch religious frescoes) and generously sized thin pizzas mark this place out. They're slightly on the expensive side – around €12 – but specials on the weekly changing lunch menu start at €7.50. The Sunday brunch buffet (10am–3pm) is €22 but comes with a glass of sparkling wine and a hot drink.

ALT LUXEMBURG

Windscheidstr. 31 ⓤ Sophie-Charlotte-Platz
☎ 030 32 38 730, ⓦ www.alt-luxemburg.de.
Mon–Sat 5pm–late. MAP P.130–131,
POCKET MAP A6

Located in a renovated customs house, *Alt Luxemburg* boasts antique furnishings, attentive service and a great menu of traditional German cuisine, plus a good wine list. There are four- or five-course fixed-price menus (€74 and €79) and a daily happy hour (5–7pm) with a fifteen percent reduction.

ENGELBECKEN

Witzlebenstr. 31 ⓤ Sophie-Charlotte-Platz
☎ 030 61 52 810, ⓦ www.engelbecken.de.
Mon–Fri 5pm–1am, Sat 4pm–1am, Sun
noon–1am. MAP P.130–131, POCKET MAP A6

A high-quality restaurant that serves Bavarian and Alpine cuisine – *schnitzel*, goulash – with an emphasis on organic products and home-made sauces. Vegetarian and vegan options are available, and the park-facing terrace is nice in the summer.

FIRST FLOOR

Hotel Palace, Budapester Str. 45
ⓤ Kurfürstendamm ☎ 030 25 02 10 20,
ⓦ firstfloor.hotel-palace.biz. Tues–Sat
6.30–11pm. MAP P.130–131, POCKET MAP C7

Matthias Diether is the mastermind behind one of Berlin's most celebrated restaurants. His inventive French/European menu is seasonal and changes regularly, and though not cheap (mains €24–54) you get your money's worth. The menus are four, six or nine courses (€109–159).

FLORIAN

Grolmanstr. 52 ⓢ Savignyplatz ☎ 030 31 39
184, ⓦ www.restaurant-florian.de. Daily
6pm–3am. MAP P.130–131, POCKET MAP A6

The two female chefs who run *Florian*, on an upmarket residential street, have been in charge for 33 years, serving fine south German food. The dishes are hearty and innovative, the interior coolly bland and the service excellent. Typical dishes include sour kidneys from the daily changing menu (mains €15.20–28.90).

GLASS

Uhlandstr. 195 ⓤ Uhlandstrasse ☎ 030 54 71
08 61, ⓦ www.glassberlin.de. Tues–Sat
6–11pm. MAP P.130–131, POCKET MAP B6

Run by talented young Israeli chef Gal Ben Moshe, this restaurant blends a relaxed, low-key interior with affordable high-end cuisine in the shape of six- or eight-course menus. Vegan versions are available but whatever you do, save some room for the fabulous deconstructed dessert.

GOOD FRIENDS

Kantstr. 30 ⓢ Savignyplatz ☎ 030 31 32 659,
ⓦ www.goodfriends-berlin.de. Daily
noon–1am. MAP P.130–131, POCKET MAP A6

Possibly the best-known Cantonese restaurant in town, though don't expect anything fancy, or even extravagantly Chinese in terms of decor. It's a large, minimal place, with dishes from €6.90 at lunch and €9.80 in the evening. Aside from the classics they serve jellyfish and spiced paunch – not for the faint-hearted.

JULES VERNE RESTAURANT

Schlüterstr. 61 ⓢ Savignyplatz ☎ 030 31 80
94 10, ⓦ www.jules-verne-berlin.de. Daily
9am–1am, kitchen till 11.45pm. MAP P.130–131,
POCKET MAP A6

The interior feels classic French but the menu is aptly global, ranging from *Flammkuchen* (*tarte flambée*) and *schnitzel* to *couscous* and *satay*. Lunchtime deals change daily.

MARJELLCHEN

KUCHI

Kantstr. 30 Ⓢ Savignyplatz ☎ 030 31 50 78 15, Ⓦ www.kuchi.de. Daily noon–midnight. MAP P.130–131, POCKET MAP A6

With a sister restaurant in Mitte, this place sells the same range of innovative *sushi*, *sashimi*, *yakitori*, as well as some Thai, Chinese and Korean recipes. Busy at peak times so it's best to reserve a table. Happy hour from 5pm includes noodle soups for €6 and *sushi* for €7.

MARJELLCHEN

Mommsenstr. 9 Ⓢ Savignyplatz ☎ 030 88 32 676, Ⓦ www.marjellchen-berlin.de. Daily 5pm–midnight. MAP P.130–131, POCKET MAP A7

It's obvious from the window displays – books, photos and other paraphernalia – that this is a time warp kind of place. Indeed, *Marjellchen* specializes in cuisine from East Prussia, Pomerania and Silesia, all served up in a cosy, traditional atmosphere. Portions are generous and service is friendly (mains €10.50–20.20).

OTTENTHAL

Kantstr. 153 Ⓢ Savignyplatz ☎ 030 31 33 162, Ⓦ www.ottenthal.com, Daily 5pm–1am. MAP P.130–131, POCKET MAP B6

White-clothed tables and relatively sparse white walls lend this place an unfussy, classic feel that ties in well with the Austrian cuisine – which is simple yet some of the best in the area. Organic ingredients feature on the menu, which includes fish dishes, risotto and a famed *Wiener schnitzel*. Good Austrian wine list too.

PARIS BAR

Kantstr. 152 Ⓢ/Ⓤ Zoologischer Garten ☎ 030 31 38 052, Ⓦ www.parisbar.net. Daily noon–1am. MAP P.130–131, POCKET MAP B6

There's still something tangibly bohemian about the *Paris Bar*, once one of the centres of West Berlin's art scene until the Wall fell and the East took over. Interesting artworks vie for your attention and the somewhat pricey food takes second place to the social networking action. Lunch €15–28, dinner mains €28–40.

RESTAURANT BREL

Savignyplatz 1 Ⓢ Savignyplatz ☎ 030 31 80 00 20, Ⓦ www.cafebrel.de. Daily 10am–1am. MAP P.130–131, POCKET MAP A6

This well-established bistro has a comfortable, friendly but sophisticated feel, with a long wooden bar, black-and-white photos and grand piano. It's matched by excellent French food and wines; try the three-course lunch menu for just €11.50.

WOHLFAHRT'S & DRESSLER

Kurfürstendamm 206–208 Ⓤ Uhlandstr. ☎ 030 88 33 530, Ⓦ www.restaurant -dressler.de. Daily 8am–1am, (kitchen till midnight). MAP P.130–131, POCKET MAP A7

This German take on a French brasserie enjoys something of a time warp ambience thanks to its Art Nouveau interior, formal but friendly service and very good seasonal food. The main dining area might be a bit stiff for some, but the small front bar is perfect for a quick coffee or lunch if you're on Ku'damm.

Cheap eats

ASHOKA

Grolmanstr. 51 Ⓢ Savignyplatz ☎ 030 31 01 58 06. Daily 11am–midnight. MAP P.130–131, POCKET MAP A6

Ashok Sharma opened this restaurant in 1975 as he was missing the food from his home in Punjab. It offers well-priced, decent quality food in a small *Imbiss*-style place. Vegetarian options and friendly staff.

BIER'S KU'DAMM 195

Kurfürstendamm 195 Ⓤ Uhlandstr. ☎ 030 88 18 942. Mon–Thurs 11am–5am, Fri & Sat 11am–6pm, Sun noon–5pm. MAP P.130–131, POCKET MAP A7

One of several spots claimed as the "best in Berlin" for *Currywurst*. It also serves meat skewers and meatballs, and is generally busy all night; if you feel like splashing out ask for champagne with your *Wurst*.

DAO

Kantstr. 133 Ⓢ Savignyplatz ☎ 030 37 59 14 14, Ⓦ www.dao-restaurant.de. Daily noon–midnight. MAP P.130–131, POCKET MAP A6

Opened by a Berliner and his Thai wife Dao in the 1970s, this Thai spot serves dishes brimful of flavour. Alongside *pad Thai* (€9.90) and fish and duck dishes (up to €20) there are specials like "Bloodnoodlesoup".

LON-MEN'S NOODLE HOUSE

Kantstr. 33 Ⓢ Savignyplatz ☎ 030 31 51 96 78. Daily noon–11pm. MAP P.130–131, POCKET MAP A6

A relaxed, tiny Taiwanese noodle shop run by friendly grandmas who make mean dumplings and noodle soups. Try the "Chinese Maultaschen" – fried ravioli-style parcels filled with pork and vegetables (€5–6). Ask for the home-made noodles (not on the menu).

Cafés and bars

CAFÉ IM LITERATURHAUS

Fasanenstr. 23 Ⓤ Uhlandstr. ☎ 030 88 25 414, Ⓦ www.literaturhaus-berlin.de. Daily 9am–midnight. MAP P.130–131, POCKET MAP B7

This place is every bit as classic and elegant as its name suggests. The spacious interior or beautiful summer garden are great spots for coffee and cake, lunch or dinner: the largely organic menu changes regularly and has vegetarian options.

CAFÉ SAVIGNY

Grolmanstr. 53 Ⓢ Savignyplatz ☎ 0157 52 00 48 10. Daily 9am–midnight. MAP P.130–131, POCKET MAP A6

A small, classic spot that's been serving great breakfasts and coffee for over a decade. Lunches start at €5.50 (soups) with hearty Burgundy stew for €13.50. Service is good and it's also nice for an evening drink.

DIENER

Grolmanstr. 47 Ⓢ Savignyplatz ☎ 030 88 15 329, Ⓦ www.diener-berlin.de. Daily 6pm–3am. MAP P.130–131, POCKET MAP A6

This Berlin ale house is a local institution – not only because it was opened in 1954 by former German heavyweight boxer Franz Diener, but because it serves dishes like *Königsberger Klopse* (meatballs in white sauce with capers, €10.50) and

CAFÉ IM LITERATURHAUS

SCHWARZES CAFÉ

has an atmosphere as old school as the menu.

EINHORN

Mommsenstr. 2 Ⓢ Savignyplatz ☎ 030 88 14 241, Ⓦ einhorn-catering.de. Daily Mon–Fri 10am–5pm. MAP P.130–131, POCKET MAP A7

A great place if you're seeking a tasty veggie lunch. There's a buffet selection including antipasti and and dishes like lentils with goat's cheese. Mostly priced by weight (€1.50/100g).

MONKEY BAR

Budapesterstr. 40 Ⓤ/Ⓢ Zoologischer Garten ☎ 030 12 02 21 210, Ⓦ www.25hours-hotels. com. Mon–Thurs & Sun noon–1am, Fri & Sat noon–2am. MAP P.130–131, POCKET MAP B6

Part of the buzz for the new *25hours* hotel (see p.156) has been that there's finally a decent rooftop bar in West Berlin. The floor-to-ceiling windows make for great sundowner vibes.

SCHWARZES CAFÉ

Kantstr. 148 Ⓢ Savignyplatz ☎ 030 31 38 038. Daily 24hr. MAP P.130–131, POCKET MAP A6

The slightly ragged charm of the "Black Café" makes it feel like it would be better placed in the east. The downstairs is small and intimate, but upstairs the large, airy room has a relaxed, convivial vibe. Food is served 24 hours, including breakfasts (from €4.50) – but this is a night-owl place really.

UNIVERSUM LOUNGE

Kurfürstendamm 153 Ⓤ Adenauerplatz ☎ 030 32 76 47 93, Ⓦ www.universumlounge .com. MAP P.130–131, POCKET MAP A7

Located in the stunning Bauhaus-era Universum Cinema, this place is an oddity even by Berlin standards. A curved main bar decorated in golds and browns and lunar-themed wallpaper lend it a futuristic feel. Good cocktails.

Clubs and venues

A TRANE

Bleibtreustr. 1 Ⓢ Savignyplatz ☎ 030 31 32 550, Ⓦ www.a-trane.de. Daily from 9pm, music from around 10pm. MAP P.130–131, POCKET MAP A6

Good jazz and decent cocktails in a classic jazz-style interior (small and smoky). Often hosts major international acts.

PURO SKY LOUNGE

Tauentzienstr. 9–11 Ⓤ Kurfürstendamm ☎ 030 26 36 78 75, Ⓦ www.puro-berlin.de. Thurs 10pm–6am, Fri 9pm–6am, Sat 11pm–6am MAP P.130–131, POCKET MAP C7

Ensconced on the twentieth floor of the ugly Europa Center, the *Puro Sky Lounge* is filled with eye candy thanks to the beautiful people who flock here for the jaw-dropping views. What it lacks in musical edge – think 1980s classics– it makes up for with an upbeat crowd.

QUASIMODO

Kantstr. 12A Ⓤ Savignyplatz ☎ 030 31 80 45 60, Ⓦ www.quasimodo.de. MAP P.130–131, POCKET MAP B6

A classic jazz bar, *Quasimodo* (underneath the Delphi Cinema) features black-and-white photos, low ceilings and intimate tables. Aside from jazz there's funk, blues and Latin and the odd international star.

Schöneberg

Famous during the 1920s as the centre of Berlin's decadent nightlife scene and again in the 1970s when it was home to David Bowie during his dissipated sojourn in the city, Schöneberg's star waned in the 1990s as the cool kids moved east. But while East Berlin has become increasingly slick and unaffordable, this part of town has – as they say – kept it real. Nowadays the hipsters are heading back, attracted by the still-low rents and the burgeoning gallery scene in Potsdamer Strasse, and it maintains its reputation as the pinkest borough in Berlin, especially around Nollendorfplatz. It's also long-been a popular spot for writers – Christopher Isherwood had his digs in Nollendorfstrasse back in the day, and a new generation of writers including Helen DeWitt and Ida Hattemer-Higgins today call the neighbourhood home. Though it lacks any major sights, the charming Winterfeldtplatz hosts a highly popular farmers' market (Sat 8am–4pm).

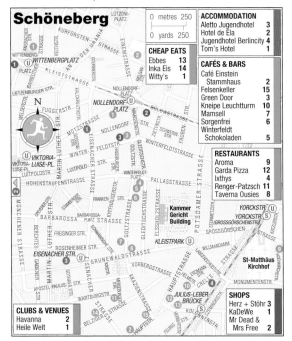

Schöneberg

ACCOMMODATION	
Aletto Jugendhotel	3
Hotel de Ela	2
Jugendhotel Berlincity	4
Tom's Hotel	1

CHEAP EATS	
Ebbes	13
Inka Eis	14
Witty's	1

CAFÉS & BARS	
Café Einstein Stammhaus	2
Felsenkeller	15
Green Door	3
Kneipe Leuchtturm	10
Mamsell	7
Sorgenfrei	6
Winterfeldt Schokoladen	5

RESTAURANTS	
Aroma	9
Garda Pizza	12
Ixthys	4
Renger-Patzsch	11
Taverna Ousies	8

CLUBS & VENUES	
Havanna	2
Heile Welt	1

SHOPS	
Herz + Stöhr	3
KaDeWe	1
Mr Dead & Mrs Free	2

Shops

HERZ + STÖHR

Winterfeldtstr. 52 Ⓤ Nollendorfplatz ☎ 030 21 64 425. Mon–Fri 11am–7pm, Sat 11am–4pm. MAP OPPOSITE, POCKET MAP D8

Intelligent, elegant designs from this German fashion duo – the dresses and suits are grown-up but not dowdy, and everything can be altered to fit.

KADEWE

Tauentzienstr. 21–24 Ⓤ Wittenbergplatz ☎ 030 21 210, Ⓦ www.kadewe.de. Mon–Thurs 10am–8pm, Fri 10am–9pm, Sat 9.30am–8pm. MAP OPPOSITE, POCKET MAP C7

If you're tired of Berlin's austere side, check out KaDeWe (Kaufhaus Des Westerns), a temple to conspicuous consumption. The largest department store in continental Europe, it sports designer gear alongside some surprisingly affordable accessories and homewares. The legendary sixth-floor food hall will leave all but the most jaded of foodies starry-eyed.

MR DEAD & MRS FREE

Bülowstr. 5 Ⓤ Nollendorfplatz ☎ 030 21 51 449. Mon–Fri noon–7pm, Sat 11am–4pm. MAP OPPOSITE, POCKET MAP D7

A dusty little legend of a music shop crammed full of everything from the latest imports to rare vintage albums.

Restaurants

AROMA

Hochkirchstr. 8 Ⓢ/Ⓤ Yorckstr. ☎ 030 78 25 821, Ⓦ www.cafe-aroma.de. Mon–Fri from 5pm, Sat from 2pm, Sun brunch 11am–2pm, from 2pm a la carte. MAP OPPOSITE, POCKET MAP E9

Tucked into a sleepy residential street, this rustic Italian gem is the unofficial headquarters for Berlin's slow food movement.

The antipasti spread at Sunday brunch (€14.50) is legendary, while classic pastas (€9–12), pizzas (€6–9) and changing seasonal specials (€15–20) satisfy the dinner crowd. The terrace is a peaceful haven.

GARDA PIZZA

Crellestr. 48 Ⓢ Julius-Leber-Brücke ☎ 030 78 09 79 70. Mon–Sat 11.30am–9pm. MAP OPPOSITE, POCKET MAP D9

Locals flock to *Garda Pizza* for their trays of thin-crust Roman-style *focaccia*. Their most popular slice (€2) combines fresh aubergine, mushroom, sheep's salami and artichokes. A tray (€15) will feed a hungry group of four. Join the crowd on the pavement, or mosey down a few metres and let your children burn off the calories in the neighbouring playground.

IXTHYS

Pallasstr. 21 Ⓤ Nollendorfplatz ☎ 030 81 47 47 69. Mon–Sat noon–10pm. MAP OPPOSITE, POCKET MAP D8

A tiny café run by two Korean widows (who've festooned the walls with biblical slogans), this places is all about great home-style cooking. Guests squeeze in to enjoy the home-made noodles with vegetables (€5) or seafood (€7.50) and the fiery, sizzling *bibimbap* (€7.50).

KADEWE

RENGER-PATZSCH

Wartburgstr. 54 Ⓤ Eisenacher Str. ☎ 030 78
42 059, Ⓦ www.renger-patzsch.com. Daily
6–11.30pm. MAP P.140, POCKET MAP D9

An interior of dark wood and
white tablecloths forms the
backdrop to an expertly
prepared selection of German
dishes (starters €6–11; mains
€16–21.50; *tartes flambées*
€8–11). In spring, look for the
dandelion salad with lardons;
in winter, the braised ox cheeks
with bacon-wrapped plums,
turnips and mashed potatoes.

TAVERNA OUSIES

Grunewaldstr. 16 Ⓤ Eisenacher Str. ☎ 030
21 67 957, Ⓦ www.taverna-ousies.de. Daily
from 5pm. MAP P.140, POCKET MAP D9

This kitschy, raucous Greek
taverna is a perennial favourite.
There are no real duds, so go
wild with the meze menu
(€4–7) and be entertained by
the jolly staff. Reservations
essential at weekends.

Cheap eats

EBBES

Crellestr. 5 Ⓢ Julius-Leber-Brücke
☎ 030 70 09 48 13. Mon–Fri 10am–7.30pm,
Sat 9am–4pm. MAP P.140, POCKET MAP D9

This quirky Swabian deli is
crowded with rings of venison
salami and trays of fresh *spätzle*
(noodles). Owner Wolfgang
Steppes finds his suppliers on
trips to southern Germany. Buy
a picnic and wander north to
Kleistpark, or grab a stool
outside and try one of the daily
specials (€2.50–5), such as
Maultaschen (ravioli) in broth.

INKA EIS

Belziger Str. 44 Ⓤ Eisenacher Str. ☎ 030 78
09 70 50. Daily: summer 11am–8pm; winter
11am–7pm. MAP P.140, POCKET MAP D9

A little taste of Latin America
in a quiet corner of

Schöneberg, *Inka Eis* serves
scrumptious scoops of
tamarind ice cream, Peruvian
grilled chicken (€6.50) and
empanadas (€4.50).

WITTY'S

Wittenbergplatz 5 Ⓤ Wittenbergplatz ☎ 030
21 19 496, Ⓦ www.wittys-berlin.de. Mon–Sat
11am–midnight, Sun noon–midnight. MAP P.140,
POCKET MAP C7

One of the city's first and finest
organic sausage stands, *Witty's*
has customers lined up along
the square for their *Currywurst*
and crispy fries.

Cafés and bars

CAFÉ EINSTEIN STAMMHAUS

Kurfürstenstr. 58 Ⓤ Nollendorfplatz ☎ 030
26 39 19 18, Ⓦ www.cafeeinstein.com. Daily
8am–1am. MAP P.140, POCKET MAP D7

Set in a beautiful historic villa,
this classic coffeehouse and
restaurant offers fantastic
breakfasts, *schnitzels* and cakes.
On sunny days make a beeline
for the spacious garden and sip
bellinis while the shadows
lengthen.

FELSENKELLER

Akazienstr. 2 Ⓢ Julius-Leber-Brücke ☎ 030
78 13 447. Mon–Fri 4pm–1am, Sat noon–2am.
MAP P.140, POCKET MAP D9

The perfect destination when
you're nostalgic for old Berlin.
Founded in 1923, this bar is
famous for its eight beers on
tap; they're drawn the
old-fashioned way, so be
prepared to wait. There's hearty,
simple food (dishes from €5),
such as lentil soup and swede
stew. No music, but plenty
of atmosphere.

GREEN DOOR

Winterfeldtstr. 50 Ⓤ Nollendorfplatz ☎ 030
21 52 515, Ⓦ www.greendoor.de. Mon–Thurs
& Sun 6pm–3am, Fri & Sat 6pm–4am. MAP
P.140, POCKET MAP D8

GREEN DOOR

This gay-friendly café will take you straight back to the 1950s. There's Hawaiian-style toast on the menu and Bing Crosby on the speakers. The Bakelite radios and kidney-shaped tables aren't just for decoration – most of the items are for sale.

WINTERFELDT SCHOKOLADEN

Goltzstr. 23 Ⓤ Nollendorfplatz ☎ 030 23 62 32 56. Mon–Fri 9am–8pm, Sat 9am–6pm, Sun noon–7pm. MAP P.140, POCKET MAP D8

Once an apothecary, this café-chocolate shop serves a lovely selection of pastries to cure all your ills. Scones with clotted cream and jam and warm chocolate fondant cake are popular.

Ring the bell and enter one of Berlin's best-loved cocktail bars. The expert but unpretentious staff will recommend the perfect drink. An older crowd fills the cosy room. Happy hour till 9pm (cocktails €7).

KNEIPE LEUCHTTURM

Crellestr. 41 Ⓤ Kleistpark ☎ 030 78 18 519, Ⓦ www.leuchtturm-kneipe.de. May–Sept daily 4pm–late; Oct–April Mon–Fri & Sun 6pm–late, Sat 8pm–late. MAP P.140, POCKET MAP D9

If you think beer just isn't the same without a cigarette, head for the "Lighthouse", with its unpretentious, welcoming atmosphere favoured by former hippies and locals. The wines can be middling so go for one of the beers on tap.

MAMSELL

Goltzstr. 48 Ⓤ Eisenacher Str. ☎ 030 92 12 29 00. Mon–Fri 10am–7pm, Sat 10am–5pm, Sun 2–6pm. MAP P.140, POCKET MAP D8

Those with a penchant for pink will be delighted by this sweet café/shop. The addictive real hot chocolate is served with a dusting of freshly grated ginger.

SORGENFREI

Goltzstr. 18 Ⓤ Nollendorfplatz ☎ 030 30 10 40 71, Ⓦ www.sorgenfrei-in-berlin.de. Tues–Fri noon–7pm, Sat 10am–6pm, Sun 1–6pm. MAP P.140, POCKET MAP D8

Clubs and venues

HAVANNA

Hauptstr. 30 Ⓢ Julius-Leber-Brücke ☎ 030 78 48 565, Ⓦ www.havanna-berlin.de. Wed from 9pm, Fri & Sat from 10pm. MAP P.140, POCKET MAP D9

With four floors and seven bars, this magnet for Latin American music fans draws a diverse clientele. Serious salsa and tango fans will find like-minded devotees to shake it on the dancefloor.

HEILE WELT

Motzstr. 5 Ⓤ Nollendorfplatz ☎ 030 21 91 75 07. Daily from 6pm. MAP P.140, POCKET MAP D7

A much-beloved destination for gay men and the women who love them. Music runs the gamut from soul and dance to house and home-brewed "Schlager". During the week, enjoy one of the friendly bar staff's famously strong cocktails and settle into a comfortable sofa. The action picks up at the weekend, when it gets too crowded for some, and just right for others.

Day-trips from Berlin

There's so much to do in Berlin that it's easy to forget there's a world outside the city. Berlin's surroundings are surprisingly sparse and beautiful – a bucolic swathe of lakes, forests and small villages. Amidst the vast landscape lie some of the city's highlights, many of them less than an hour from the centre. Easily accessible by public transport, areas such as Dahlem, Potsdam and Wannsee make for enjoyable and edifying visits (as well as memorials to the darker side of the city's past). The most popular day-trip is Potsdam, which includes Schloss Sanssouci and Babelsberg film studios as well as a town centre distinct from anything in Berlin. The Wannsee area offers lakeside beaches as well as historical villas and the magical Pfaueninsel, while Dahlem has botanical gardens and some excellent ethnological museums. History buffs will find journeys to Sachsenhausen concentration camp, Villa Wannsee and Hohenschönhausen Stasi prison both chilling and instructive.

SACHSENHAUSEN

Str. der Nationen 22, Oranienburg ⓢ Oranienburg (end of S1 line, then follow signs for Gedenkstätte Sachsenhausen) ⓣ 033 01 20 00, ⓦ www.stiftung-bg.de. Daily: March 15–Oct 14 8.30am–6pm; Oct 15–March 14 8.30am–4.30pm. Museums, archive and library closed Mon, but the open-air exhibition, "Station Z" memorial and visitor information centre remain open. Free. Guided tours available for groups (€15–25) in a range of different languages.

Located in Oranienburg, 35km north of the city, Sachsenhausen ranks among Berlin's most emotionally wrenching wartime memorials – which is saying a lot for a city like this. Established in 1936, it was first used as a prison for political opponents. It became a training ground for SS officers, and from 1938 to 1945 the central administration for all concentration camps was located here. After the war started, tens of thousands of prisoners were brought here. In 1943 a small gas chamber was added. By 1944 some 200,000 people had passed through the prison, with tens of thousands dying of starvation, disease, mistreatment and systematic extermination. In April 1945 more than 33,000 prisoners were sent on the notorious death marches, during which more than a thousand

SACHSENHAUSEN

POTSDAM

died – those who collapsed en route were routinely shot. When the camp was liberated by Russian soldiers on April 22, 1945 only three thousand prisoners remained, many of whom who died in the days afterwards. The camp became a Soviet-run prison and in 1948 it was renamed "Special Camp No. 1". Sixty thousand people were interned here over five years, including six thousand German officers transferred from Western Allied camps. By the time the camp closed in the spring of 1950, twelve thousand had died of malnutrition and disease. In 1956, the GDR turned the site into a memorial, removing many of the original buildings and constructing an obelisk, statue and meeting area. Today the memorial is a place of commemoration as well as a museum that includes a wealth of information on the camp, artwork by inmates, models, pictures and more. Following the discovery in 1990 of mass graves from the Soviet period, a separate museum was opened about the Soviet-era history.

POTSDAM

Direct line to Wannsee, then change on S1 (20–30min; ticket for zones A,B and C); or regional trains (RE1) to Potsdam and Babelsberg. You can cover most of Potsdam by foot, though the Berlin and Potsdam WelcomeCard (see p.162), available from the tourist centre at the train station, includes transport and gives discounts on over two hundred attractions.

Located 24km southwest of Berlin, Potsdam makes for an easy and pleasant day-trip, with plenty to see and do, from the wonderful Schloss Sanssouci and its gardens to the Babelsberg film studios (see p.146). There are two quaint historic quarters in the city itself that are worth seeking out.

The **Russian Colony Alexandrowka** (Alexandrowka 2; ☎0331 817 02 03, ⓦwww .alexandrowka.de; Tues–Sun 10am–6pm, June–Sept Fri till 9pm; €3.50), created in 1826–27 on the request of Friedrich Wilhelm III in memory of his friend Tsar Alexander I, is an artist's village with twelve picturesque wooden houses and a small Russian Orthodox chapel (1829) on Kapellenberg hill to the north. Check out the Russian tearoom in the warden's house. The **Holländisches Viertel**, or Dutch quarter (ⓦwww.hollaendisches-viertel .net), consists of around 150 three-storey redbrick houses, and was built between 1734 and 1742 for Dutch craftsmen invited to Potsdam by Friedrich Wilhelm I. The houses are built in the classic Dutch style with shuttered windows and slanted roofs; at Mittelstrasse 8 the **Jan Bouman Haus** preserves a typical house of the era (☎0331 28 03 773; Mon–Fri 1–6pm, Sat & Sun 11am–6pm; €2), while the **Potsdam Museum** at Alter Markt 9 (☎0331 289 68 03; daily 10am–6pm; €3) displays historic paintings and photos of the city.

SCHLOSS SANSSOUCI AND PARK

Park Sanssouci ⑤ Potsdam. Around 5km from Potsdam train station; bus #695 goes from the train station, with stops at Schloss Sanssouci, the Orangerie and Neues Palais (among others). ☎ 033 19 69 42 00, ⌨ www .spsg.de. Palace Tues–Sun: April–Oct 10am–5pm; Nov–March 9am–4pm, timed guided tours only. Park daily 9am–dusk. Admission to palace €12 (€8 in winter); other attractions individually priced, or €19 day ticket for all buildings. Park: free.

The highlight of any trip to Potsdam, Schloss Sanssouci was built for Frederick the Great by the magnificently titled Georg Wenzeslaus von Knobelsdorff between 1745 and 1747. It was his summer residence – the place he came for some peace and quiet and to be with his beloved dogs (*Sans Souci* means "without worries" in French); the parkland, buildings and palaces dotted around it were added by later Prussian kings. Having survived unscathed from the War, the palace is considered one of the most significant examples of Rococo architecture – much of the original artworks were moved to Rheinsberg during the War or were transferred as booty to the Soviet Union, though

Frederick's library and 36 oil paintings were returned and can be viewed today alongside furnishings and decorations from the original rooms. The adjacent **picture gallery** exhibits works by Rubens, van Dyck, Caravaggio and other renowned artists, and the historic windmill – built in the Dutch style and rebuilt in 1993 – is worth a visit, as is the **Chinese Teahouse** (same times as Sanssouci; €3) and the **New Palace** (Neues Palais; Mon & Wed–Sun 10am–5/6pm; €8), a larger Baroque-style palace intended to display Frederick's power to the world. Best of all is the surrounding **park**, an inspiring display of terraced vineyards, flamboyant flower beds, hedges and abundant fruit trees. Note that the palaces are highly popular in summer and tours inside the main palace are limited, so arrive early or book ahead.

FILMPARK BABELSBERG

August-Bebel-Str. 26–53 (entrance Grossbeerenstr. 200) ⑤ Babelsburg, then bus #601, #619, #690 to Filmpark or RE1 to Medienstadt ☎ 033 17 21 27 50, ⌨ www .filmpark-babelsberg.de. April 1 to Nov 1 daily 10am–6pm. €21.

SCHLOSS SANSSOUCI

Some of Germany's most famous films were created at Studio Babelsberg, including masterpieces such as *Metropolis* (1927) and *The Blue Angel* (1930), starring Marlene Dietrich – in its heyday the studios were Europe's version of Hollywood. This associated theme park allows visitors to roam sets from old films, witness stuntmen in action and marvel at the special effects. It's especially good (if not better) for kids, who will enjoy the Jungle Playground and the Animal Farm.

DAHLEM MUSEUMS

ⓘ Dahlemdorf ☎ 030 83 01 438, ⓦ www .smb.museum. Tues–Fri 10am–5pm, Sat & Sun 11am–6pm, €8 (free Thurs 2–6pm).

The district of Berlin-Dahlem, located in the south of the city, is a green and pleasant place. It offers a collection of museums that comprise one of Germany's best ethno-cultural collections, as well as a splendid botanical gardens (see p.148).

The main **Ethnological Museum** (Ethnologisches Museum) holds around a million items, including artworks from Africa, exhibits from North-American Indians, full-scale wooden huts and boats from the South Pacific, a large collection of ceramic and stone sculptures from the Mayas, Aztecs and Incas and an intriguing assemblage of pre-Columbian relics, including gold objects and antiquities from Peru. There's also a great **Department of Music** where you can hear folk music recordings from around the globe.

The **Museum for Asian Art** includes both the Far Eastern collection and the Museum of Indian Art. It is devoted to one thousand years of Asian culture, and features lots of porcelain and lacquer from Korea, China and Japan, green jade, a seventeenth-century imperial throne from China and Japanese woodblock prints – all plundered during a massive "shopping expedition" the Germans undertook in Asia. Outside the main complex (a 5min walk away), the **Museum of European Cultures** (Museum Europäischer Kulturen) is devoted to the German people themselves – not the aristocrats but the middle class and the peasant stock who built the country. The exhibits go back four centuries, tracing how artisans and homemakers lived and worked. Household items are displayed along with primitive industrial equipment such as a utensil for turning flax into linen. Furnishings, clothing, pottery and even items used in religious observances are shown, along with some fun and whimsical exhibits, including depictions of pop culture from the 1950s to 1980s.

DOMÄNE DAHLEM

Königin-Luise-Str. 49 ☎ 030 66 63 000, ⓦ www.domaene-dahlem.de. Daily except Tues 10am–6pm. €3.

Just over the road from the museums is a working farm and handicraft centre known as Domäne Dahlem. Intended to showcase something of Germany's pre-industrial era, the complex includes an old estate house, a collection of agricultural instruments and demonstrations of artisan trades such as woodcarving, ceramics and wool spinning. The best time to come is at the weekend when more of the machines and workshops are on display and there's a small organic market (8am–1pm).

DAHLEM BOTANIC GARDENS

Königin-Luise-Str. 6–8 ⓤ/Ⓢ Rathaus Steglitz, and 15min walk or bus #X83 to Königin-Luise-Str./Botanischer Garten. ☎ 030 83 85 01 00, ⓦ www.bgbm.org. Daily: museum 10am–6pm; garden Jan, Nov & Dec 9am–4pm; Feb 9am–5pm; March & Oct 9am–6pm; April & Aug 9am–8pm; May, June & July 9am–9pm; Sept 9am–7pm. Gardens €6; museum €2.50.

Founded as an extension to the kitchen garden of the Berlin palace by the Elector of Prussia, by 1815 the royal herbarium had developed hugely thanks to extensive botanical research by C.L. Willdenow. The collection was moved to Dahlem in 1907 and today hosts 22,000 species of plants over 43 hectares, making it one of the largest and most diverse botanical gardens in the world. The sixteen green-houses (Gewächshäuser) feature an array of specialist areas such as a garden of aquatic and marsh plants, an aroma and touch garden and medicinal plants. The attached museum features sections of preserved fossils and plantformations on artificially constructed landscapes.

PFAUENINSEL

Ⓢ Wannsee, then bus #208 to the passenger ferry (€2). Museum: April–Oct Tues–Sun 10am–5.30pm. Island: April & Sept 9am–7pm; May–Aug 9am–8pm, Oct 9am–6pm. €4.

STRANDBAD WANNSEE

Formerly known as *Kanninchenwerder* ("Rabbit Island"), Peacock Island features a castle built by Prussian king Frederick William II in 1793 for him and his mistress Wilhelmine Enke. His successor Frederick William III turned the island into a model farm and from 1821 had the park redesigned by Peter Joseph Lenné and Karl Friedrich Schinkel, who planned several buildings (one of which now houses a small museum). The king also laid out a menagerie modelled on the Ménagerie du Jardin des Plantes in Paris, in which exotic animals and birds including peacocks were housed. In addition to several free-ranging peacocks, other native and exotic birds can be found in captivity, comple-mented by a rich variety of flora. The entire island is designated as a nature reserve.

HOUSE OF THE WANNSEE CONFERENCE

Ⓢ Wannsee, then bus #114 (direction "Krankenhaus Heckeshorn") to Haus der Wannsee-Konferenz ☎ 030 80 50 010, ⓦ www.ghwk.de. Daily 10am–6pm. Free (guided tour €2, German only).

It's hard to imagine that this handsome villa at Wannsee lake has an iniquitous history, but it was here that the "Final Solution of the Jewish Question" was discussed – and decided – by fifteen high-ranking Nazi officials, who agreed to exterminate the entire Jewish population of Europe. Since 1992 it has served as a memorial and documentation centre, with a permanent exhibit that draws on detailed historical research to profile the conference and the process of deporting Jews to the ghettoes and camps. A library on the second floor (named after Joseph Wulf, an Auschwitz survivor and campaigner for this memorial) holds thousands of books on Nazism, anti-Semitism, the Holocaust, as well as Nazi-era documents such as children's books promoting Nazism. However, the most spine-tingling experience is simply standing in the room where the plans were made for the murder of millions.

STRANDBAD WANNSEE

Wannseebadeweg 25 ⓢ Wannsee/Nikolaisee ⓦ www.berlinerbaeder.de. Daily April–Sept; check website for exact times. €5.50.

Strandbad Wannsee's impressive 1275m long (and 80m wide) sweep of sandy beach has long been a venerable summer destination for Berliners. Officially the largest lido in Europe, it's located on the eastern side of the Wannsee, just a twenty-minute train ride from the city centre. Its current "look" was formulated by architects Martin Wagner and Richard Ermisch. Today the "Mother of all Lidos" attracts up to 230,000 visitors per year and has been designated a cultural heritage site. Between 2004 and 2007, it underwent a €12.5 million refurbishment for its centenary celebrations.

MAX LIEBERMANN VILLA

Colomierstr. 3 ⓢ Wannsee then either bus #114 toward Heckeshorn to Liebermann-Villa (5min) or 20min walk ☎ 030 80 58 59 00, ⓦ www.liebermann-villa.de. April–Sept Mon, Wed, Fri & Sat 10am–6pm, Thurs & Sun till 7pm; Oct–March daily except Tues 11am–5pm. Winter €6, summer €7.

German Impressionist Max Liebermann's "castle by the sea", built in 1909, and particularly its expansive, 7000-square-metre garden, was the subject of more than two hundred of his paintings. An exhibition documents Liebermann's life here, with prints and photographs. On the upper floor are around forty paintings, pastels and prints that revolve around his Wannsee works – pictures of the flower terrace, perennial garden, birch grove and the lawn leading down to the lake – plus portraits of family and personalities. The garden has been reconstructed today as it was originally planned by Liebermann, and brims with rare and diverse species.

GEDENKSTÄTTE BERLIN-HOHENSCHÖNHAUSEN

Genslerstr. 66 ⓢ Freienwalder Str. (then 10min walk) or #M6 from Hackescher Markt Genslerstr. (then 10min walk) ☎ 030 98 60 82 30, ⓦ stiftung-hsh.de. Daily 9am–4pm, English tours 11.30am & 2.30pm €5.

With its intact buildings, equipment and furniture, the Stasi prison at Hohenschön-hausen provides a particularly authentic – and grisly – portrait of public persecution during GDR times. The Stasi used it to detain and physically and psychologically torture dissenters. The prison, which remained largely a secret until the Wall fell in 1989, was turned into a memorial in 1994, and since 2000 has been an independent foundation that researches the history of the prison and produces exhibitions, events and publications. The only way to see the memorial is via a guided tour, available in German, English and other languages; tours with former inmates are also available, though mostly in German. The tour includes a survey of the older and newer prison blocks and detailed descriptions of daily life in the prison.

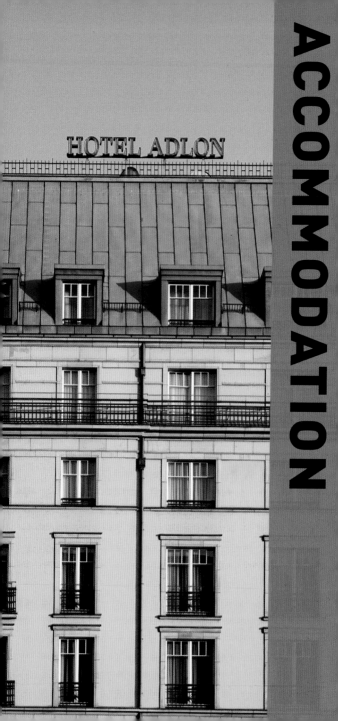

Accommodation

Berlin's accommodation options run the gamut from cheap and cheerful hostels to corporate hotels, super-deluxe five stars and intimate boutique and "art" hotels. Prices quoted usually include taxes and service charges, though breakfast and parking are sometimes extra – it's worth double-checking when booking. While there are many rooms in the city, there are also a lot of visitors; booking ahead in the warmer, more popular months is recommended, especially during large events such as the film festival (see p.165).

Spandauer Vorstadt

CIRCUS HOSTEL > Weinbergsweg 1a ⓤ Rosenthaler Platz ☎ 030 20 00 39 39, ⓦ circus-berlin.de. MAP P.32–33, POCKET MAP D11. One of the most popular hostels in the city, *Circus* offers pleasant, clean dorms, private rooms – even penthouse apartments – and a convivial, upbeat vibe right on buzzing Rosenthaler Platz. Bicycles for rent, free walking tours and their own microbrewery add to the appeal. Buffet breakfast €5. **Dorms from €19, doubles from €85**

CIRCUS HOTEL > Rosenthalerstr. 1 ⓤ Rosenthaler Platz ☎ 030 20 00 39 39, ⓦ circus-berlin.de. MAP P.32–33, POCKET MAP E10. The sister establishment of the *Circus* hostel (located just over the road) is a more upmarket and more eco-friendly place. Sixty rooms include junior suites and apartments, decorated in striking colours with wooden floors and antique furniture. Restaurant *Fabisch* serves organic and locally sourced German cuisine. Buffet breakfast €9. **Doubles from €95**

HEART OF GOLD > Johannisstr. 11 ⓢ Oranienburger Str. ☎ 030 29 00 33 00, ⓦ heartofgold-hostel.de. MAP P.32–33, POCKET MAP C12. Good-value and friendly hostel near one of the busiest strips in Mitte. Dorms and rooms are basic but clean, and staff go the extra mile to make staying here fun. Expect lots of space-themed decorative touches. Buffet breakfast €4. **Dorms from €9, rooms from €45**

KASTANIENHOF > Kastanienallee 65 ⓤ Senefelderplatz ☎ 030 44 30 50, ⓦ kastanienhof.biz. MAP P.32–33, POCKET MAP H2. This recently renovated hotel has 44 rooms in an elegant house, with decor that nods to Berlin's fascinating history, including photos, illustrations and maps. Great location for Prenzlauer Berg and Mitte. Breakfast (€9) not included. **Doubles from €87**

SOHO HOUSE > Torstr. 1 ⓤ Rosa-Luxemburg-Platz ☎ 030 40 50 440, ⓦ www.sohohouseberlin.com.

Apartment rentals

Private apartments are a popular, and often good-value choice for many travellers to Berlin, and a plethora of options exist all over the city. The best apartments offer value for money, are well-located and usually stylish or interestingly decorated. ⓦ www.oh-berlin.com, ⓦ www.be-my-guest.com and ⓦ www.brilliant-apartments.de all have a good spread of apartments and regular special deals.

MAP P.32–33, POCKET MAP F11. Private members' club in a restored Bauhaus building with twenty swanky apartments, four huge lofts and forty hotel rooms that range from tiny to extra large. Decor is quirky and fun, and hints at the faded glamour of the late 1920s. There's also a lovely spa, gym, rooftop pool, restaurant, bars, screening room and private dining area. **From €210**

WEINMEISTER > Weinmeisterstr. 2 ⓤ Weinmeisterstr. ☎ 030 75 56 670, ⓦ the-weinmeister.com. MAP P.32–33, POCKET MAP E11. This new hotel features 84 spacious rooms with large beds, a stylish design ethic – Apple TVs in the rooms – plus a decent bar and lounge, a rooftop bar and a sixth-floor beauty spa. Breakfast €18. **Doubles from €129**

Unter den Linden and the government quarter

ADLON KEMPINSKI > Unter den Linden 77 ⓤ/Ⓢ Brandenburger Tor ☎ 030 22 610, ⓦ hotel-adlon.de. MAP P.54–55, POCKET MAP B14. Probably the most famous hotel in the city, and definitely one of the most luxurious, the *Hotel Adlon Kempinski* matches a wealth of history (previous guests include Emperor Wilhelm II, Albert Einstein and Michael Jackson, who famously dangled a baby from one of the hotel balconies) with serious five-star swagger and an enviable location overlooking the Brandenburg Gate on Pariser Platz. Breakfast €42. **Doubles from €260**

ARCOTEL JOHN F > Werderscher Markt 11 ⓤ Hausvogteiplatz ☎ 030 40 50 460, ⓦ arcotelhotels.com. MAP P.54–55, POCKET MAP D14. Close to Gendarmenmarkt, this 190-roomed hotel is a slightly cheaper option than the neighbouring big guns but has all the facilities you'll need – gym, sauna, meeting rooms, restaurant, bar. Breakfast not included. **Doubles from €117**

ARTE LUISE KUNSTHOTEL > Luisenstr. 19 ⓤ/Ⓢ Friedrichstr. ☎ 030 28 44 80, ⓦ luise-berlin.com. MAP P.54–55, POCKET MAP B12. Within

walking distance of the Reichstag and Unter den Linden, this art hotel has fifty charmingly appointed and highly individual rooms, Dutch sculptures in the large lobby and an in-house restaurant serving German-Mediterranean cuisine. Breakfast €11. **Doubles from €99**

HOTEL DE ROME > Behrenstr. 37 ⓤ Französische Str. ☎ 030 46 06 090, ⓦ roccofortecollection.com. MAP P.54–55, POCKET MAP C14. Occupying a nineteenth-century former Dresdner Bank building, this high-class hotel mixes history with a swanky interior, luxurious rooms, an expansive spa and a fantastic restaurant (*La Banca*) and rooftop terrace. Breakfast €35. **Doubles from €295**

WESTIN GRAND > Friedrichstr. 158–164 ⓤ Französische Str. ☎ 030 20 270, ⓦ westingrandberlin.com. MAP P.54–55, POCKET MAP C13. Built during the GDR, this large hotel, well positioned on Friedrichstrasse and close to the Brandenburg Gate, has been refurbished to feature a refined *belle époque* interior and beautifully appointed rooms and suites. Breakfast €32. **Doubles from €189**

Alexanderplatz and the Nikolaiviertel

ART'OTEL > Wallstr. 70–73 ⓤ Märkisches Museum ☎ 030 24 06 20, ⓦ www.artotel.com. MAP P.65, POCKET MAP F14. With its impressive range of paintings by Georg Baselitz (and others), this design hotel has reasonable rates, good in-house food and drink options and friendly staff. Breakfast €17.50. **Doubles from €89**

CITYSTAY HOSTEL > Rosenstr. 16 Ⓢ Hackescher Markt ☎ 030 23 62 40 31, ⓦ citystay.de. MAP P.65, POCKET MAP E12. Close to Hackescher Markt, the *Citystay* is a big, loft-style space in a nineteenth-century building with dorms and private rooms. No leisure facilities but the bar serves craft beer, coffee and home-made cake, and there's a nice courtyard (until 10pm). Breakfast buffet (partly organic) is €5.50. **Dorms from €10 (bedding €2.50), doubles from €40**

LUX 11 > Rosa-Luxemburg-Str. 11 ⓤWeinmeisterstr. ⓣ030 93 62 800, ⓦlux-eleven.com. MAP P.65, POCKET MAP F12. This designer apartment-hotel oozes style and has big, comfy rooms (with kitchenettes and spacious, open bathrooms), a decent restaurant–bar (*Prince*) and a concept store with a milk bar. Breakfast buffet €18. **Doubles from €109**

PARK INN > Alexanderplatz 7 ⓤ/ⓢAlexanderplatz ⓣ030 23 890, ⓦparkinn-berlin.de. MAP P.65, POCKET MAP F12. This towering 37-floor GDR-era building looks better on the inside than the out. Unexciting but comfortable rooms feature cosy beds, marble bathrooms and, past the twentieth floor, panoramic views across Berlin. Gym, sauna and top-floor casino too. Breakfast not included. **Doubles from €79**

Potsdamer Platz and Tiergarten

BERLIN MARRIOTT HOTEL > Inge-Beisheim-Platz 1 ⓣ030 22 00 00, ⓦwww.berlinmarriott.de. MAP P.74–75, POCKET MAP A15. This business hotel is a surprisingly dynamic spot for leisure travellers too. Located right on Potsdamer Platz, it boasts a slick "fashion bar" designed by local star Michael Michalsky (with DJs at weekends), an excellent restaurant (*Midtown Grill*), plus a pool and comprehensive fitness centre. **Doubles from €129**

GRAND HOTEL ESPLANADE > Lützowufer 15 ⓤNollendorfplatz ⓣ030 25 47 80, ⓦwww .esplanadeberlin.com. MAP P.74–75, POCKET MAP D6. Smack between Ku'damm and Unter den Linden, this large, fancy hotel has two restaurants, a New York-style cocktail bar and spa – you can even rent a private yacht, the MS *Esplanade*. Breakfast €22. **Doubles from €89**

HOTEL ALTBERLIN AT POTSDAMER PLATZ > Potsdamer Str. 67 ⓤ/ⓢPotsdamer Platz ⓣ030 26 06 70, ⓦwww.altberlin.de. MAP P.74–75, POCKET MAP E7. A turn-of-the-twentieth-century, Wilhelminian-era hotel with "grandma" style rooms, old-world decor and long-forgotten Berlin specialities served at its restaurant, *Rike's*. Breakfast included. **Rooms from €83**

HOTEL HANSABLICK > Flotowstr. 6 ⓤTiergarten ⓣ030 39 04 800, ⓦhansablick.de. MAP P.74–75, POCKET MAP B5. The *Hansablick*, located right on the water, has rooms with balconies and/ or river views and a traditional interior that features artworks by the likes of Otmar Alt and Heinrich Zille. Rates include breakfast, wi-fi and parking. **Doubles from €79**

RITZ CARLTON > Potsdamer Platz 3 ⓢ/ⓤ Potsdamer Platz ⓣ030 33 77 77, ⓦritzcarlton.com. MAP P.74–75, POCKET MAP A15. This distinctive skyscraper hotel has 303 rooms with expensive cherry wood closets and watercolour paintings. There are also bars, a tea lounge, a great brasserie, and fantastic five-star service. Breakfast included. **Doubles from €220**

Prenzlauer Berg

HOTEL TRANSIT LOFT > Immanuelkirchstr. 14 ⓤ/ ⓢAlexanderplatz ⓣ030 48 49 37 73, ⓦtransit-loft.de. MAP P.86–87, POCKET MAP K3. A modern hotel set in a nineteenth-century, yellow-brick factory and well located for Kollwitzplatz (see p.88). The 47 rooms (dorms included) are airy and well lit with basic furnishings and en-suite showers. The same owners run *Hotel Transit* in Kreuzberg (see p.156). Breakfast included. **Dorms from €21, doubles from €59**

LETTE'M SLEEP > Lettestr. 7 ⓢPrenzlauer Allee ⓣ030 44 73 36 23, ⓦbackpackers.de. MAP P.86–87, POCKET MAP J3. Located directly on Helmholtzplatz, this vaguely hip backpacker hostel has basic but clean dorms (four-to-seven bed) as well as twins and private apartments. There's a common room with DVD evenings, kitchen (but no breakfast), free wi-fi and a beer garden in summer. **Dorms from €15, doubles from €49**

MYER'S HOTEL > Metzer Str. 26
Ⓤ Senefelderplatz Ⓣ 030 44 01 40,
Ⓦ www.myershotel.de. MAP P.86–87,
POCKET MAP J3. Set in a nineteenth-
century Neoclassical building, this
tasteful "boutique" hotel has 51 rooms
in a range of shapes and sizes, a
glass-roofed courtyard with lounge and
gallery with changing exhibitions. There's
also a garden with terrace. Breakfast not
included. **Doubles from €67**

Friedrichshain

A&O HOSTEL FRIEDRICHSHAIN
> Boxhagener Str. 73 Ⓢ Ostkreuz
Ⓣ 030 80 94 75 400, Ⓦ aohostels.
com. MAP P.102–103, POCKET MAP
B17. *A&O* is especially good for families,
since, alongside dorms, singles and
doubles it has family rooms plus a
children's game-room and large garden
with volleyball and basketball courts.
Breakfast €7. **Dorms from €12, doubles
from €24**

ANDEL'S HOTEL BERLIN >
Landsberger Allee 106 Ⓢ Landsberger
Allee Ⓣ 030 45 30 530, Ⓦ andelsberlin.
com. MAP P.102–103, POCKET MAP
M3. This sprawling design hotel has
557 small and retro-ish rooms with full
amenities and spacious bathrooms. The
top-floor *SKYKITCHEN* restaurant/bar has
great city views and there's a 550-square
metre spa. Breakfast included. **Doubles
from €99**

JUNCKER'S HOTEL GARNI >
Grünberger Str. 21 Ⓤ Frankfurter Tor
Ⓣ 030 29 33 550, Ⓦ junckershotel
.de. MAP P.102–103, POCKET MAP A16.
A small, family-run hotel with medium
sized but good-quality rooms, friendly
staff and a quiet atmosphere only
occasionally interrupted by the hostel
next door. Breakfast €8. **Doubles
from €59**

MICHELBERGER > Warschauer Str.
39 Ⓤ Warschauer Str. Ⓣ 030 29 77
85 90, Ⓦ michelbergerhotel.com.
MAP P.102–103, POCKET MAP M7.

Creative, welcoming and trendy, the
119 rooms here are imaginatively and
individually designed, the stylish lounge
area has regular gigs and the drinks and
food are good. A sauna, kitchen and new
apartments are in the pipeline. **Doubles
from €60**

NHOW > Stralauer Allee 3
Ⓢ Warschauer Str. Ⓣ 030 29 02 990,
Ⓦ nhow-hotels.com. MAP P.102–103,
POCKET MAP M7. This four-star concept
hotel merges a music theme with
designer hotel rooms. Recreational
amenities include a health club, sauna
and fitness facility and some rooms have
great views over the river. Breakfast
included. **Doubles from €139**

NU HOTEL BERLIN > Gubener Str. 46
Ⓤ Frankfurter Tor Ⓣ 030 68 81 12 20,
Ⓦ nu-hotel.de. MAP P.102–103, POCKET
MAP M6. Close to the East Side Gallery
and O2 World, this 28-room, three-star
hotel has rooms that are functional but
feature lots of natural light and decent
amenities. Breakfast included. **Doubles
from €71**

OSTEL > Wriezener Karree 5
Ⓤ Ostbahnhof Ⓣ 030 25 76 86 60,
Ⓦ www.ostel.eu. MAP P.102–103,
POCKET MAP L6. This shrine to "*Ostalgie*"
– nostalgia for the old Communist
GDR – is kitted out with a wealth of GDR
memorabilia like brown floral wallpaper,
1970s radio clocks and photographs
of GDR leaders. Prices will satisfy
contemporary communists too. **Doubles
from €39**

West Kreuzberg

ANGLETERRE HOTEL > Friedrichstr.
31 Ⓤ Kochstr. Ⓣ 030 34 34 73 300,
Ⓦ hotel-angleterre.de. MAP P.109,
POCKET MAP G7. Close to Checkpoint
Charlie and the Jewish Museum, the
"English Hotel" has a restaurant and bar/
lounge, and lots of charming old detailing,
including restored murals, stuccoed
ceilings, wood finishes and wall mirrors.
Breakfast not included. **Doubles from €88**

JOHANN HOTEL > Johanniterstr. 8
Ⓤ Prinzenstr. Ⓣ 030 22 50 740,

W hotel-johann-berlin.de. MAP P.109, POCKET MAP H8. Close to Bergmannstrasse. and the Jewish Museum, the *Johann* is a fairly nondescript but friendly hotel, with spacious rooms and a peaceful garden. Breakfast included. **Doubles from €95**

MÖVENPICK HOTEL > Schöneberger Str. 3 S Anhalter Bahnhof ☎ 030 23 00 60, W moevenpick-hotels. com. MAP P.109, POCKET MAP F7. This former Siemens office has a unique mix of contemporary and industrial decor: Philippe Starck pieces in the rooms, wood and glass in abundance and a pleasant courtyard restaurant (*Hof zwei*) and bar. Breakfast €22. **Doubles from €99**

RIEHMERS HOFGARTEN > Yorckstr. 83 U Mehringdamm ☎ 030 78 09 88 00, W riehmers-hofgarten.com. MAP P.109, POCKET MAP F8. There's a low-key, residential atmosphere at this hotel in a historically protected building. The 22 rooms and apartments have a correspondingly nineteenth-century feel and there's a delightful living room for relaxation. **Doubles from €131**

HOTEL TRANSIT > Hagelberger Str. 53 U Mehringdamm ☎ 030 78 90 470, W hotel-transit.de. MAP P.109, POCKET MAP F8. This bright, breezy hostel occupies a former factory building and has basic but decently sized rooms and an upbeat atmosphere. Breakfast included. **Doubles from €59**

East Kreuzberg

BAXPAX KREUZBERG HOSTEL > Skalitzer Str. 104 U Görlitzer Bahnhof ☎ 030 69 51 83 22, W baxpax.de. MAP P.116–117, POCKET MAP K7. This artsy, laidback hostel offers themed rooms (check the bed inside a VW Beetle in the Berlin room), a casual vibe and dorm and private rooms. **Dorms from €7, doubles from €74**

MOTEL ONE BERLIN-MITTE > Prinzenstr. 40 U Moritzplatz ☎ 030 69 56 71 740, W motel-one .com. MAP P.116–117, POCKET MAP J7.

Well located for Alexanderplatz and the Oranienstrasse scene, this functional hotel has comfortable enough rooms with all necessary conveniences, a bar for snacks and drinks and free wi-fi. Breakfast €9.50. **Doubles from €77**

ROCK'N'ROLL HERBERGE > Muskauer Str. 11 U Görlitzer Bahnhof ☎ 030 61 62 36 00, W www .rnrherberge.de. MAP P.116–117, POCKET MAP K7. With seven rooms designed by local artists, billiards and table football and vegan and non-vegan breakfasts and snacks, this budget hangout is especially set up for musicians and music lovers – as the graffiti of Falco and Joe Strummer testify to. Rooms for up to five people (not dorms) are available (from €34 per person). **Doubles from €49**

Charlottenburg

25HOURS HOTEL BIKINI BERLIN > Budapester Str. 40, U / S Zoologischer Garten, ☎ 030 12 02 210, W www.25hours-hotels.com. MAP P.130–131, POCKET MAP B6. The hotel that single-handedly funked up West Berlin, the *25hours* comes with a playfully cool design aesthetic, quirky bedrooms and a fabulous rooftop restaurant and bar (see p.139). The Kaiser Wilhelm Church (see p.132) is right across the street. **Doubles from €110**

AM SAVIGNYPLATZ HOTEL > Kantstr. 22 S Savignyplatz ☎ 030 50 18 17 36, W www.am-savignyplatz-hotel.de. MAP P.130–131, POCKET MAP A6. A beautiful old building that has been thoroughly modernized, the *Am Savignyplatz* is surprisingly stylish – its eleven rooms are spacious and modern, and one of them even has a small garden. **Doubles from €69**

ASKANISCHER HOF > Kurfürstendamm 53 S Savignyplatz ☎ 030 88 18 033, W askanischer-hof .de. MAP P.130–131, POCKET MAP A7. *Askanischer Hof* exudes an authentically vintage atmosphere with period rooms (sixteen in total), eccentric decor – gramophones, Prussian-era furnishings

– and drawings and photos on the walls. Breakfast included. **Doubles from €80**

DORMERO HOTEL > Eislebener Str. 14 Ⓤ Augsburger Str. ☎ 030 21 40 50, Ⓦ www.brandenburger-hof .com. MAP P.130–131, POCKET MAP B7. A mixture of modern Bauhaus and romantic intimacy, this beautiful hotel offers impeccable service, amazing (if expensive) Scandinavian dining in the Michelin-starred *Quadriga* restaurant and a Japanese-inspired Winter Garden Lounge. Breakfast €9–36. **Doubles from €109**

HOTEL OTTO > Knesebeckstr. 10 Ⓤ Ernst-Reuter-Platz ☎ 030 54 71 00 80, Ⓦ www.hotelotto.com. MAP P.130–131, POCKET MAP A6. *Otto* eschews the traditional for a cheery, modern experience that's all blues, magentas and greens. The 46 rooms are chic and individually designed and the organic food at the restaurant is good too. Breakfast €15. **Doubles from €100**

HOTEL Q! > Knesebeckstr. 67 Ⓤ Uhlandstr. ☎ 030 81 00 660, Ⓦ www.loock-hotels.com. MAP P.130–131, POCKET MAP A6. One of west Berlin's swankiest hotels, the *Q!* has bathtubs built into bed frames, elegantly minimal rooms, chocolate massages and the *Fox Bar*. **Doubles from €110**

PENSION DITTBERNER > Wielandstr. 26, Ⓤ Adenauerplatz ☎ 030 88 46 950, Ⓦ hotel-dittberner.de. MAP P.130–131, POCKET MAP A7. This tastefully designed pension, made up of two connected apartments, has been run by Frau Lange since 1958. It's friendly and intimate with an antique charm and some very large and grand rooms. **Doubles from €115**

SWISSÔTEL > Augsburger Str. 44 Ⓤ Kurfürstendamm ☎ 030 22 01 00, Ⓦ swissotel.com. MAP P.130–131, POCKET MAP B7. A short stroll from the Kaiser-Wilhelm-Gedächtnis-Kirche (see p.132) and Berlin Zoo (see p.128), this eco-friendly corporate hotel has 316 rooms, restaurant and a bar/lounge, sauna and fitness facilities. **Doubles from €125**

HOTEL ZOO > Kurfürstendamm 25 Ⓤ Kurfürstendamm ☎ 030 88 43 70, Ⓦ www.hotelzoo.de. MAP P.130–131, POCKET MAP B6. This historic hotel re-opened to great fanfare in 2014. Its 145 rooms are sumptuously appointed with tasteful fashion photographs and high-quality wooden floors and furnishings. There's a restaurant and lounge, and two sixth-floor penthouse suites if you feel like splashing. **Doubles from €150.**

Schöneberg

ALETTO JUGENDHOTEL > Grunewaldstr. 33 Ⓤ Eisenacher Str. ☎ 030 21 00 36 80, Ⓦ aletto.de. MAP P.140, POCKET MAP E9. Singles, doubles and dorms for up to eight people at this colourful and lively hostel – table football, video games and a large DVD library keep customers entertained. Breakfast included. **Dorms from €19, doubles from €50**

HOTEL DE ELA > Landshuter Str. 1 Ⓤ Viktoria-Luise-Platz ☎ 030 23 63 39 60, Ⓦ hotel-de-ela.de. MAP P.140, POCKET MAP C8. A mix of twenty-first-century design in a nineteenth-century Victorian building, *De Ela* has large, comfortable rooms with a classic feel for decent prices. Family friendly too. Breakfast and wi-fi included. **Doubles from €40**

JUGENDHOTEL BERLINCITY > Crellestr. 22 Ⓤ Kleistpark ☎ 030 78 70 21 30, Ⓦ jugendhotel-berlin .de. MAP P.140, POCKET MAP E9. With 170 plain but comfy beds in a renovated factory building, this is a good option for budget-conscious travellers. Pool tables, decent rooms and a convivial bar. **Dorms from €21, doubles from €65**

TOM'S HOTEL > Motzstr. 19 Ⓤ Nollendorfplatz ☎ 030 21 96 66 04, Ⓦ toms-hotel.de. MAP P.140, POCKET MAP C7. This friendly gay hangout has a great bar (*Tom's*), a vibrant café and is close to the gay scene of Nollendorfplatz. Rooms are comfortable and artistically decorated and apartments feature a flat-screen TV and free wi-fi. Breakfast €6.50. **Doubles from €79**

Arrival

By air

Flying is, predictably, the cheapest and most convenient way to get to Germany from overseas, as well as from many other European countries thanks to the proliferation of discount airlines.

Both Berlin's airports (wwww .berlin-airport.de) are within Berlin public transport's zone AB, so normal single (€2.70) or day tickets apply. From Berlin's **Schönefeld airport** (SXF) S-Bahn line S9 runs (every 20min) to Alexanderplatz (38min), the Hauptbahnhof (44min) and Bahnhof Zoo (50min); bus #X7 (N7 at night) runs (every 20min) to nearby U-Bahn Rudow. From **Tegel airport** (TXL) the frequent #TXL express bus runs to the Hauptbahnhof and Alexanderplatz, while #X9 express or local #109 and #128 buses run to Bahnhof Zoo. **Taxis** from Tegel tend to cost €20–35, depending on which part of the city you want to get to; from Schönefeld expect to pay more like €30–50.

In 2017/2018 Tegel is due to close and Schönefeld extended into **Berlin Brandenburg International** airport.

By train

Germany is well connected by train with destinations throughout continental Europe. Check Deutsche Bahn's excellent website (wwww .bahn.de) for international routes. From the UK, a slow but comfortable option is via Paris, with the overnight sleeper departing a couple of times a week from Paris Est (total travel time from London around 16hr); a quicker daytime route is via Brussels and Cologne (from 10hr 30min).

The huge **Hauptbahnhof** northeast of the Brandenburg Gate is well connected to the rest of the city by

S- and U-Bahn. Many long-distance routes also stop at Ostbahnhof, convenient for Friedrichshain, or Bahnhof Zoo, for Charlottenburg. All are well connected by S-Bahn.

By bus

Several private bus companies, such as BerlinLinienBus (wwww .berlinlinienbus.de) and Eurolines (wwww.eurolines.com/en) run routes from as far afield as Barcelona and Bucharest.

Most international buses stop at the bus station (ZOB), linked to the centre by express buses #X34 and #X49, as well as regular buses #104, #139, #218, #349 and #M49; U-Bahn #2, from Kaiserdamm station; S-Bahn from Messe-Nord/ICC.

Getting around

U- and S-Bahn

BVG (wwww.bvg.de) operate an efficient, integrated system of U- and S-Bahn train lines, buses and trams. U- and S-Bahn trains run daily 4.30am–12.30am (Fri & Sat all night).

Buses and trams

The city bus network – and the tram system mainly in eastern Berlin – covers most of the gaps left by the U-Bahn; several useful **tram** routes centre on Hackescher Markt, including the M1 to Prenzlauer Berg.

A night-time network of buses and trams operates, with buses (around every 30min) often following U-Bahn line routes; free maps are available at most stations.

Buses #100 and **#200** drive past many famous Berlin sights en route from Zoologischer Garten to Alexanderplatz, providing a cheap alternative to a sightseeing tour.

City tours

Original Berlin Walks ☎ 030 30 19 194, ⌨ www.berlinwalks.de. Offers a range of walking tours of between three and six hours, many of which cover the main sights and beyond. Prices vary according to tour.

Trabi Safaris ☎ 030 30 20 10 30, ⌨ trabi-safari.de. Drive around the city (slowly) in a Trabant, the car of choice for the GDR (with guides and without) with live information delivered to you via radio. Day and night "safaris" available. Around €60 depending on numbers (maximum four in a car).

Slow Travel Berlin ⌨ slowtravelberlin.com. English-speaking cultural/historical walking tours (2hr), mostly run by long-term residents. €20

Alternative Berlin ☎ 0162 81 98 264, ⌨ www.alternativeberlin.com. Street art tours, pub crawls and other "alternative culture" trawls.

Fritz Music Tours ⌨ www.musictours-berlin.com. For a musical perspective on the city, covering everything from Bowie to *Berghain*.

Tickets and passes

Tickets are available from machines at U-Bahn stations, on trams (machines on trams only take coins) or from bus drivers. Zone AB **single tickets** cost €2.70; zone ABC single €3.30; **short-trip tickets** (*Kurzstreckentarif*) are available for three train or six bus/tram stops for €1.70; zone AB **day tickets** cost €6.90. Validate single tickets in the yellow machines on platforms before travelling.

For two, three or five days the **WelcomeCard** (see p.162) is good value.

Bike rental and tours

Cycling in Berlin is very easy, safe and very popular. Not only is the city (mostly) as flat as a pancake, there are dedicated cycle lanes throughout.

There are also numerous rental places, including: Fat Tire (daily: March–Nov 9.30am–6pm; mid-April to Sept till 8pm; call or email out of season ☎ 030 24 04 79 91, ⌨ fattirebiketours.com/berlin), beneath the TV tower at Alexanderplatz. They also offer half-day **bike tours** (4hr 30min; €26/students €24). Nearly all hostels rent bikes for around €12/day.

Taxis

Taxi fares are €3.40 flag fall plus €1.79/km for the first 7km, then €1.28/km thereafter; if you hail a taxi on the street – rather than at a stand or by phone – you can ask for a short-trip price (*Kurzstreckentarif*) before the trip starts and pay €4 for a 2km ride. Taxi firms include: Taxi Funk ☎ 030 44 33 22 and Funk Taxi ☎ 030 26 10 26.

Fly less – stay longer!

Rough Guides believes in the good that travel does, but we are deeply aware of the impact of fuel emissions on climate change. We recommend taking fewer trips and staying for longer. If you can avoid travelling by air, please use an alternative, especially for journeys of under 1000km/600miles. All Rough Guides' flights are carbon-offset, and every year we donate money to a variety of environmental charities.

Directory A–Z

Addresses

If you are looking for an address in the former East, bear in mind house numbers run in different directions on each side of the street, as opposed to the usual odd/even system.

Children

Berlin is a surprisingly child-friendly city. There are public playgrounds all over the city (many created from transforming bombed-out areas), plenty of green areas to play in such as Tiergarten, Volkspark Friedrichshain and Viktoriapark, and, in the colder months, kindercafés (see *Kiezkind*, p.96) where parents can enjoy a frothy coffee while their kids enjoy the toys.

Cinema

Movies in English play everyday at Babylon Kreuzberg (ⓦwww.yorck.de), Cinemaxx Colloseum (ⓦwww.cinemaxx.de), Cinestar Originals (ⓦwww.cinestar.de) and in the Sony Center (ⓦwww.sonycenter.de).

Crime and emergencies

Serious crime is relatively low in Berlin, though petty crime such as bike theft can be rife. You can get help at any police station where English is usually spoken. Reporting thefts at local police stations is straightforward, but inevitably there'll be a great deal of bureaucracy to wade through.
Emergency numbers are: Police ☎110; fire and ambulance ☎112.

Discount passes

The **WelcomeCard** (Berlin AB: 48hr €19.50; 72hr €26.70; 5-day €34.50; Berlin and Potsdam ABC: 48hr €21.50; 72hr €28.70; 5-day €39.50; ⓦwww.berlin-welcomecard.de) includes public transport and up to fifty percent off at many of the major tourist sights. Though the standard card doesn't cover the Museum Island, a version that does include these museums is available (see p.48). Many of the discounts are the same as student prices.

Electricity

230 V, 50 Hz. The Continental two-round-pin plug is standard.

Embassies and consulates

Australia, Wallstr. 76–79 ☎030 88 00 880; Canada, Leipziger Platz 17 ☎030 20 31 20; Ireland, Jaegerstr. 51 ☎030 22 07 20; New Zealand, Friedrichstr. 60 ☎030 20 62 10; South Africa, Tiergartenstr.18 ☎030 22 07 30; UK, Wilhelmstr. 70–71 ☎030 20 45 70; US, Pariser Platz 2 (postal address Clayallee 170) ☎030 83 050.

Gay and lesbian Berlin

Berlin's diverse gay scene is spread across the city, but with a focus of sorts in Schöneberg, especially around Nollendorfplatz. The magazine *Siegessäule* (ⓦwww.siegessaeule.de) has listings and can be picked up in many cafés and shops. Club nights by GMF (ⓦwww.gmf-berlin.de) at various venues, including Sundays at *House of Weekend* (see p.71), are always worth checking out. The Christopher Street Day Gay Pride festival takes place every year in June (see p.165; ⓦcsd-berlin.de).

Health

There's an emergency room at Campus Charité Mitte (entrance Luisenstr. 65/66), ☎030 45 050. Doctors generally speak English. Pharmacies (Apotheken) can deal with many minor complaints; all display a rota of local pharmacies open 24hr, including Apotheke Hauptbahnhof, at the Hauptbahnhof.

Internet

Free wi-fi at the Sony Center, and in many hotels; internet access in all hostels (around €1.50/30min).

Listings and websites

ExBerliner is a monthly English-language magazine focusing on arts and music listings in Berlin (ⓦ www.exberliner.com). The two main listings magazines in German are *Tip* (ⓦ www.tip-berlin.de) and *Zitty* (ⓦ www.zitty.de); all are widely available in cafés and bars. For adverts and classifications also check Craig's List Berlin (ⓦ berlin.de.craigslist.de). Useful English-language websites include ⓦ berlin.unlike.net and ⓦ www.slowtravelberlin.com.

Lost property

Allegedly only 25 percent of lost items in Berlin turn up again, but it's worth contacting Zentrales Fundbüro, Platz der Luftbrücke 6 (ⓣ 030 75 60 31 01), who will help you with the search (there are six such offices around the city). Left or lost luggage can also be reclaimed at both airports and at the Lost & Found section at the Deutsche Bahn. Look for the "Fundbüro" at Hauptbahnhof if you lost something in the subway or tram, or contact BVG-Fundbüro Potsdamer Str. 180–182 (BVG-Callcenter ⓣ 030 19 449).

Money and banks

The German currency is the euro (€). Exchange facilities are available in most banks, post offices and commercial exchange shops called **Wechselstuben**. The Reisebank has branches in most main train stations (generally open daily, often till 10/11pm) and ATMs are widespread. Basic **banking hours** are Monday to Friday 9am to noon and 1.30 to 3.30pm, Thursday till 6pm. **Credit cards** are fairly widely accepted – but certainly not universally; independent or smaller restaurants and cafés often don't take them. There can be a surcharge in hotels and smaller hotels.

ATMs and exchange are at the airports, and major stations including: Reisebank, at the Hauptbahnhof (daily 8am–9pm), Zoo station (daily 8am–9pm), Friedrichstr. station (Mon–Fri 7.30am–8pm, Sat & Sun 8am–8pm) and Ostbahnhof (Mon–Fri 7am–9pm, Sat & Sun 8am–8pm).

Opening hours

Larger shops open at 8am and close around 6 to 8pm weekdays and 2 to 4pm Saturday, and often close all day Sunday; smaller shops often open at 11am/noon and keep quite erratic hours. Pharmacies, petrol stations and shops in and around train stations stay open late and at weekends. Museums and historic monuments are, with a few exceptions, closed on Monday.

Phones

Call shops are the cheapest way to phone abroad, though you can also phone abroad from all payphones except those marked "National"; phonecards are widely available. The operator is on ⓣ 03.

Post offices

Post offices are open Monday to Friday 8am to 6pm and Saturday 8am to 1pm. There's a convenient branch at Dircksenstr. 2, Mitte.

Smoking

After a wave of restrictions on smoking in all bars was introduced, a lawsuit from a small bar owner resulted in the law being loosened, and Berlin bars are pretty much almost all back to being smoky or having smoking areas. Expect to get smoke in your eyes in almost all bars that don't serve food. All restaurants are smoke free but many offer a smokers' lounge somewhere.

Sports and outdoor activities

Bundesliga football (🌐 www .bundesliga.de) is the major spectator sport in Germany, with world-class clubs playing in top-notch stadiums, many revamped for the 2006 World Cup such as the Olympic stadium (see p.133). Important matches sell out well in advance; tickets can be purchased from the clubs' websites.

Time

Berlin is on Central European Time (CET), one hour ahead of Britain and six hours ahead of EST, with the clocks going forward in spring and back again in autumn on the same dates as the rest of the EU. Generally speaking, Berliners, like the rest of Germany, use the 24-hour clock.

Toilets

There are a few public toilets (*Öffentliche Toilette*, WC) some of which you'll find in the almost romantic-looking toilet huts in parks and close to the subway. In some, you have to put a €0.50 coin in the slot to open the door. There are mostly free toilets at petrol stations, where you have to ask the clerk for the key. Also big shopping centres

have public toilets normally with a maintenance woman, who you should tip around €0.30–50. Gentlemen should head for *Herren*; ladies should head for *Damen*.

Tipping

If you're in a group, you'll be asked if you want to pay individually (*getrennt*) or all together (*zusammen*). In general, round your bill up to the next €0.50 or €1 and give the total directly to the waiter when you pay (rather than leaving it on the table afterwards).

Tourist offices

The main contact details are: ☎ 030 25 00 25, 🌐 www.visitberlin.de. Tourist offices at: Hauptbahnhof (daily 8am–10pm), Brandenburg Gate (daily 9.30am–7pm) and Kurfürstendamm 21 (Mon–Sat 9.30am–8pm, Sun 10am–8pm).

Travellers with disabilities

Buses and trams marked with a wheelchair symbol are equipped for disabled passengers, and a footnote on the printed schedule provided at every stop indicates which trams and buses are so equipped. Look for the words *behindert* (disabled) and *ausgestattet* (outfitted). Both buses and trams also have seat-belt-like straps to prevent a wheelchair from rolling during transit.

Festivals and events

BREAD & BUTTER

January Ⓦ www.breadandbutter.com

Held in Tempelhof, the city's most prestigious fashion event features a dizzying range of brands, labels and designers – and plenty of parties in the evening.

LONG NIGHT OF THE MUSEUMS (LANGE NACHT DER MUSEEN)

January and August Ⓦ www.lange-nacht -der-museen.de

There are two Long Nights of the Museums, when many of Berlin's museums stay open late into the night – usually until midnight or later – with special programmes and events.

BERLINALE

February Ⓦ www.berlinale.de

For two weeks each year, Berlin turns into Hollywood as the Berlinale international film festival takes over the town. Around four hundred films are shown every year as part of the Berlinale's public programme, the vast majority of which are world or European premieres.

IMPRO

Ten days in March Ⓦ www.improfestival.de

Running since 2001, this event is the biggest improvisation theatre festival in Europe. Its goal is to show international developments and take part in an intercultural exchange with different ensembles.

GALLERY WEEKEND

End April/early May Ⓦ www .gallery-weekend-berlin.de

Fifty-plus galleries and small venues dedicated to design and art open for one weekend to present exclusive exhibitions and contemporary international art.

MY FEST

May 1 Ⓦ www.myfest36.de

Kreuzberg open-air festival, with music and cultural events and a lot of food stalls (especially around Kottbusser Tor). Note that May Day demonstrations in the evening in the same area have a tendency to turn ugly, though the daytime is usually very safe and fun.

BERLIN FESTIVAL/ BERLIN MUSIC WEEK

May Ⓦ www.berlinfestival.de, Ⓦ www.berlin-music-week.de

Acclaimed three-day dance and pop festival held at Tempelhof. The guests tend to be world renowned – Moby, Peaches, Björk – and the event coincides with other music events such as Music Week, which feature additional shows in clubs across town.

CARNIVAL OF CULTURES

May Ⓦ www.karneval-berlin.de

This colourful weekend street festival has been running since 1996, with four music stages featuring acts from around the world, plus culinary delights and handmade arts and craft stands. The peak of the festivity is a street parade with around 4800 participants from eighty nations on Whitsunday.

CHRISTOPHER STREET DAY (CSD)

June Ⓦ www.csd-berlin.de

Held in memory of the first big gay uprising against police assaults in Greenwich Village (the Stonewall riots), Berlin's biggest celebration of gay pride has been running since 1970 and draws around half a million people.

FÊTE DE LA MUSIQUE

June Ⓦ www.fetedelamusique.de
Over ninety concerts are put on all over town to celebrate the Fête de la Musique, a hugely ambitious event that happens across 520 cities.

CLASSIC OPEN AIR

July Ⓦ www.classicopenair.de
Five days of classical music at the beautiful Gendarmenmarkt. Previous events have included London's Royal Philharmonic Orchestra performing the complete James Bond title themes and The Scorpions performing with the German Film Orchestra Potsdam.

INTERNATIONAL LITERATURE FESTIVAL

September Ⓦ www.literaturfestival.com
Berlin's biggest literary event celebrates "diversity in the age of globalization" and features an eclectic and international selection of writers over twelve days.

BERLIN ART WEEK

Mid-September Ⓦ www.berlinartweek.de
Started in 2012, Berlin Art Week offers an exciting and richly varied programme of outstanding exhibitions, openings and events at ten participating institutions.

BERLIN MARATHON

Late September Ⓦ www.bmw-berlin -marathon.com

First held in 1974, Berlin's marathon traditionally takes place on the last weekend in September. With around fourty thousand participants from around one hundred countries, it's one of the largest and most popular road races in the world.

FESTIVAL OF LIGHTS

Mid-October Ⓦ www.festival-of-lights.de
Every autumn, Berlin's famous sights are transformed into a sea of colour and light, including the Brandenburg Gate, the Berlin TV Tower, Berliner Dom and more. The nightly light show comes with art and cultural events around the topic of light.

BERLIN JAZZ FESTIVAL

Early November Ⓦ www.berlinerfestspiele.de
Running since 1964, the Berlin Jazz Festival is a world-renowned event that presents all the diverse styles of jazz. The full and varied programme is traditional and progressive in equal parts, and has tended to focus in particular on big bands and large ensembles.

INTERNATIONAL SHORT FILM FESTIVAL

Mid-November Ⓦ www.interfilm.de
The five-day International Short Film Festival Berlin was founded in 1982 and is today Berlin's second largest international film festival. The event showcases numerous competitions across all genres, as well as workshops and parties.

Public holidays

January 1, January 6 (regional), Good Friday, Easter Monday, May 1, Ascension Day, Whit Monday, Corpus Christi (regional), August 15 (regional), October 3, November 1 (regional) and December 25 and 26.

CHRISTMAS MARKETS

December
Many public locations in Berlin, such as Gendarmenmarkt, Alexanderplatz and the Schloss Charlottenburg, are taken over by Christmas markets selling arts, crafts, Glühwein, *Wurst*, pancakes and more.

Chronology

720 > The region known today as Berlin is settled by Slavic and Germanic tribes.

948 > Germans take control over the area of present-day Berlin.

983 > The Slavs rebel (successfully) against German rule.

Twelfth century > Germans take over the land again.

1244 > Berlin is first mentioned in written records.

1247 > The city of Cölln is founded right next to Berlin.

1307 > Cölln and Berlin become known simply as "Berlin", the larger of the two cities.

1451 > Berlin becomes the royal residence of the Brandenburg electors and has to give up its status of a free Hanseatic city.

1539 > The city becomes officially Lutheran.

1576 > Nearly five thousand inhabitants of Berlin are wiped out by the bubonic plague.

1618 > The Thirty Years' War begins. It has a devastating impact on Berlin with a third of houses damaged and half of the population left dead.

1685 > Friedrich Wilhelm offers asylum to the Huguenots. More than fifteen thousand come to Brandenburg and six thousand settle in Berlin.

1699 > Inauguration of Schloss Charlottenburg, commissioned by Sophie Charlotte, wife of Friedrich I.

1701 > Berlin becomes the capital of Prussia.

1740 > Friedrich II – known as Frederick the Great – comes to power and rules until 1786. He turns Berlin into a centre of Enlightenment.

1745–47 > Sanssouci Palace is built as the summer palace of Frederick the Great.

1788–91 > The Brandenburg Gate is built by Carl Gotthard Langhans.

1806 > Napoleon conquers Berlin but grants self-government to the city.

1810 > Humboldt University is founded by Prussian educational reformer and linguist Wilhelm von Humboldt.

1841 > The Museum Island is dedicated to "art and science" by Friedrich Wilhelm IV of Prussia.

1861 > Wedding, Moabit and several other suburbs are incorporated into Berlin.

1871 > Berlin becomes the capital of a unified German Empire, under Otto von Bismarck's chancellorship.

1894 > The Reichstag opens.

1918 > Berlin witnesses the end of World War I and the proclamation of the Weimar Republic.

1920 > Berlin is established as a separate administrative zone with the Greater Berlin Act. A dozen villages and estates are incorporated into the city to expand it.

1923 > Tempelhof is officially designated an airport.

1933 > Adolf Hitler comes to power shortly after the Reichstag is set on fire.

1939 > The beginning of World War II.

1938–45 > Thousands of Jews (and other minorities) living in Berlin are sent to death camps.

1943–45 > Seventy percent of Berlin is destroyed in air raids.

1945 > The Allies take Berlin, and divide it into four zones.

June 1948 > The Berlin airlift begins, with Allied planes delivering essential supplies to an isolated West Berlin.

1949 > The Federal Republic of Germany is founded in West Berlin and German Democratic Republic in East Berlin.

June 1953 > An uprising of industrial workers against the Communist regime is brutally put down.

August 1961 > The tension between East and West culminates in the building of the Berlin Wall.

June 1963 > US President John F. Kennedy visits West Berlin, delivering his famous speech, "*Ich bin ein Berliner*".

1972 > Access is guaranteed across East Germany to West Berlin with the Four Powers Agreement.

1982 > US President Ronald Reagan visits Berlin for the first time.

1987 > During his second Berlin visit, Reagan makes a speech in front of the Brandenburg Gate, demanding Mr Gorbachev "tear down this wall!".

1989 > Following mass demonstrations across East Berlin, the border crossings are finally opened on November 9.

October 3, 1990 > The two parts of Berlin are unified as part of the Federal Republic of Germany.

1997 > Peter Eisenman's controversial design for a Memorial to the Murdered Jews of Europe (see p.58) is chosen.

1999 > Berlin becomes capital of reunified Germany and the German government and parliament begin their work in Berlin.

2005 > Openly gay mayor Klaus Wowereit dubs Berlin "poor but sexy", which becomes a slogan for the city.

2006 > Demolition begins on the former East German parliament, the Palast der Republik (see p.50).

2006 > The new Hauptbahnhof is opened.

2008 > Tempelhof airport is officially closed; the surrounding area is later turned into a public park (see p.112).

2009 > Twenty years since the fall of the Wall is celebrated with a "Festival of Freedom". Visiting dignitaries include Mikhail Gorbachev and Bill Clinton.

2014 > Structural work on new Stadtschloss (City Palace) completed; expected to open 2019.

German

Being the cosmopolitan city it is, it's fairly easy to get around Berlin using English. That said, it's worth learning some basics in case you find yourself needing to communicate in the native language. Needless to say, any attempt at speaking German often goes a long way.

Alphabet

Umlaut: ä, ö, ü are the letters that have the mysterious Umlaut in the German language, which can also be spelled as ae, oe or ue. The ä is pronounced like the English a, the others are comparable to speaking the German o or u with a ping-pong ball in the mouth.

The "Sharp S": Whenever the s is supposed to be emphasized in German, the "sharp s", **ß**, is used, which is pronounced like the English double s. Since the spelling reform in 1996 there have been some discussions about whether to retain ß or use ss, but for now both variations are accepted.

Pronunciation

Consonants: "w" is pronounced like the English "v"; "sch" is pronounced "sh"; "z" is "ts". The German letter "ß" is basically a double "s".

Vowels: "ei" is "eye"; "ie" is "ee"; "eu" is "oy".

Basic words and phrases

Yes	Ja
No	Nein
Please	Bitte
Thank you	Danke
Good morning	Guten Morgen
Good evening	Guten Abend
Hello/Good day	Güten Tag

Goodbye	Tschüss, ciao, or auf Wiedersehen
Excuse me	Entschuldigen Sie, bitte
Today	Heute
Yesterday	Gestern
Tomorrow	Morgen
Day	Tag
Week	Woche
Month	Monat
Year	Jahr
Weekend	Wochenende
Monday	Montag
Tuesday	Dienstag
Wednesday	Mittwoch
Thursday	Donnerstag
Friday	Freitag
Saturday	Samstag/ Sonnabend
Sunday	Sonntag
I don't understand	Ich verstehe nicht
How much is...?	Wieviel kostet...?
Do you speak English?	Sprechen Sie Englisch?
I don't speak German	Ich spreche kein Deutsch
I'd like a beer	Ich hätte gern ein Bier
Where is?	Wo ist?
entrance/exit	der Eingang/der Ausgang
Toilet	das WC/die Toilette
Women	Damen
Men	Herren
Hotel	das Hotel
HI hostel	die Jugendherberge
Main train station	der Hauptbahnhof
Bus	der Bus
Plane	das Flugzeug
Train	der Zug
Cheap	billig
Expensive	teuer
Open	offen/auf
Closed	geschlossen/zu
Entrance	Eingang
Exit	Ausgang
Smoking/no smoking	rauchen/nicht rauchen

GERMAN

1	Eins
2	Zwei
3	Drei
4	Vier
5	Fünf
6	Sechs
7	Sieben
8	Acht
9	Neun
10	Zehn
11	Elf
12	Zwölf
13	Dreizehn
14	Vierzehn
15	Fünfzehn
16	Sechzehn
17	Siebzehn
18	Achtzehn
19	Neunzehn
20	Zwanzig
21	Ein-und-zwanzig
22	Zwei-und-zwanzig
30	Dreissig
40	Vierzig
50	Fünfzig
60	Sechzig
70	Siebzig
80	Achtzig
90	Neunzig
100	Hundert
1000	Tausend

Food and drink

TERMS AND PHRASES

Breakfast	Frühstück
Lunch	Mittagessen
Coffee and cakes	Kaffee und Kuchen
Dinner	Abendessen
Knife	Messer
Fork	Gabel
Spoon	Löffel
Plate	Teller
Cup	Tasse
Glass	Glas
Menu	Speisekarte
Starter	Vorspeise
Main course	Hauptgericht
Dessert	Nachspeise

The bill	Die Rechnung
Organic	Bio
Vegetarian	Vegetarisch

BASICS

Brot	bread
Brötchen	bread roll
Butter	butter
Ei	egg
Essig	vinegar
Honig	honey
Joghurt	yoghurt
Käse	cheese
Kuchen	cake
Marmelade	jam
Milch	milk
Öl	oil
Pfeffer	pepper
Reis	rice
Sahne	cream
Salz	salt
Scharf	spicy
Senf	mustard
Sosse	sauce
Suppe	soup
Zucker	sugar

DRINKS

Bier	beer
Eiswürfel	ice cube
Flasche	bottle
Kaffee	coffee
Leitungswasser	tap water
Mineralwasser	mineral water
Saft	juice
Sprudelwasser	sparkling mineral water
Stroh	straw
Tee	tea
Teekanne	teapot
Wein	wine
Weissbier/ Weizenbier	wheat beer

MEAT (FLEISCH) AND FISH (FISCH)

| Currywurst | sausage served with a curry powder and tomato ketchup |

Forelle	trout
Garnelen	prawns
Huhn, Hähnchen	chicken
Kabeljau	cod
Lachs	salmon
Lamm	lamb
Lammkotelett	lamb chop
Leber	liver
Leberkäse	meatloaf
Makrele	mackerel
Rindfleisch	beef
Schinken	ham
Schweinefleisch	pork
Speck	bacon
Thunfisch	tuna
Wiener Schnitzel	breadcrumb-coated cutlet, usually veal but sometimes pork
Wurst	sausage
Zander	pikeperch

VEGETABLES (GEMÜSE)

Blumenkohl	cauliflower
Bohnen	beans
Bratkartoffeln	fried potatoes
Erbsen	peas
Gurke	cucumber or gherkin
Grüne Bohnen	green beans
Karotten, Möhren	carrots
Kartoffel	potatoes
Knoblauch	garlic
Lauch (or Porree)	leeks
Maiskolben	corn on the cob
Paprika	peppers
Pilze or Champignons	mushrooms
Pommes frites	chips or fries
Rosenkohl	Brussels sprouts
Rotkohl	red cabbage
Salat	salad
Salzkartoffeln	boiled potatoes
Sauerkraut	pickled cabbage
Spargel	asparagus (white asparagus is particularly popular in season)

Tomaten	tomatoes
Zwiebeln	onions

FRUIT (OBST)

Ananas	pineapple
Apfel	apple
Aprikose	apricot
Banane	banana
Birne	pear
Erdbeer	strawberry
Himbeer	raspberry
Kirsch	cherry
Melone	melon
Orange	orange
Pfirsch	peach
Pflaum	plum
Trauben	grapes
Zitrone	lemon

DESSERTS AND CAKES

Eis	ice cream
Keks	biscuits
Käsekuchen	cheesecake
Kuchen	cake
Schokolade	chocolate
Torte	cake/tart

GERMAN SPECIALITIES

Knödel/Klösse	Poached or boiled potato or bread dumplings
Maultaschen	stuffed noodles similar to ravioli
Quark	A type of strained fresh cheese
Sauerbraten	Pot roast, usually beef
Schweinsbraten	Pot-roasted pork
Spätzle	Egg noodles of soft texture

PUBLISHING INFORMATION

This third edition published January 2016 by **Rough Guides Ltd**

80 Strand, London WC2R 0RL

11, Community Centre, Panchsheel Park, New Delhi 110017, India

Distributed by Penguin Random House

Penguin Books Ltd, 80 Strand, London WC2R 0RL

Penguin Group (USA) 345 Hudson Street, NY 10014, USA

Penguin Group (Australia) 250 Camberwell Road, Camberwell, Victoria 3124, Australia

Penguin Group (NZ) 67 Apollo Drive, Mairangi Bay, Auckland 1310, New Zealand

Penguin Group (South Africa) Block D, Rosebank Office Park, 181 Jan Smuts Avenue, Parktown North, Gauteng, South Africa 2193

Rough Guides is represented in Canada by

Tourmaline Editions Inc., 662 King Street West, Suite 304, Toronto, Ontario, M5V 1M7

Typeset in Minion and Din to an original design by Henry Iles and Dan May.

Printed and bound in China

© Rough Guides 2016

Maps © Rough Guides

180pp includes index

A catalogue record for this book is available from the British Library

ISBN 978-0-24120-419-1

1 3 5 7 9 8 6 4 2

MIX
Paper from responsible sources
FSC™ C018179
www.fsc.org

ROUGH GUIDES CREDITS

Editor: Neil McQuillian

Layout: Pradeep Thapliyal

Cartography: James Macdonald

Picture editor: Phoebe Lowndes

Photographers: Diana Jarvis, Roger d'Olivere Mapp

Proofreader: Anita Sach

Managing editor: Monica Woods

Production: Jimmy Lao

Cover design: Nicole Newman, Chloe Stickland and Pradeep Thapliyal

Editorial assistant: Freya Godfrey

Senior pre-press designer: Dan May

Publisher: Keith Drew

Publishing director: Georgina Dee

THE AUTHOR

Paul Sullivan is an itinerant British writer and photographer who's been based in Berlin since 2008. His words and images have appeared in *The Guardian*, *The Sunday Times Travel*, *The Telegraph* and *National Geographic* and he's authored several guidebooks for publishers like Time Out, Hg2, Cool Camping and Wallpaper*, as well as a couple of books on Icelandic and Jamaican music. He runs local travel site www.slowtravelberlin.com and also runs photography tours in the city. This is his first Rough Guide.

ACKNOWLEDGEMENTS

Paul Sullivan would like to thank Laura Harker for additional research and writing. Thanks also to Nicola Brown and Lewis Bush for their assistance on this title.

HELP US UPDATE

We've gone to a lot of effort to ensure that the second edition of the **Pocket Rough Guide Berlin** is accurate and up-to-date. However, things change – places get "discovered", opening hours are notoriously fickle, restaurants and rooms raise prices or lower standards. If you feel we've got it wrong or left something out, we'd like to know, and if you can remember the address, the price, the hours, the phone number, so much the better.

Please send your comments with the subject line "**Pocket Rough Guide Berlin Update**" to mail@roughguides.com. We'll credit all contributions and send a copy of the next edition (or any other Rough Guide if you prefer) for the very best emails.

Find more travel information, connect with fellow travellers and book your trip on Ⓦ roughguides .com

PHOTO CREDITS

Index

Maps are marked in **bold**.

R

SO NOW WE'VE TOLD YOU
ABOUT THE THINGS NOT TO
MISS, THE BEST PLACES TO
STAY, THE TOP RESTAURANTS,
THE LIVELIEST BARS AND THE
MOST SPECTACULAR SIGHTS,
IT ONLY SEEMS FAIR TO
TELL YOU ABOUT THE BEST
TRAVEL INSURANCE AROUND

WorldNomads.com
keep travelling safely

RECOMMENDED BY ROUGH GUIDES